SOCIAL MOVEMENTS AND THE LEGAL SYSTEM

A Theory of Law Reform and Social Change

This is a volume in the

Institute for Research on Poverty Monograph Series

A complete list of titles in this series appears at the end of this volume.

SOCIAL MOVEMENTS AND THE LEGAL SYSTEM

A Theory of Law Reform and Social Change

JOEL F. HANDLER

Institute for Research on Poverty
University of Wisconsin—Madison
Madison, Wisconsin

ACADEMIC PRESS   New York   San Francisco   London
A Subsidiary of Harcourt Brace Jovanovich, Publishers

This book is one of a series sponsored by the Institute for Research on Poverty of the University of Wisconsin pursuant to the provisions of the Economic Opportunity Act of 1964.

ACADEMIC PRESS, INC.
111 Fifth Avenue, New York, New York 10003

United Kingdom Edition published by
ACADEMIC PRESS, INC. (LONDON) LTD.
24/28 Oval Road, London NW1 7DX

Library of Congress Cataloging in Publication Data

Handler, Joel F
    Social movements and the legal system:
    A theory of law reform and social change.

    (Institute for Research on Poverty monograph series)
    Bibliography: p.
    Includes index.
    1. Law––United States. 2. Sociological jurisprudence.
3. Social movements–United States. I. Title.
II. Series: Wisconsin. University––Madison. Institute
for Research on Poverty. Monograph series.
KF384.H27   340.1'15   78–11151
ISBN 0–12–322840–9

PRINTED IN THE UNITED STATES OF AMERICA

78 79 80 81 82   9 8 7 6 5 4 3 2 1

To Cindy and Buddy, Lynn and Bill

The Institute for Research on Poverty is a national center for research established at the University of Wisconsin in 1966 by a grant from the Office of Economic Opportunity. Its primary objective is to foster basic, multidisciplinary research into the nature and causes of poverty and means to combat it.

In addition to increasing the basic knowledge from which policies aimed at the elimination of poverty can be shaped, the Institute strives to carry analysis beyond the formulation and testing of fundamental generalizations to the development and assessment of relevant policy alternatives.

The Institute endeavors to bring together scholars of the highest caliber whose primary research efforts are focused on the problem of poverty, the distribution of income, and the analysis and evaluation of social policy, offering staff members wide opportunity for interchange of ideas, maximum freedom for research into basic questions about poverty and social policy, and dissemination of their findings.

Contents

Foreword

For several decades, social scientists and legal scholars had debated a large but crude question: Can the legal system be used to change society? The obverse question was: Is the law "merely" a codification of societal practices? Depending on ideological predispositions, one could select an illustration here, an example there, that seemed to prove both cases. Finally, in the last quarter century, social reality has provided us with enough instances of lawyers attempting to change society through the courts that we can begin to give a sophisticated answer to a crude question. Since the 1950s we have seen a large number of attempts to use the courts to effect specific remedies for group problems and social wrongs. This large number of cases can be systematically compared and contrasted. The sophisticated question becomes: Under what conditions can the law and judicial action be used to effect change? What are the favorable and unfavorable conditions for the use of the courts and judicial remedies?

Joel Handler has made an important attack on the problem. In *Social Movements and the Legal System*, Handler examines the attempts of social movements to use court action to achieve concrete changes. He reviews the course of thirty-five cases drawn from four major areas—environmental protection, consumer protection, civil rights, and social welfare. In many ways his monograph is pathbreaking. Most prior work relating to the use of law for social change has dealt with single issues in great detail. They are historical case descriptions. By examining a large number of cases, Handler moves us to a comparative approach and hence to conditional propositions and generalizations.

Reviewing a large number of cases does not automatically lead to comparison. One can skip from case to case, either describing or loosely using the cases to illustrate an idea here, a guess there. Systematic comparison depends on having a theory. Here, Handler makes a major contribution. He presents us with five interconnected clusters of concepts that, taken together, explain the outcome of attempts to effect change: (1) the characteristics of groups that are conducive to the mobilization of resources for collective action; (2) the benefit–cost distribution of specific actions that contribute to group mobilization; (3) the structure of the law reformers—their technical and political skills and their funding base, which affects their staying power over the course of a suit; (4) the nature and effectiveness of judicial remedies; and (5) the nature of the bureaucratic situation that facilitates or inhibits the implementation of the social movement goals.

In developing this model, Handler has drawn heavily on recent work on the conditions for collective action and resource mobilization in social movements. The advantage of this approach is that it recognizes that social movements have differential ability to mobilize resources for sustained action. As it is rare that the opponents of social change are quickly persuaded of the justice of the social movement's claims, social movements must often sustain battles over extended time periods. Indeed, the course of a single case, or line of cases (e.g., school desegregation), can last a generation. A weak or fragmented social movement cannot sustain the battles by itself.

It remains to be seen whether Handler's theoretical presentation is in fact the most inclusive and parsimonious that can be developed. He articulates most fully the model of resource mobilization. His model of judicial remedies and of bureaucratic contingencies is less fully developed and justified. Moveover, it may be that a more parsimonious approach would rearrange his conceptual analysis. For instance, the distribution of benefits and costs is one of the factors that influence the mobilization of resources for change and resources for opposition. For some purposes it should be treated as part of the characteristics of social movement and countermovement. (Handler's focus on the proponents of change leads him to slight, though not ignore, the organization of the opponents of change.) Although one might want to rearrange his analysis, however, it is clear that Handler has firmly grasped the major factors that influence outcomes.

In some ways, the most illuminating parts of the manuscript are his discussions of the relation of judicial remedies to bureaucratic contingencies. Here one sees the difficulties of using judicial remedies to change the behavior of field staff making case-by-case decisions or in monitoring a large project such as the Trans-Alaskan pipeline. On the other hand, one sees the effectiveness of on–off decisions in prohibiting construction or in changing a universally applied benefit formula in a welfare case.

Handler presents his discussion of bureaucratic contingencies without much reference to organization theory or to the emerging policy science of implementation. Yet he has wide acquaintance with these matters, and his discussion is sophisticated and sensitive to nuance. Students of policy implementation can read his discussion with profit.

Although center stage is given to the outcomes of judicial remedies, Professor Handler recognizes that litigation is used for indirect purposes—to raise consciousness, to dramatize the cause, to raise money. The legal case may be a tactical choice for the movement—failure in the case may be better for the long-range goals of the movement than success. Moreover, he recognizes that there are a number of political and economic processes outside the courtroom and the bureaucracy that must be weighed in measuring effectiveness of attempts to change society and specific aspects of it.

Most of this study deals with the attempt of social movements to use the legal system before the society at large and the legislature has accepted and implemented the movement's goals. For purposes of exposition here, bureaucratic agencies are treated as enemies, and the social movement and its allies rarely are aided by the government. Or where so aided, the legislature and the courts have not been successful in affecting the priorities of the entrenched bureaucratic agents. Handler identifies with the "outs" and has studied situations where the "outs" have not become the "ins"; he has not studied situations where the social movement or its legatees control bureaucratic agencies. He worries that the process of institutionalization of social movements will not increase pluralism, but only increase corporatism. Yet corporatism is not a dirty word, and from the point of view of a social movement on the outside, it is probably better to be included in the corporate state, to be consulted and included in the decision making process, than to be left outside completely. Moreover, the historical record shows many successful cases of the use of bureaucratic agencies to implement social change. Although my own prognosis is far less gloomy than Handler's, I, along with many others, am in his debt for his incisive analysis of attempts to use the courts for social change.

Mayer N. Zald
UNIVERSITY OF MICHIGAN
ANN ARBOR, MICHIGAN

Acknowledgments

The work on this book extended over a long period of time and drew on diverse sources of intellectual and financial support. During most of my academic career, I have been a staff member at the Institute for Research on Poverty, which not only provided financial resources but also enabled me to work in a most congenial multidisciplinary climate. The past director, Robert Haveman, and the present director, Irwin Garfinkel, have always been encouraging and sympathetic to my efforts. Of particular significance at the Institute was the study of lawyers' careers in legal rights activities; work on that study provided a great deal of background and insight into the present work. I would like to thank my principal collaborators on that study, Ellen Jane Hollingsworth and Howard Erlanger. Working with them intensively for 4 years greatly deepened my understanding of the issues that I have dealt with in this book. In addition, both read substantial portions of the manuscript and were of great help.

For many years I worked closely with Sanford Jaffe of the Ford Foundation in the development of the public interest law program. This experience proved invaluable in that there was probably no other way that I could have learned about the inner workings of the firms and the financial and organizational issues of public interest law. During this period, many public interest lawyers gave generously of their time and were of great importance to me. While I cannot list all of them, I would especially like to thank the lawyers who worked at the Center for Law and Social Policy and Public Advocates.

A third important source came from the economic evaluation of public interest law, also financed by the Ford Foundation, under the direction of Burton Weisbrod. I was an intimate participant of that project and gained an empirical and theoretical perspective on the subject. Many students and faculty participated in that project, but I am especially indebted to Burton Weisbrod, Neil Komesar, and David Trubek.

Betsy Ginsberg worked with me on all three projects and provided me with thoughtful, penetrating criticisms. From time to time, I received help on specific aspects of the book. My debt extends to Lawrence Friedman, Gloria Handler, Joseph Hartley, Harold Jordan, Kenneth McNeil, Pauline Tesler, and William Whitford. Mayer Zald read the entire manuscript and offered many helpful suggestions.

During the academic year 1974–1975, I received a John Simon Guggenheim Memorial fellowship to work on the book. I gratefully acknowledge that support.

Anyone who has undertaken major research projects knows the value of a good secretary, and I have the best. Many thanks to Violette Moore.

Joel F. Handler
SCHOOL ROCK FARM,
VERONA, WISCONSIN

SOCIAL MOVEMENTS AND THE LEGAL SYSTEM

A Theory of
Law Reform and Social Change

A Theoretical Perspective

The Problem

Americans have always resorted to the courts to challenge the action of government, but only from the late 1950s on has the use of litigation as an instrument of social reform become so widespread that it can be called a movement. Most notable has been the work of civil rights groups, particularly the litigation activities of the National Association for the Advancement of Colored People (NAACP) and the NAACP Legal Defense and Education Fund, Inc. (LDF). *Brown* v. *Board of Education*[1] (the school desegregation case) came at the outset of the Warren Court, a period of judicial activism during which the federal courts opened their doors to the claims of the disenfranchised and minorities in American society.[2]

The apparent successes in civil rights litigation and the receptivity of the Supreme Court and the lower federal courts encouraged other groups and organizations to adopt a law-reform strategy. In the late

[1] 347 U.S. 483 (1945).
[2] See for further information on court activity, Vose (1972), McCloskey (1972), and Horowitz (1977, chap. 1).

1960s, the War on Poverty (OEO) Legal Services advocated law reform (test-case litigation) as a strategy to help eliminate poverty. Ralph Nader emphasized law, if not litigation, as an instrument of social change. Nader used publicity, reports, and exposure in an attempt to force agencies to carry out laws already on the books and to get legislatures to enact additional laws. Then, starting about 1970, came the foundation-supported *public interest law firm.* Public interest law firms are known primarily for representing environmentalists and consumers, but, in fact, they also represent many other interests—the physically and mentally ill, children, women, juveniles, and TV viewers.[3]

Thus, from the late 1950s on, we have witnessed three interrelated phenomena. There was a period of judicial activism that stimulated and encouraged the use of litigation as a tool of social reform. There was a growth in the number of client groups turning to lawyers and the courts. At first the most prominent groups were blacks, who were joined later by other minorities; then there were the poor, followed by environmentalists, consumers, women, and a whole range of others. And, there was a rise in lawyer organizations interested in law reform, that is, test-case litigation, which attracted a steady stream of professional recruits.

This book sets forth a theoretical framework for evaluating the 25-year experience of social-reform groups and law-reform lawyers. What were the law reformers and their clients trying to do? What was their theory on what was wrong with society, and what was their prescription for change? Under what circumstances did social-reform groups and law reformers succeed in their efforts?

Despite diversity among law-reform organizations, one can identify certain common, underlying themes. For the most part, the lawyers in these organizations want more of society's goods for their clients. Often they justify their work in terms of procedural justice, but substantive goals are far more important. NAACP and LDF lawyers are committed to blacks; Legal Services lawyers to the poor; public interest lawyers to preserving the environment, or protecting consumers, or other groups and interests. These social reformers differ from other social reformers or political entrepreneurs in that they happen to be lawyers who use their professional skills to work toward social reform.[4]

The principal method that these reformers use is advocacy: They

---

[3] For descriptions of how various kinds of law reformers developed, see Handler, Hollingsworth, and Erlanger (1978, chap. 2), James (1973, Intro.), Kazanijian (1972), Moonam and Goldstein (1972), and Vanderwicken (1971).

[4] This, of course, is a unique and important difference. See Leone (1972, pp. 43, 46).

wish to alter the adversary system to strengthen its capacity to suit their needs and desires and those of their clients. Benefits will be obtained through representation in court of groups and interests who, they feel, have been unrepresented or underrepresented. But advocacy is not restricted to courts; it takes place wherever important decisions are made affecting the interests of client groups—in all branches and levels of government, in the media, in the private sector. In the words of one of the founders of public interest law, "[T]he underlying commitment of the new practice is . . . to the principle that everyone affected by corporate and bureaucratic decisions should have a voice in those decisions [From Halpern and Cunningham, 1971, p. 1095]." Other themes in law-reform activity are consciousness-raising and legitimization. The legal system is used as a vehicle to make clients and the community aware of goals and issues. Court decisions, statutes, and administrative rules legitimate the values of law reformers and their clients.[5]

Most of the activity of law-reform lawyers is directed against the government. Test-case litigation and other forms of advocacy representation seek to make the state live up to its promises by enforcing laws already on the books. These tactics also aim at a balance in the flow of information so that agencies exercising discretionary power will modify their views of the public interest in the direction of the definitions that the lawyers advocate.

Underlying these efforts at strengthening the adversary system and reforming government is the basic assumption that benefits will be redistributed to social-reform groups through the revitalization of pluralism. The law-reform lawyers accept the pluralist interpretation of American government, are aware of the serious shortcomings of pluralism, and seek to remedy these shortcomings.

The core of pluralist thought is that society is composed of many autonomous interest groups (including government) creating multiple centers of power, and that the public interest is served through the competition of the various groups. Society is diverse; hence, groups arise to represent various interests. Pluralists believe that as long as there are many competing groups, government will not be controlled by any one interest. The pluralist model is one of accommodating demands for change, equilibrium, and stability. The normal operation of the political system is responsive to change in that the articulation of demands by dissatisfied groups is facilitated through the competition of political parties, the multiple points of access in the political system,

[5] For a complete description of law reformers and especially the new public interest lawyers, see Handler, Hollingsworth, and Erlanger (1978), Weisbrod, Handler, and Komesar (1978), and Rabin (1976). For a discussion of the tactics, including litigation, used by social-reform groups in one community, see McNeil (1973).

the seeking out of allies by existing interest groups, and normative commitments to open access (Gamson, 1975, pp. 5–9; Truman, 1959, pp. 481–497). At the same time, overlapping membership in different and sometimes competing groups, as well as the potential for the rise of opposition groups, tends to modify demands; there is always the potential for countervailing power. These forces push toward equilibrium and stability.

Critics of pluralism argue that interest groups have been taken into partnership with government and have become "institutionalized." Instead of competition among groups vying for government benefits, there is consensus politics. Government deals with the most powerful, best-organized interests in society and tends to sanction and support bargains already struck, which further strengthens the entrenched groups. The partnership system fails to take into account unarticulated interests or weak and poorly organized groups. The present system, instead of fostering change, increases benefits and advantages for elites and perpetuates the status quo (Lowi, 1971; Connolly, 1969).

There are a number of ways to remedy institutionalized pluralism. However, law reformers choose to use the legal system to strengthen the position of weak, poorly organized, or unarticulated interests in society. The prescription of the law reformers for making pluralism work is to strengthen the "out" groups. As Ralph Nader put it, "A primary goal of our work is to build countervailing forces on behalf of citizens. . . . Must a just legal system not accord victims the power to help themselves, and deter those forces which victimize them? [*Harvard Law School Record, 1969*]". Although as we shall see, the activity of law reformers is centered mostly in the courts and administrative agencies, where in theory it strengthens the advocacy position of the out groups, it applies wherever important decisions are made affecting their interests. The law reformers seek *access* for their clients, meaning not only that the views and interests of their clients will be heard, but that they will be *listened* to (Rabin, 1976, p. 230). Government and other decision-making bodies will become responsive to other demands, and social change will come through a revitalized pluralist system.

The law-reform strategy seeks to increase the power of the client groups. Why have these groups been so powerless? And how can law reformers change the situation? To answer these questions, we will examine characteristics of the groups. Then, we must look at characteristics of the law reformers. Why do they take certain kinds of actions? How appropriate are their actions in light of the needs and problems of their clients? As we shall see, the law reformers are litigation-oriented, but how much can courts really accomplish? Finally, we must consider what we mean by success. How do we evaluate whether law-reform activity is successful?

In this chapter, I try to identify the variables of a partial theory that would explain the success of law-reform activity by reform groups.[6] These variables are: (a) the characteristics of social-reform groups; (b) the distribution of the benefits and costs of activity by social-reform groups; (c) the nature of the bureaucratic contingency confronting the social-reform group; (d) characteristics of judicial remedies; and (e) characteristics of the law reformers. First, I will discuss the characteristics of each of the variables, then I will specify the relationships.

Characteristics of Social-Reform Groups

Social-reform groups face the central task of mobilizing resources to pursue goals. Without resources, social-reform groups are nothing. But how do groups mobilize resources? What leads people to become members of groups or to contribute money, political support, or services? The ability of a group to mobilize resources depends primarily on size, on its ability to attract elite support, or on its capacity to provide meaningful selective incentives to its leaders and staff.

A common assumption about mobilization is that people with mutual interests join together to further those interests since all members of the group are better off acting together. Group action is rational, self-interested behavior on the part of individuals. Mancur Olson, Jr. (1965) has challenged this assumption. In his view, unless the group is either small or coercive, rational, self-interested individuals will not join together to further common interests.[7]

The key to Olson's analysis is the distinction between collective and selective goods, and the concept of the free rider. Collective goods or public goods are goods that any member of a group can consume even if the member has not paid any of the cost of producing the goods. A consumer who does not pay is called a *free rider*. As rational, self-interested individuals, there is no economic reason why consumers should pay for the cost of producing goods when they can enjoy a free ride. Olson uses as an example factory working conditions. An individual worker would not pay union dues unless required to by a

[6] The theory is partial because it takes as given certain factors or parts of a complete theory. See McCarthy and Zald (1977, pp. 1212–1214). The factors that are taken as given are identified in the text.

[7] See also Salisbury (1969, p. 1) and Welch and Walter (1975, p. 81) on this point.

union shop because the worker enjoys the benefits of good working conditions that are negotiated by the union, regardless of whether he pays any dues.

Olson's free-rider analysis applies to large groups where an individual's potential contribution has no effect on whether the collective goods will be produced. If the group is sufficiently small, an individual's contribution will make a difference, and the individual will contribute so long as the benefits of receiving the collective goods outweigh the costs.[8] Collective goods will also be supplied in a large group if it contains within it an hierarchical organization (i.e., small subgroups) and the leaders obtain either a disproportionate share of the collective goods or additional, selective goods, such as salaries or side payments. In either case, the leaders will continue to pay for the cost of producing the collective goods only as long as the benefits exceed the costs. Olson argues that the larger the group, the more unlikely that a small subgroup would be willing to pay for the costs of supplying the collective goods. A third reason why large groups have difficulty in organizing to provide collective goods is that organizing has high costs (*resource* or *transaction* costs), which, of course, will vary with the size of the group.

Olson's theory is important for the analysis in this book because most of the social-reform groups discussed have a large, dispersed membership; they seek collective goods (environmental amenities, safe products, school desegregation) and appear to be highly vulnerable to the free-rider problem. According to Olson, these groups have the least chance of success in organizing and achieving their goals.

Olson stresses that his subject is economic organizations. He thinks that his theory would apply as long as rational individuals are interested in common goals. He does not think the theory is useful in describing religious or philanthropic groups, or for groups "with a low degree of rationality—that is, working for lost causes [p. 37]." He has a strong skepticism about the sufficiency of ideological appeals for the purposes of mobilization.

Other social scientists think that Olson concedes too much in thinking that groups not motivated by self-interest also do not have to overcome the free-rider problem. According to William Gamson (1975), "An individual, imbued with a sense of responsibility to the group, might recognize the necessity of personal sacrifice, not in spite of, but *because* of the full force of Olson's argument [p. 26]." It does not follow

---

[8] For criticisms and qualifications of the point that size alone determines the supply of collective goods, see Chamberlin (1974) and Smith (1976). In a later paper, Fireman and Gamson (forthcoming) question the validity of Olson's theory, and think that nonutilitarian incentives such as solidarity, loyalty, responsibility, and a sense of efficacy are more important in mobilization.

logically from Olson's theory that appeals to loyalty, ideology, and solidarity are insufficient to mobilize a group; the theory does mean that "to be successful, groups must find *some* way of overcoming the free-rider problem [Gamson, 1975, p. 27]." Gamson argues that there are no differences between self-interested groups and groups where the major beneficiaries are different from the constituency, such as philanthropic organizations. Both types of groups must overcome the free-rider problem.[9]

If Olson's theory is correct, how do we explain the fact that groups do exist? What incentives do groups use to mobilize resources? Many people join organizations (charities, fraternal, religious, and ethnic organizations) for reasons of solidarity or for a sense of satisfaction when the benefits go to the larger society or groups other than the joiner (for example, an organization to abolish the death penalty). Although these purposive incentives are important, James Q. Wilson (1973, pp. 45–51) thinks that leaders have difficulties in maintaining purposive organizations, if for no other reason than that the organizations rarely attain their goals, and, that to survive, such organizations usually have to develop supplementary systems of incentives or become staff led, a form of organization that will be discussed shortly.[10]

Selective incentives are usually classified in concrete terms, such as specific material rewards or benefits, prestige, and increased career opportunities. The most powerful selective incentives are material ones, and, according to Gamson (1975, pp. 60–69), organizations that are successful in supplying material selective incentives have the best success rates.[11] Olson also argues that large economic organizations can provide collective goods only if the collective goods are a "by-product" of the organization. A union, for example, can supply lobbying efforts (a collective good) because it has the capacity to overcome free riders through coercion or by providing selective incentives to members. Material incentives, of course, can take many forms depending on the organization—wages, salaries, low-cost insurance, charter air flights, or tennis courts. Wilson, however, points out that while such incentives prove useful in attracting members to an organization, addi-

[9] Anthony Oberschall (1973, p. 114) is of the same view as Gamson, arguing that Olson's theory applies logically to noneconomic groups who also face the free-rider problem.

[10] Gamson (1975, pp. 61–63) attempts to compare the success rates of groups with and without selective incentives; the latter he calls universalistic groups that are defined as groups where the major beneficiaries and constituencies are different. His results are inconclusive.

[11] See Gamson (1975, pp. 68–69). In his study of 53 social-reform groups, he found that while all used appeals to values and loyalty to mobilize their constituencies, those organizations fared better that were able to offer selective incentives to their members. But see Fireman and Gamson (forthcoming).

tional benefits are usually needed to induce members to perform new tasks; however, granting selective incentives often violates organizational norms of equity. Therefore, groups have to employ solidary incentives to supplement material incentives. Wilson (1973) thinks that the particular usefulness and limitations of material incentives are most acute for organizations with lower-income members. Lower-income people, he argues, want material incentives or other selective incentives that are "immediate, substantial, and personal" (they are closest to Olson's rational, economic man), and lower-income organizations quickly fade when these kinds of incentives are no longer available (1973, pp. 36–39, 64–73).[12] A prominent example is that of the National Welfare Rights Organization, which is discussed in Chapter 5.

Selective incentives also can be provided to a small, privileged group within a large organization—to the leadership, for example. Leaders of groups, especially if the groups are successful, have the chance to obtain significant rewards, such as prestige and political office or other career opportunities (Oberschall, 1973). McCarthy and Zald (1973, 1977) argue that selective incentives for leaders combined with the use of outside (nonmembership) support have given rise to an important type of social-reform organization that they call *funded social movement organizations*. Many of these organizations develop a professional full-time staff. Their distinguishing feature is that the professional leadership does not have to depend on a mass membership for financial support. Leaders of such organizations use the mass media to attract members, gather support, and influence elites. The size and activity of these organizations may depend more on media coverage than on the size of membership, intensity of feelings, or nature of grievances. Many of these organizations raise money by mail solicitation; they require nothing else for membership. Dues may be small, and as they pour in, the leaders, who are full time, can claim to "speak" for a large constitutency that may actually be only moderately interested in the cause. As noted, Wilson thinks that many purposive organizations survive only when they adopt funded social-movement characteristics and are, in effect, led by staff with little more than a letterhead.

Although leaders of funded social movements are not dependent on members, they are dependent on outside contributors, who McCarthy and Zald call a *conscience constituency*, donors who participate by paying for the collective goods but who do not consume them. The task of the leaders is to persuade these donors to contribute.

---

[12] For a case study supporting Wilson, see O'Brien (1974).

Their funding tends to be highly unstable. In many of these organizations, most who contribute do not directly experience the grievances of the group; their relationship is tenuous and they have other demands on their money.

Several of the organizations discussed in this book resemble the type described by McCarthy and Zald. They have large or paper memberships. Their leaders use the media to attract outside support from elites and contributing beneficiaries. Of particular interest to us is the use of law to promote and legitimize the organization in attracting this support.

Although organizational structures and incentives are discussed taxonomically, in real life it is rare to find pure types; most organizations as they pass through different periods of time have varying kinds of structures and rely on several kinds of incentives (Wilson, 1973, p. 51).[13] For example, Common Cause started with substantial amounts of seed money obtained from wealthy individuals, foundations, and businesses. It developed a full-time, highly skilled and experienced professional staff, and then a mass membership. The organization devotes a great deal of its resources to developing and maintaining a membership. However, despite the fact that the membership tends to be white and middle class, university educated, with many professionals, most members do little more than contribute their $15; less than a quarter even bother to respond to questionnaires from the national office. In short, Common Cause is a purposive organization that has so far overcome the free-rider problem through a combination of strategies—selective incentives for the leaders, outside backers, and appeals for modest monetary contributions from a mass middle-class membership. It is a staff-led organization with the members playing no serious role in the determination of policy (McCarthy and Zald, 1973, p. 22; Friedman and Macaulay, 1977; Gamson, 1975).

The continued existence and apparent prosperity of Common Cause and other similar organizations (for example, Ralph Nader's) illustrate the difficulties in trying to be precise about theories of social-reform groups. At present, there is agreement that Olson's concept of the free rider is the starting point for all groups, but that there are a variety of incentives available to overcome free riders. Beyond this, the theory is vague; it emphasizes matters of degree rather than clear-cut categories. From time to time, particular incentives have been used to attract support, but the crucial questions are how much support and for how long. The National Welfare Rights Organization flourished but

[13] For the kinds of resources and incentives needed for a "constituency" organization, see Sabatier (1975, pp. 301–342, 319–20).

failed to last because it wasn't able to develop the kinds of resources that support Common Cause. A local environmental group raised $55,000 to challenge a utility at the state level, but was unable to continue the fight before the Federal Power Commission.[14] Litigation and administrative proceedings for technical and complex matters can be lengthy and expensive, and even the largest social-reform groups have to be very selective in picking causes.

In sum, the ability of an organization to mobilize resources depends on a number of characteristics, most of which are matters of degree. Organizations will tend to do better to the extent that they are small or can attract outside funding or can provide meaningful selective incentives to leaders and members. Organizations will tend to face difficulties in mobilizing resources to the extent that they are large and without internal, privileged groups, or cannot attract outside support or provide meaningful selective incentives, but only can offer collective goods. Selective incentives are crucial; they vary in type (material, solidary, or purposive) and effectiveness depending on their content, the type of members, and the kind of leadership.

The distribution of the supply of incentives for social-reform groups is summarized in Table 1.1. For purposes of analysis, I am assuming dichotomous categories, that is, the supply of collective goods and selective incentives are classified in terms of "high" and "low" even though, in fact, amounts supplied will vary on a continuum. The supply of collective goods that an organization is interested in providing determines the severity of the free-rider problem. Thus, with small economic organizations (for example, trade associations dominated by a few large firms), some collective goods may occasionally be provided in the course of the organization's everyday work, but the main business of the organization is supplying material selective incentives to its principal members. To the extent that it is successful, there will be high levels of material selective incentives supplied to the staff and leadership. There can be solidary selective incentives, but they will not be significant; purposive incentives will not be important. The same analysis applies to large economic organizations if we assume that they fit Olson's principal exception, namely, that the supply of collective goods is only a by-product of the organization, which through coercion or other means can supply high amounts of material selective incentives to its members and staff.

Fraternal organizations are also not primarily concerned with supplying collective goods, although they do engage in such activities from time to time. The free-rider problem is not severe. Material selective in-

14 See U.S. Senate (1977).

Table 1.1 *Social-Reform Groups: Collective Goods and Incentives*

Type of organization	Supply of collective good	Supply of Selective Incentives					
		Material		Solidary		Purposive	
		Members	Staff	Members	Staff	Members	Staff
Economic							
Small (e.g., trade association)	Low	High	High	Low	Low	—	—
Large (e.g., union)	Low (by-product)	High	High	Low	Low	—	—
Fraternal	Low	Low	Low	High	High	Low	Low
Charitable	High	—	High	—	High	High	High
Environmental	High	—	High	—	High	High	High
Consumer							
Middle class	High	—	High	—	High	High	High
Social welfare							
Lower class	High (benefits not exclusive)	—	High	—	High	Low	High
Political reform							
Middle class	High	—	High	Low	High	High	High
Lower class	High	—	High	—	High	Low	High

centives are supplied in low amounts to members and staff (for example, contacts that may lead to business for aspiring professionals), but the main incentives are solidary for both members and staff. Fraternal organizations also can have some purposive incentives.

The remaining organizations on the chart are primarily concerned with supplying high amounts of collective goods and thus must devise strategies to overcome free riders. Charitable organizations do not provide any material selective incentives for members. If they are successful in McCarthy and Zald's terms, then they do supply high amounts of material selective incentives to the staff. The staff attracts the outside support and membership contributions but is largely independent of the membership, and its members are building full-time, professional careers that can lead to other opportunities. It is the success in supplying these incentives that keeps these organizations alive. There is no solidarity between the dispersed, mass membership, but there may be among the staff. To the extent that the staff is successful in supplying outside resources and membership contributions, it follows that there are high amounts of purposive incentives among both staff and members of the organization that surmount the free-rider problem. But how much the free-rider problem is overcome and for how long a period of time depends on whether the supply of material and purposive incentives can be successfully maintained.

Environmental and consumer groups (middle class) can be analyzed in a similar way to charitable organizations. They can overcome free-rider problems only insofar as they are successful in raising money from members through purposive incentives or insofar as the leaders can raise outside funding that gives them material selective incentives. Since membership is dispersed, there are no solidary incentives, although such incentives could be strong among the staff.

Social welfare organizations, such as welfare rights organizations, tenants' unions, and the like, seek to better the conditions of their members (material selective incentives), but because they typically cannot restrict the benefits to members, they become collective goods. The organization cannot supply any material selective incentives to its membership, a characteristic that Wilson regards as virtually fatal. If the leaders and staff could attract outside support, they would receive material selective incentives (including power and prestige) that could keep the organization going. There would also be high amounts of solidary and purposive incentives among the staff. Most commentators think that purposive incentives are low among members of these organizations.

The purpose of political-reform organizations is to supply collective goods. At the same time, political-reform organizations provide high amounts of material selective incentives to the leaders and the staff—success can lead to great rewards. There are probably significant amounts of purposive incentives, at least with political-reform organizations whose membership is middle class, and there might be solidary incentives as well. Purposive and solidary incentives are probably not significant with political-reform organizations composed of lower-class members.

Looking at Table 1.1 as a whole, only the economic organizations supply significant amounts of material selective incentives to members and, at the same time, are not primarily concerned with supplying collective goods. With the exception of fraternal organizations (which do not constitute a significant group for purposes of this book), all of the other organizations are in the business of supplying high amounts of collective goods, but supply no material, selective incentives to their members. Yet Gamson found that the ability to supply the selective material incentives was significantly related to organizational success. The organizations do have purposive incentives, but Wilson, as well as other commentators, doubts the efficacy of these incentives in sustaining an organization (Jenkins and Perrow, 1977).[15] However, this conclusion has to remain a doubt rather than a certainty in view of the apparent continued success of Common Cause and Ralph Nader; although there are outside resources for both organizations, membership support continues to be significant.

The results of the table illustrate the importance of the McCarthy–Zald thesis, namely, the critical role that outside support plays in maintaining these organizations. It is the outside support that supplies the material selective incentives to the staff of the organization. And for many social-reform groups, such as Common Cause, there is a considerable overlap between the appeals needed to obtain outside support and maintaining the purposive incentives of membership. Both the McCarthy–Zald thesis and this monograph deal with the use of law reformers and the legal system by social-reform groups to enhance the

[15] An empirical study comparing the success of the UFW from 1965 to 1972 with the failure of the National Farm Labor Union from 1946 to 1952 is consistent with the general conclusion concerning the varying importance of incentives in mobilization. The Jenkins and Perrow (1977) study concluded that the difference was due primarily to outside support for the United Farm Workers from liberals and unions that was not forthcoming for the National Farm Labor Union, and a change in the government from hostility to divided neutrality. The outside support was mostly through purposive incentives (for example support for the table grape boycott) that began to fade after 1972, which is when the fortunes of the UFW also began to decline.

ability of the groups to mobilize outside resources and to maintain purposive incentives. The availability of law reformers and the legitimacy
bestowed by favorable judicial or administrative rules are both outside
resources and means of acquiring more resources.

Thus far, I have examined only the characteristics of social-reform
groups and have illustrated how incentive structures are related to
chances of success. Obviously, many more factors in the environment
of an organization determine whether success will be attained.

Distribution of Benefits and Costs of Activity by Social-Reform Groups

According to Wilson (1973, 1974), the distribution of benefits and
costs also helps predict whether organizational activity will be successful. There is a variety of scattered evidence supporting the proposition that individuals and organizations are more *threat-oriented* than
opportunity-oriented. By this, Wilson means that they are more likely to
respond if they think they will suffer losses (increased costs or loss of
benefits) than if they think that unless they act they will lose a chance
to increase benefits or reduce costs. There are a number of historical
examples to support the proposition that interest-group activity is much
more likely to be aroused when there are direct, visible, and immediate
threats to group interests. Many important regulations in transportation, communications, and particular industries came about to contain
crises produced by severe instabilities. As we shall see, much of current
social-reform activity poses this kind of threat to adversaries. This is
especially true in the consumer and environmental areas, but may also
apply in social welfare programs when special interest groups, such as
bureaucracies, professionals, and job holders face threats of loss of
budgets or power or benefits if social-reform groups succeed.

The distribution of benefits and cost can affect mobilization to the
extent to which it is concentrated or diffused. This distinction rests
heavily on Olson's concept of the free rider. In some programs, benefits
are concentrated, and costs distributed (for example, tariffs or subsidies for shipbuilding or agricultural price supports). In these situations, beneficiary groups organize and form partnership arrangements
with government. Opposition groups are weak either because of the
free-rider problem, or, if they are purposive organizations, because
they have no direct stake in the matter. These are the cases that critics
cite as failures of pluralism to promote the public interest. In this kind
of situation, the small beneficiary group (for example, the producers or

occupational licensees) can make substantial gains by capturing the regulatory process and the costs that it imposes on the consumer will be unobtrusive. To preserve their position and prevent the formation of opposition groups, the industry and the agency will keep a low profile.

Where both benefits and costs are concentrated, there is continuing struggle and regulation. Wilson's examples are conflicts between labor and management, particularly over union security; wholesalers, retailers, large chain stores, and small, independent sellers over resale price maintenance; and railroads and truckers. These situations tend to be visible since the contending groups try to seek allies and appeal to the courts, but no one group is able to completely capture the regulatory apparatus.

Where benefits and costs are widely distributed (for example, in Social Security), programs become institutionalized quickly and benefits increase without a great deal of organizational activity. These programs are enacted by political entrepreneurs or as the result of dramatic events. Because of the wide distribution of benefits and costs, it is difficult to mount successful organized activity either for or against the program. The cost to each taxpayer is so small, that, in effect, efforts to curtail these programs become purposive rather than a matter of economic self-interest. Benefits are so widely distributed that they are almost like collective goods; beneficiaries will enjoy the benefits, but only make small contributions to their retention or growth. Political scientists, such as Wilson, point to the steady rise of these broadly based social welfare programs. From time to time, there is budget-cutting (for example, in education and welfare), but only on the edges, and often temporarily at that. The most influential actors may be members of the bureaucracy, which has strong selective incentives to expand the program.

Product safety and environmental programs are examples in which benefits are distributed and costs are concentrated. Opposition tends to become intense; consumer and environmental groups have difficulty in organizing because of the free-rider problem and purposive incentives. On the other hand, many consumer and environmental programs have been enacted over a long period of time, starting with antitrust laws in 1890 and food, drug, and meat regulation after the turn of the century. Wilson points out that between 1962 and 1970 Congress passed 20 consumer protection bills, as well as significant environmental legislation. In light of Olson's theory, what is the explanation of the apparent triumph of large, purposive groups over small, powerful interest groups facing concentrated losses? Although some of the legislation came in the aftermath of scandal, Wilson thinks it is misleading to focus on any one set of events. Rather, he notes that much consumer and environmental legislation is initiated by members of Congress, particularly presidential hopefuls, rather than the Executive and that the former, at least perhaps until the present administration, has been more in tune with widespread popular concern about consumer and environmental issues. Congressional chairmen in particular have public interest constituencies, and they have adroitly used hearings and the media to publicize their causes.

A distinction, however, must be made between the enactment of the substantive goals of a reform and the procedural mechanisms for implementing the goals. The characteristics of the mobilization effort, and especially the use of the media, make compromise on the substantive goals difficult; the appeal is moralistic and designed to intensify purposive incentives. Procedural mechanisms often have less visibility, and it is here that the groups facing concentrated costs will focus their efforts. The enactment of the basic legislation does not, according to Wilson, often represent organizational triumphs; rather the laws are usually the product of temporary coalitions aided by either entrepreneurs or particularly dramatic events and the media. It is after the statement of the goals that the struggle starts over the procedural mechanisms and the future of the administration; here, staying power becomes crucial since the opposition groups have strong incentives (concentrated costs) to work to undermine the program and the reform groups face the free rider.

Wilson offers a number of reasons, which are important to us, about why, in situations where costs are concentrated and benefits dispersed, industry can capture the enforcement machinery of the program. Foremost is the fact that much of this legislation requires countless implementation decisions on a continuing basis—for example, the inspection of meat, the producing and storing of drugs, the prevention of false and misleading advertisements. At the minimum, this means that officials have to exercise discretion as to what will be enforced and how much enforcement there will be. Agencies in this position have to take samples, which can be biased. Quite often there are no hard and fast measures of performance, the personnel lack the experience and training to do the tasks, and in the case of inspectors they often operate in a hostile environment. Under these circumstances, there will be considerable differences in the enforcement capabilities depending on the characteristics and effects of the rules. A rule will be enforced if it is highly visible, entails little cost, and does not affect competition. The example Wilson gives is the warning label on cigarette packages. Meat inspection is the opposite. It is of low visibility, consumers cannot readily detect violations, and because of competition, it is profitable for firms to sell meat that falls below standard. In this situation, a great deal of effort will be needed to ensure administrative compliance.

What this means to Wilson is that although the passage of regulation where costs are concentrated and benefits dispersed can be accomplished through the use of the media together with coalitions of consumer and/or environmental groups and presidential hopefuls, it is unclear whether the reform organizations have the staying power to produce lasting social change. He thinks the general rule still holds that organizations, both private and public, seek first and foremost to maintain themselves. This means that they will resist policies that impose costs and that the problem of the free rider remains an important issue where dispersed benefits are involved.

Wilson's typology illustrates the congruence in the three theories of mobilization by social-reform groups. McCarthy and Zald's funded social movements are influential in getting programs on the national agenda and manipulating the media and elites. This approach aids purposive organizations and helps enact legislation. On the other hand, Olson's analysis of the applicability of the free-rider problem is used by Wilson to explain his most important examples, the weakness of social-reform groups where benefits are distributed but costs are concentrated. The introduction of noneconomic incentives and McCarthy and Zald's contributing beneficiaries refine and make more subtle Olson's analysis; they complicate and enrich the analysis, but do not significantly weaken the major point. All theorists agree on the difficulties of the out groups in organizing and staying organized until programs are enacted and implemented. In many of the examples that I will be discussing, social-reform groups face difficulties either because of the distribution of the benefits and costs of their activity or because the groups are purposive. The two variables—the structural characteristics of the groups and the distribution of the benefits and costs of activity—interact; they are closely related and are major determinants of the success of social-reform groups in gaining access to the political system.

The effects of the distribution of the costs and benefits of social action on the ability of groups to mobilize resources are summarized in Table 1.2. Distribution (a) is the classic case of institutionalized pluralism—special interest groups have strong incentives (i.e., benefits are concentrated) to capture government and institute programs that benefit the small groups and impose costs that are widely distributed; groups that seek to mobilize in opposition face the free-rider problem.

Table 1.2 *Effects of Distribution of Benefits and Costs on Ability of*
Groups to Mobilize Resources

Effects	Distribution	
Favorable	(a)	Benefits concentrated; costs distributed
	(b)	Benefits distributed; costs distributed
	(c)	Benefits concentrated; costs concentrated
Unfavorable	(d)	Benefits distributed; costs concentrated

Distribution (b) is also favorable *once* the program is enacted; this is the example for Social Security and other broadly based welfare benefits. Distribution (c) is the highly visible, continuous struggle. Distribution (d) is the most important situation for purposes of this monograph. Environmental and consumers groups are key examples of social-reform groups that attempt to impose concentrated costs on small interest groups that yield benefits that are collective goods. A great deal of other activity such as civil rights and welfare also falls into Distribution (d). This is the situation that is least favorable to mobilization by social-reform groups, and one of the strategic tasks of the social-reform groups is to alter the distribution of benefits and costs to move up the "effects" ladder. For example, alliance with special interest groups that would benefit from the environmental cause (for example, tourism) provides concentrated benefits. There are also ways of distributing the costs of environmental and consumer protection. Either or both of these changes would ease the task of mobilization.

The Bureaucratic Contingency

Most activity by social-reform groups is directed at government. Groups seek to have existing laws enforced, or new laws enacted and enforced. This activity involves all levels of government, although the level that we are concerned with is that of the working bureaucracy. The challenge is to administrative rules or policies, and to their implementation (or lack of it) in the field. Getting a bureaucracy to obey an order is not always easy. It depends on the nature of the order, and the structure of the bureaucracy. In most cases, a negative order (for example, an injunction) does not present great difficulties; the bureaucracy is commanded to stop whatever it is doing or planning to do. The directive is often unambiguous and easily monitored. Thus, if an environmental group can get a court order stopping a bulldozer, there is no great problem in enforcing the order.

Quite different are orders commanding a bureaucracy to take

positive steps to change the way in which it performs its task. Many agencies are large, decentralized, and a great deal of discretion exists at the field level. Orders, to be effective, require obedience from independent agencies of government scattered around the country. The classic example is the school desegregation problem. It was extremely difficult to enforce the *Brown* decision, and even the particular court orders in various school districts in the South could not be brought easily into effect (United States Civil Rights Commission, 1963). Wilson's example of enforcing the meat inspection laws is another illustration; there are large numbers of inspectors making hundreds of decisions each day in meat processing plants throughout the country; it is extremely difficult to monitor their actions, let alone change their behavior. The police, welfare agencies, hospitals, mental institutions, and prisons are also hard to control for similar reasons.

Problems of enforcement are also severe when affirmative orders deal with technically complex matters, which usually require actions extending over a considerable period of time. These orders are seldom totally unambiguous. Officials who are opposed to such orders have numerous opportunities for evasion. An example that will be discussed in Chapter 2 is the construction of the Trans-Alaskan Pipeline; the environmentalists fought bitterly to impose standards of construction that would minimize environmental risks, but monitoring the actual construction required considerable financial and technical resources. It is questionable whether even government agencies, such as the General Accounting Office, were able to keep tabs on performance. With technically complex matters that are long term, monitoring requires skill and expertise, as well as staying power.

Visibility is another factor. Some agencies make large numbers of decisions—the Food and Drug Administration, the United States Forest Service, the Federal Communications Commission, social benefit agencies, and criminal justice systems. It is often hard to keep up with what these agencies are doing, let alone change their behavior.

Why is it so difficult to control administrative discretion? In most large agencies, the organizational chart gives an imperfect picture of what actually goes on. Public agencies are massive, dense, complex organizations. They possess enormous discretion; they cannot be controlled by management or legislative or policymaking organs of government. Although agencies often have not been given clear substantive goals, we expect agencies to be accountable to political leaders, to deal in an equitable manner with their clients, to be efficient and responsive to clients who fall outside of the rules, and to maintain fiscal integrity. These goals conflict with one another (Wilson, 1973). Within the organizations themselves, there are distinctive and often conflicting goals among individuals, the various units, and the groups who have different sources of information, attitudes, expertise, and perceptions. Conflicting goals make it difficult to measure performance or to persuade others to change their behavior. The structure of complex organizations produces different sources of power and conflict.[16] There is constant conflict between line officers in charge of getting the work out, and the staff, which is supposed to be supportive of the line. Conflicts arise over threats to established ways of doing business and the desire to innovate and prove relevance to the organization. Differences in training, age, experience, and job security are also sources of conflict. Conflicts arise between professionals and organizational members. In addition to customary rewards, professionals seek recognition from fellow professionals and resent evaluations from managers; as a result, organizations often experience difficulty in exercising control over professionals and usually have to delegate autonomy. As organizations grow, they need different types of experts such as accountants, research scientists, management consultants, and lawyers, all of whom usually have different perspectives on problems, issues, and goals. Power in organizations gravitates to those units that perform the most critical functions for the organization. Organizations contain cliques and coalitions that constantly form and reform as groups and individuals attempt to gain or retain power.

Of particular importance is the power of lower-level participants. In study after study, it has been demonstrated that the field-level officials have within their power the ability to thwart or accept changes in administration (Scheff, 1961; Hall, 1972). According to David Mechanic (1962), in some instances the source of power of lower-level participants is expertise; persons at the field level become indispensable because of their skill and knowledge and can use this power to make or break superiors to the extent that superiors are hesitant to discipline such lower-level participants. Other sources of power of lower-level participants include having a location and position in the organization from where one can control sources of information or resources. Cliques and coalitions among lower-level participants can increase power. An important source of power is the rules of an organization; lower participants can thwart operations by rigidly adhering to overly strict rules. Because of the various sources of power, organizations "are, in a sense, continuously at the mercy of their lower participants (Mechanic, 1962, p. 350)."

The varying sources of power and conflict within complex organizations usually force superiors who want to implement policy to

---

[16] For a concise description of the literature on power and conflict within complex organizations, see Hall (1972, chap. 7).

resort to a bargaining process that extends throughout the organizations, and includes relations between the clients of the organizations and the lower-level officials (Katz, 1977; Handler and Hollingsworth, 1971; Handler, 1973). In the continuous bargaining process, rules are used as poker chips rather than as commands.

Given this model of organizational behavior, social-reform groups and law reformers typically demand an adminstrative change that consists of a series of decisions occurring over a long period of time, and which may be technically complex; one-time, isolated decisions are relatively rare. Long-term decisions have to be made and implemented throughout the bureaucracy, through the myriad sources of power and conflict. What happens at the field level is usually decisive. Thus, for a reform strategy to be effective, it must have enough scope and depth to cover a broad range of administrative activity and to penetrate below the top level of management. It must have staying power to insure that initial changes are not subverted, technical competence, and a broad range of political skills.

On the other hand, the fact that bureaucracies are large and complex and are arenas of internal political conflict often means that social-reform groups, though attacking the organization, can find allies within the organization. Consumer and environmental organizations often receive sympathetic information from intermediate levels of agencies they are investigating or attacking. If the bureaucracy is divided over the issues confronting it, the problems faced by social-reform groups are somewhat lessened. In addition, some agencies are created to further the goals of social-reform groups—consumer and environmental protection are examples. To the extent that the activities of these agencies coincide with the goals of the social-reform groups, there is an alliance rather than a conflict.

It is important, then, to see what kinds of demands social-reform groups are making on the bureaucracy. Some demands will be met with only limited effort required from the social-reform group. Others will require much work by the social-reform group. For the purposes of this monograph, I take as a given a relatively hostile bureaucracy. This is the usual situation facing most social-reform groups, especially since even those agencies that are created to further the goals of social-reform groups often find themselves in conflict with those groups.[17]

The different effects of the demands made on the bureaucracy are

[17] Quite often it does not take long before former comrades in arms find themselves at loggerheads when some join agencies established to further the cause. Joan Claybrook, formerly head of Congress Watch, Nader's main lobbying group, was appointed head of the National Highway Traffic Safety Administration by President Carter. On December 1, 1977, Ralph Nader demanded her resignation, charging that she paid more attention to auto industry officials than to consumer interests. See also *The New York Times* (1977b) and DiMento (1977, p. 436).

summarized in Table 1.3. One-time decisions, such as the abandonment of a construction site, will require less social-reform group effort than a decision that is long term (for example, the construction of the Trans-Alaskan Pipeline). A decision that can be made at the top will require less effort than one that requires lower-level changes in behavior. And, obviously, technically complex decisions make greater demands on the resources of social-reform groups than decisions that are technically simple, and decisions that reduce discretion require less monitoring than decisions that continue to be discretionary. An example would be where a quantitative measure of water or air quality can be substituted for a vague standard such as "pure" or "clean."

Table 1.3 *Effect of Type of Bureaucratic Response Demanded on Ability of Social-Reform Group to Succeed*

Favorable to success	Unfavorable to success
One time	Long term
Can be solved at the top	Requires field-level penetration
Technically simple	Technically complex
Discretion can be reduced	Discretion required

Judicial Remedies

It is because social-reform groups lack the power to seek their demands through the normal political processes or through direct action that they turn to the legal system for help. Courts have always been used by those who find the balance of political forces against them. The powerless seek to neutralize inequities in bargaining power or at least to extract some concessions from their opponents. The use of the courts often appears to be a less dangerous and less costly means than nonlegal struggles against formidable opponents (Sarat and Grossman, 1975; Turk, 1976; Dolbeare, 1967).

But how much can litigation accomplish? As noted, the judicial system helped social-reform groups press for their demands. The legal rules opening courts to reformers expanded greatly. There were new statutory rights, but courts also made use of constitutional doctrines. The due process clause, for example, helped people who claimed welfare benefits, or who wanted employment tenure, or security of tenancy in low-income housing. Courts held that government could not take rights away or revoke privileges without holding hearings.[18] In reviewing administrative agency decisions, courts were less willing to defer to claims of agency expertise and discretion; they scrutinized the decision-making processes of the agencies. Courts also expanded the doctrine of standing that comprises the rules governing what persons or groups can challenge government decisions either before the agencies or in court.[19] In the 1970s, the Supreme Court has retreated somewhat from the doctrines created during the activist period, but the pendulum has not swung back very far. Compared with the situation before the 1950s, courts now are available to hear many social-reform claims that previously would have had no forum.

Nevertheless, agencies can still thwart the will of the courts, and hence, that of social-reform groups. As stated my premise is that agencies are usually hostile to the claims of social-reform groups. Agencies become sponsors and developers in partnership with their regulated clients; they want to carry out their programs without interference from outsiders. When ordered to do otherwise, an agency will often do the absolute minimum needed to comply with the letter of the order.[20]

Bureaucratic hostility is important because, despite the availability of judicial remedies, social-reform groups are still forced to seek relief first and foremost from the agencies. Only rarely can a claimant persuade a court to act against an agency before the claimant has first gone to the agency. At its core, this attitude makes sense; agencies have primary responsibility for making and maintaining policy and it is disruptive for courts to intervene in matters that are committed to agency discretion, especially before the agency has had a chance to consider the matter. Therefore, unless the claimant can show that it will suffer irreparable harm and that it is hopeless (or virtually so) to go to the agency, the court will usually tell the claimant to go to the agency first. This deference has enormous practical consequences for social-reform groups. They are subject to delays, complex administrative procedures, problems of moot arguments, and other difficulties in fighting their ways through the decision-making processes of the agencies (Large, 1972).

After the agency has acted (or refused to act), judicial review is usually available. Yet, for a variety of reasons, judicial review may be

---

[18] *Green* v. *McElroy*, 360 U.S. 474 (1959); *Thorpe* v. *Housing Authority of Durham*, 393 U.S. 268 (1969); *Shelton* v. *Tucker*, 364 U.S. 479 (1960); *Goldberg* v. *Kelly*, 397 U.S. 254 (1970).

[19] *Edwards* v. *South Carolina*, 372 U.S. 229 (1963); *NAACP* v. *Alabama*, 357 U.S. 449 (1958); *New York Times* v. *Sullivan*, 376 U.S. 254 (1964). See Horowitz (1977, ch. 1) and Stewart (1975).

[20] However, factions within agencies sometimes welcome pressure by social-reform groups and courts; it gives them strength to overcome internal or external opposition to change. But this is not the usual situation.

an inadequate remedy. Many cases involving social-reform groups, particularly in matters of environmental and consumer protection, focus on procedures; they ask for a hearing or for the agency to consider additional factors in reaching its decision. "Victory," then, means that the claimants must return to the agency for a hearing. Even though a claimant can persuade an appellate court to overturn an administrative decision on the ground that it was arbitrary and capricious, the court will rarely make a substantive decision. In matters committed to agency discretion, reviewing courts are very reluctant to substitute their judgments for the agencies (Handler, 1966). Courts also consider themselves overburdened and, especially in technical and complex areas, would rather delegate substantive responsibility than handle such matters.

Perhaps the most serious problem with judicial remedies has to do with enforcement. Traditionally, courts tend to avoid regulatory or structural injunctions, which are those seeking to control or direct behavior over a long period of time or alter the relationship between people, groups, or institutions. Under extreme situations, activist courts have reorganized voting districts, supervised the formulation and implementation of school desegregation and busing plans, and framed programs for patients in mental hospitals. But these are extraordinary situations. In the usual case, the court will not set up elaborate machinery to enforce its orders.[21] Lawyers and judges have great faith in the propensity of court orders (as well as other rule changes) to change behavior and compliance is usually taken for granted (Horowitz, 1977). This is an unfortunate assumption as far as social-reform groups are concerned. Many of the things that the groups want are either technically complex or require behavior changes in decentralized bureaucracies where, as we have seen, supervisors even experience great difficulty in implementing lower-level change. With court orders, as with administrative rules, as the number of units whose behavior must change expands, so do the occasions to evade the orders. Courts become almost impotent when confronted with supervising difficult problems of enforcement. They lack the machinery or the will to engage in these tasks; often judges express irritation or weariness when litigation becomes protracted. Reliance, then, is usually placed on the original parties. This not only makes enforcement sporadic, but, more importantly for our purposes, it places great strain on the staying power of the social-reform groups (Horowitz, 1977).

Monetary relief, in contrast, is readily susceptible to monitoring, except where extensive calculations are required, or where small sums

[21] See *Yale Law Journal* (1975) on this issue.

must be disbursed to large numbers of claimants who lack the information and resources with which to pursue their claims (for example, welfare recipients, consumers entitled to refunds, and taxpayers).

The judicial remedy is most effective if the court can substitute its decision for the agency's, that is, if it need not defer to agency discretion, or can solve the matter for the social-reform group by a preventive injunction, or, otherwise render a decision that is readily monitored (monetary orders, for example). A permanent injunction against a construction program satisfies all three tests. But this is not typical. Social reform groups usually will need remedies that call for administrative discretion, are long term, technically complex, and require lower-level implementation. The effects of the type of judicial remedy on the probabilities of success of social-reform groups are summarized in Table 1.4.

Table 1.4 *Effects of Type of Judicial Remedy on Probability of Success of Litigation by Social-Reform Groups*

Favorable	Unfavorable
Preventive injunction	Regulatory or structural injunction
Court can impose solution	Matter has to be referred back to agency
Order readily monitored[a]	Order complex or involving large numbers of claimants

[a] For example, monetary damages.

Characteristics of Law Reformers

When social-reform groups turn to the legal system, they must use lawyers. Lawyers offer professional skills that are subject to implicit and explicit conditions. The profession has its norms, ethics, and biases; the lawyers have career goals and aspirations, relationships with colleagues and other clients and business associates. The relationship between lawyer and client varies enormously. Strong, rich, and confident clients direct their lawyers; on the other hand, lawyers dominate the relationship when clients are poor, or deviant, or unsophisticated. Lawyers offer the opportunity to use the legal system, but, along with the courts and other legal institutions, exact their price.

Throughout our history, private practitioners have taken cases on behalf of social-reform groups. Sometimes the groups have sufficient resources to retain counsel on a commercial basis. Usually, however, individual lawyers undertake this work at a reduced fee or for free as part of their charitable, or *pro bono*, obligations. During the recent growth of legal action by social-reform groups, private practitioners have handled some of the cases, but the most important work on behalf of the most significant social-reform groups has been undertaken by organizations of lawyers, most of whom are supported by charitable contributions. These lawyers, whom I call *law reformers*, have histories and professional characteristics that distinguish them from the rest of the profession and affect their relations with the social-reform groups in significant ways. Because of these differences, law reformers exact a different kind of price for their services.

Although law reformers are part of the legal profession's *pro bono* activity, they constitute a reaction to that history and tradition. Until the late nineteenth century, there were no organized voluntary activities on the part of the profession; whatever charitable work was done was performed by individual private practitioners.[22] By the turn of the century, efforts were undertaken to more systematically organize *pro bono* work. There developed two basic traditions. One was the legal aid movement that primarily handled "service" cases, that is, legal matters for individual clients (for example, divorce, contract) and was traditional in orientation in the sense that legal aid lawyers accepted the existing political, economic, and social system. These lawyers believed that the legal system worked well but that some people needed better access to it.

The other tradition was more aggressive; it did not accept the status quo and sought to change the political, economic, and social system to the advantage of the clients by the use of test-case law-reform litigation. Although there were diverse strands in the aggressive tradition, the most important early influences were those of the National Association for the Advancement of Colored People (NAACP), and its subsequent creation, the NAACP Legal Defense and Education Fund, Inc. (LDF).[23] The distinguishing characteristic of these two organizations was the strategic use of test-case law-reform litigation. By 1954, the year of the LDF's famous victory, *Brown* v. *Board of Education,* the two organizations had won 34 of 38 cases in the Supreme Court. This record had an enormous influence on the development of aggressive law reform. The victories appeared to illustrate the efficacy of the law-reform route to social change; at the stroke of the judicial pen, so it seemed, the longstanding demands of blacks were met. Supreme Court

[22] There are, of course, many histories of legal aid. For a concise account, see Handler, Hollingsworth and Erlanger (1978, chap. 2).

[23] As a result of NAACP cases, the United States Supreme Court invalidated antiblack voting restrictions (1915), housing segregation ordinances (1917), and the exclusion of blacks from juries in criminal cases (1923). For the importance of the influence of the NAACP and the LDF as a role model, see Rabin (1976).

decisions gave the lawyers and their clients enormous prestige and publicity, and facilitated fund raising and the recruitment of young lawyers.

There were other influential groups, for example, the American Civil Liberties Union (see Rabin, 1976) and the Civil Rights Division of the Department of Justice under the Kennedy and Johnson administrations. However, when the War On Poverty's Legal Services program started in 1967, its law-reform emphasis was modeled on the NAACP and the LDF. Strategically planned test-case litigation would now bring about social change on behalf of the poor (Handler, Hollingsworth, and Erlanger, 1978). Thereafter, expansion of law reform to other groups in society moved rapidly. Ralph Nader, who is a lawyer, stressed the role of the lawyer on behalf of the consumer and the environmentalist. In the late 1960s and early 1970s, foundations began to fund public-interest law firms that engaged in law reform in such areas as consumer issues, environment, education, employment, and minority rights. The growth of law-reform activity in both the public and the voluntary sector, in turn, influenced law-reform organizations among the private bar. The Lawyers Committee for Civil Rights Under Law and the Law Students Civil Rights Research Council concentrated on civil rights for blacks in the South. Private law firms established separate *pro bono* departments; the American Bar Association and several local bars also supported law-reform activities (Handler, Hollingsworth, and Erlanger, 1978).

By the mid-1970s aggressive law reform could be found among private practitioners, government programs, and the voluntary sector. However, the core of the activity, and the most important for our purposes, consists of the voluntary efforts, and in particular, the foundation-supported public interest law firms. Although there is a fair amount of instability among these firms, it is probably safe to estimate that there were between 80 and 90 firms, most of which were established between 1965 and 1975.[24] Most firms had 4 or less salaried lawyers; the largest firm had 35, and the average for all of the firms was 6. Most firms had a position for 1 salaried nonlawyer. In 1975, the budgets of these firms ranged from $7000 to $4,720,000, with 56% of the budgets under $200,000. The largest source of funds came from foundations, followed by contributions and gifts.

The bulk of these firms' activity was spent in litigation, negotiation, administrative rulemaking, and monitoring. Much smaller

[24] See Handler, Ginsberg, and Snow (1977). For other histories and descriptions of public interest law, see Green (1975), Marks (1972), Auerbach (1976), Handler, Hollingsworth and Erlanger (1978), Rabin (1976), and Halpern and Cunningham (1971).

amounts of time were devoted to legislative work, for example: lobbying, testifying (10%); research, that is, information dissemination (14%); and internal administration, such as fund raising (12%). Firms tended to concentrate in particular subject areas, but, overall, the subject matter of public interest law covers a wide spectrum—civil liberties, environmental protection, consumer protection, employment, education, media reform, health care, welfare, housing, voting rights, occupational health and safety.

Although there is considerable diversity among the firms, they seem to fall into three basic organizational structures. Most firms are formally independent and self-contained. In structure, they resemble a private law firm except, of course, for the funding source. Other firms are affiliated with a parent organization, such as the League of Women Voters or the Consumers Union. Although these firms receive independent gifts and grants, they rely primarily on the parent organization for funding and direction. A third structure consists of a central office with a full-time staff and a network of participating lawyers. The principal example of this kind of firm is the LDF.

In addition to the voluntary sector, public interest law firms, there are also mixed public interest law firms, that is, firms that are in the for-profit sector but that try to devote a substantial part of their resources to what they define as public interest cases. These firms support themselves from fees generated from their commercial clients or, in some instances, fees paid by their public interest clients. There are about 65 of these firms, with an average size of just under four salaried lawyers. These firms concentrate in the same subject areas as the other public interest law firms. In addition, there are a few public interest law firms sponsored by bar associations and about a dozen Legal Services back-up centers that engage in test-case law-reform litigation.

The relationship between law reformers and their clients is very different from the relationships in private practice. In the ordinary attorney–client relationship, the client offers to purchase legal services. Although the ethics of the profession dictate that all are entitled to legal representation, subject to unusual circumstances, an individual lawyer is free to reject a client; the lawyer may be a specialist, or have a conflict of interest, or have no reason whatever. But in the usual situation, the lawyer takes the case if the client can pay the bill, and performs whatever services are necessary to advance the client's interest. These services may include the traditional litigation skills that one commonly associates with lawyers, but they may also include bargaining and negotiation, office work, lobbying, and other kinds of behind-the-scenes activity.

The attorney–client relationship for law reformers is affected by their personal characteristics, the size and resources of their offices, and their funding sources—all of which differ markedly from those found in private practice. Although people make career decisions for various reasons, the best evidence is that law-reform lawyers are committed social reformers. As compared with the rest of the bar, they are young, have proportionately better law-school records, are further to the left politically, and are taking about a 40% cut in salary to practice public interest law. Moreover, their financial sacrifice appears to be permanent rather than a temporary cut in the nature of a capital investment whereby the lawyer would recoup the loss by virtue of the public interest law experience.[25] According to these lawyers, there are many nonpecuniary reasons for engaging in public interest law work—the sense of satisfaction in doing something good, publicity and rapid exposure to high government officials or corporate executives, significant responsibility in handling big cases, working in a small office with compatible colleagues, and differences in lifestyles. Lawyers in private practice, if successful, can also achieve many of these same rewards, but after a much longer period of apprenticeship. The nonpecuniary rewards of public interest law are important to the lawyers and, as we shall see, affect the attorney–client relationship. These lawyers value their freedom to achieve these rewards through their selection of clients and cases.

Neil Komesar and Burton Weisbrod (1978), in a recent study of public interest law, have suggested that law-reform lawyers may usefully be viewed as "publicity maximizers" rather than profit maximizers. Good publicity can further the client's cause, increase the lawyer's reputation, and thereby strengthen his capacity to negotiate and deal with high officials, increase the ability of the firm and the social-reform group to raise money, satisfy the organizational needs of the firm's funding source, and, when the time comes, increase the lawyer's future employment opportunities.

Test-case litigation can more nearly fulfill the need for good publicity than most other kinds of lawyering skills. The principal contrast is between test-case litigation and lobbying, which is another important technique that lawyers use on behalf of clients. The successful lobbyist is a person who stays with a key legislative committee or a government agency for years, slowly and quietly building the relation-

---

[2] Although the public interest law movement is too young to make predictions, most lawyers who leave these firms do not go into high-paying jobs in private practice. For a full analysis of the economic aspects of public interest law jobs, see Komesar and Weisbrod (1978) and compare Handler, Hollingsworth, and Erlanger (1978, chap. 8).

ship, supplying information, and establishing confidence and mutual interests. A successful lobbyist gets a committee or agency to adopt his position sometimes without even any awareness that the lobbyist first brought the idea to the committee or agency's attention and worked for its adoption. There have been a few studies of lobbyists that have concluded that lobbyists are older and more experienced than public interest lawyers (between ages 40 and 60), have long experience, patience, and the ability to handle frustration and delay (see Komesar and Weisbrod, 1978). Public interest lawyers, in contrast, are younger, most have had no experience in this kind of work, and, have a rapid turnover, if not in their firm, then at least in the subject area. Even if they were inclined to lobby, most would lack the time to develop the contacts, and the intimate knowledge of the workings of the committees or the agencies. There also is the problem of temperament—whether young, socially committed lawyers can be patient, willing to compromise, and be of good cheer in the face of defeat. A good lobbyist does not have a sense of outrage or at least he does not reveal it.

Until recently, there have been legal restrictions on lobbying by public-interest law groups. These have eased somewhat but it is doubtful whether this change in the law will affect significantly the actual behavior of the lawyers. Prior to the change, some lawyers from time to time engaged in activities that resembled lobbying but were not technical violations. Although the experience varied, many reported that behind-the-scenes negotiations, especially if carried out over a long period of time, were not satisfactory. The lawyers felt that they were less powerful in this role, and the lack of publicity was viewed as a detriment to their interests and the interests of their clients. They felt more comfortable in the litigation setting. While the change in the lobbying restrictions may lead to the establishment of national lobbying groups on behalf of public interest law, it is less likely that individual lawyers in the firms will devote substantially more time to lobbying.

There are other reasons why public interest law firms will tend to use test-case litigation. These law firms deal in controversial questions with high stakes, such as, the environment, product safety, and discrimination. The opponents do not take kindly to these lawsuits; they question the motivations of the lawyers and their sponsors as well as the propriety of public or foundation support for this work, and have not hesitated to complain vigorously in a variety of public and governmental forums. Law reformers and foundations feel the need for legitimation from courts. One potent defense against political attack would be a favorable decision by a federal court of appeals since it would appear that the law reformers had acted properly, that their claims were justified in law.

A court decision has more public relations value than an administrative rule, a study, or a report. Law reformers have been trying to grow and become a movement; to do this, they have to become known. Publicity is also important in other ways. As McCarthy and Zald (1973) argue, leaders of weak or paper organizations must manipulate the media (and elites) to attract support. Court cases, particularly when they stop a bulldozer or unmask some outrageous practice, can be dramatic and newsworthy, and provide the legitimacy so necessary for support from elites.[26]

These tendencies toward test-case litigation fit the training and role models of the public interest lawyers. Law schools emphasize the appellate court decision, rather than the skills of the lobbyist and office negotiator. And the models for these social reformers are the great Supreme Court litigators of civil liberties cases.

On the other hand, though the law reformers tend toward litigation, the resources of their offices impose certain constraints on the type of litigation that can be undertaken. The firms cannot really afford long-term litigation that turns on complex factual matters. Neither they nor their clients can pay for the experts and related costs of such lawsuits. There is, in fact, a dramatic contrast between the small size and slender resources of these firms, and the formidable resources of their opponents, the government and the large corporations represented by the largest law firms.

Because social-reform groups usually lack the market power to pick and choose among lawyers, the public interest lawyers have greater freedom in the selection of clients and cases. What, then, are the characteristics of this attorney–client relationship? How does client and case selection fit the needs of the law reformers? Sometimes the lawyers think of a problem and contact the leaders of organizations they have dealt with before and get them to agree to the plans of the lawyers. McCarthy and Zald think that with the rise of professional leaders in funded social movements, grievances may be manufactured to attract new funding sources. Law reformers can aid in this process; they, too, create and define problems, which serve the needs of the firm as well as the social-reform group.[27] The lawyers gain from the publicity; since they deal solely with the leaders, they need expend little or no resources to persuade the membership. The leaders, in turn, have a free

---

[26] For a theoretical analysis of the relationship between outcomes or achievement and the task of mobilizing resources, see Snyder and Kelly (1978).

[27] See Edelman (1974, chap. 4), Rosenheim, (1976), and Mayhew (1975).

resource, an opportunity to gain publicity for themselves and the organization, and the opportunity to accomplish some of their goals through the legal system. The lawsuit may not be a high-priority item on their agenda, but the leaders are willing to go along because of the free or low-cost gains. This arrangement allows the law reformers flexibility in picking cases and selecting tactics and issues. They have freedom to tailor litigation to the firm's program—its substantive mission and that of its funding source.

This kind of attorney–client relationship, of course, is by no means universal. Many client groups have an active membership and an articulate leadership, willing and able to direct and control the lawyers. Nevertheless, even these strong groups lack the power of the purse; they do not pay the lawyers, who, thus, continue to operate more or less under their rules and constraints.

Other law firms are organized by and are integrated subunits of parent organizations—such as the Sierra Club, Consumers Union, and Public Citizen (Ralph Nader). The parent groups use many techniques besides litigation (for example, lobbying and information dissemination). The lawyers have available to them the resources of the organization, which may give them less of a bias toward the use of litigation exclusively.

With organizations that make extensive use of networks of participating lawyers we would expect the litigation bias to be strongest among the participating lawyers. Participating lawyers in outlying areas and local groups would lack the capacity to do anything but litigate. In addition, local groups might feel intensely about particular issues and be less amenable to compromise and negotiation.[28]

Law reformers, and especially public interest law firms, have strengths and weaknesses that may or may not serve the best interests of their clients. They favor litigation, especially the big cases, and in some situations, this can be very useful for the social-reform groups. But when problems are long-term, or complex, or require extensive changes in field-level discretion, more effective change may be brought about through lobbying. There may be need for extensive bargaining and negotiation. Law reformers then will be of most use if they can combine their litigation skills with lobbying, political, and information skills. They are of less use to social-reform groups to the extent that by choice or necessity they have only litigation skills.

Table 1.5 summarizes the characteristics of law reformers as they relate to the probable success of law-reform activity by social-reform

[28] An examination of the docket sheets of 24 public interest law firms supported these hypotheses. Fifty-four percent of the cases of independent firms involved litigation as compared with 85% of the cases of the participating firms. See Handler, Ginsberg, and Snow (1977, Table 9).

Table 1.5 *Effect of Characteristics of Law Reformers on Probabilities of Success of Social-Reform Groups*

Favorable	Unfavorable
Affiliated with parent group	Independent, foundation-supported
Have available technical resources	Lack technical resources
Have available political resources	Lack political resources

groups. It is expected that the tendencies toward litigation, toward maximum publicity, and toward fitting client needs to law reformer needs would be stronger with the independent foundation-supported law firm. At the same time, and reinforcing those tendencies, would be the lack of technical and/or political resources. These law reformers would have to select clients and cases carefully. Conversely, it is expected that affiliated law reformers would be more under the control and direction of the client organizations, and would be able to call upon technical and/or political resources; these law firms would have less of a litigation bias and less need for publicity.

Summary: The Costs of Success

The price that the social-reform group might have to pay for law reformers is a point that applies more generally. The law reformers have their instrumental goals and values which, as I have noted, may conflict with the goals and values of the social-reform group. Each of the five variables that affect the likelihood of success of a social-reform group has favorable or unfavorable characteristics and the interaction of the group with these characteristics can impose constraints. For example, in addition to the special demands of the law reformers, using the legal system itself may exact a high price. The lawyers, with the leaders, often assume a dominant position with regard to tactics and strategy once the group goes the legal route. The membership is confronted with a mysterious procedure and trade language; the specialists take over. There is a danger that the nonlegal activity of the group will languish pending the outcome of the litigation. There will be the inevitable delays that can sap the enthusiasm of the membership. Using the courts might mean framing the issues that, while legally sound, lose political and purposive appeal. And, then, there is the risk of losing.

The other variables may affect the social-reform group in a similar manner. It was noted that one possible way of altering unfavorable distribution of benefits and costs would be to seek alliances with special interest groups; this would have the effect of concentrating benefits (selective incentives). With purposive organizations, however, alliances can be troublesome insofar as moralistic members may lose their enthusiasm at what they perceive is a betrayal of the cause. The special interest groups have their program and their values, which may only partially coincide with those of the social-reform group.

Relationships with bureaucracies will also vary, especially with long-term problems that will require monitoring and continual negotiations. I have stressed that bureaucracies are not single-minded, monolithic entities but rather arenas of conflict with shifting groups and interests. Sometimes the activity of social-reform groups strikes a sympathetic chord with certain interests in the bureaucracy and cooperative arrangements can be made, often surreptitiously. But for the social-reform group to benefit, there has to be an exchange; the group has to satisfy the interests of those in the bureaucracy. Ties of cooperation often develop over monitoring procedures where little favors are often exchanged to make life easier. At each step, the adversaries have to weigh the benefits and costs of cooperating or fighting. In either event, the characteristics of the bureaucracy affect the activities of the social-reform group.

Table 1.6 summarizes the five variables that have been discussed. The presentation in the Table is not meant to convey the impression that the only analytic question is how can the social-reform group mobilize resources to overcome the sets of unfavorable characteristics of the variables. These characteristics are not inert matter waiting to be acted upon by the social-reform groups. Rather, as has been discussed, confronting these variables will, in turn, very likely affect the activities of the social-reform group. The variables are part of the social context within which the groups operate.[29]

The Dependent Variable: What is "Success"?

Five variables have been specified that seem to affect the outcome of the law-reform efforts of social-reform groups. Let's now turn to the dependent variable. What is meant by "success"? Defining organizational success is a difficult problem (see Hall, 1972). Scholars have pointed out that there is a difference between the stated or official goals of an organization and its operative goals, the goals that are actually pursued. Moreover, as noted, organizations often have multiple

[29] Snyder and Kelly (1978) strongly emphasize the theoretical importance of both the environment in which the social-reform groups operate and the consequences of their activities on the task of mobilizing resources.

Table 1.6 *Variables That Predict Outcomes of Law Reform by Social-Reform Groups*

Variables	Favorable	Unfavorable
Characteristics of groups	Small size	Large size
	Outside funding	No outside resources
	Availability of selective benefits	Collective goods only
Benefit–cost distribution of group action	Benefits concentrated; costs distributed	Benefits concentrated; costs concentrated
	Benefits distributed; costs distributed	Benefits distributed; costs concentrated
Bureaucratic contingency	One time	Long term
	Can be solved at the top	Requires field-level penetration
	Technically simple	Technically complex
	Discretion can be reduced	Discretion required
Judicial remedy	Preventive injunction	Regulatory or structural injunction
	Court can impose solution	Matter has to be referred back to agency
	Order readily monitored[a]	Order complex or involving large numbers
Structure of law reformers	Affiliated with parent groups	Independent, foundation-supported
	Have available technical resources	Lack technical resources
	Have available political resources	Lack political resources

[a] For example, monetary damages.

goals that can be inconsistent and which, in fact, require multiple in-
dicators of success. How, then, can one measure the accomplishment of
particular goals? Finally, organizations rarely completely accomplish
their goals (however defined) and are usually evaluated in terms of *effectiveness*—the degree to which an organization realizes its goals.

Defining and measuring outcomes is further complicated because
this book is concerned with contemporary organizations. Gamson
(1975), for example, in his study of social-reform groups, limited his
sample to groups that functioned prior to 1945 to be able to ascertain
whether the groups had achieved their objectives. Although some
historical examples will be used, for the most part, the groups that are
of interest to us are in the middle of their battles and the benefits of
hindsight are simply not available. In most cases, outcomes will have to
be in the nature of a forecast and the theory will not be able to be
validated. Nevertheless, judgments will have to be made. In evaluating
effects, my starting point will be groups that are seeking tangible
benefits such as better health, education, and welfare programs; these
benefits would include not only more resources but also better standards of administration. For consumer groups, tangible benefits would
mean safer and more economical products, and more information; for
environmentalists, the preservation of wilderness areas, lower levels of
pollution and conservation of energy; for minorities, the enjoyment of
civil rights, jobs, and so forth. These are specific, tangible outcomes
that, for the most part, can be identified and measured.

To achieve these results, two steps are required: First, new norms
must be established or existing ones revalidated; second, the norms
must somehow be implemented in the field. There are many examples
of laws that produce no change; these laws must (except for symbolic
rewards, which shall be discussed shortly) be regarded as unsuccessful.

In evaluating activities of social-reform groups it is unrealistic to
expect complete "victories" in political efforts. Take, for example, the
Food Stamp program. In dollar terms, the program has expanded enormously over the years, resulting in massive distributions of goods to the
poor. Yet, many potential eligibles, for one reason or another, do not
receive benefits, and there are numerous problems of inequities and
poor administration. What can we say about the "success" of those
who fought for the program? Have they accomplished their goals? The
growth in the program (particularly during an antiwelfare administration) counts as success; the potential eligibles who do not receive food
stamps count as examples of failure.

Social-reform groups do not always seek tangible goods and services. They may be interested in symbolic rewards (see Gusfield, 1963;
Edelman, 1964). The distinction between symbolic and tangible

rewards is subtle, especially since tangible benefits carry with them symbolic rewards as well. The enactment of public programs and changes in laws and administrative rules legitimate aspirations and values, and sometimes redistribute goods and services (Wilson, 1974). But there can be occasions when groups are interested in symbolic rewards only. Symbols may be important in and of themselves. Or, the group may have no hope of implementing the symbolic victory. Finally, the group may think that the symbolic victory will lead to a change in the distribution of goods and services. For example, groups will push for the enactment of a law or court decision, hoping that some further action will follow. The victory will be considered "half a loaf."

In the real world, purely symbolic rewards are rare. There is always some enforcement, or some effect on behavior. Ralph Nader succeeded in getting passed a Highway Safety Act despite the opposition of the automobile industry. If we view Nader's objective as the enforcement of the law, then mere passage was not a victory; in fact, it might have been a defeat if it lulled his supporters into thinking they had won. On the other hand, enforcement of this single piece of legislation may be too narrow a test by which to judge Nader's success. If we view his efforts as part of a long-term, broad campaign to raise the nation's consciousnesss about consumerism and the environment, then lack of enforcement of one piece of legislation is not that crucial. The enactment of legislation—the legitimization of values and aspirations—may be important in the long run (Wilson, 1974). Success or failure is a matter of degree and not based upon the "either–or" concept. In many instances, success or failure is clear; in others it is harder to assess.

Social-reform groups seek changes in the law; yet, the effects of changes in laws on social change are especially difficult to assess. Few laws bring about total compliance, but if change is detected, what is the cause? Sometimes the law sharpens perceptions and acts as an educator or moral persuader. Other times, the law may merely ratify changes that have already occurred in society. Not infrequently, changes in the law bring about unintended changes in society. In general, it is exceedingly difficult to separate the independent effects of legal changes from effects caused by the interaction of legal changes with broader societal factors such as public opinion, the effects of timing, and social and economic conditions. Because of the complexity of this issue, "Few authors have felt secure enough to attempt generalizations about necessary and sufficient conditions for a law to act as an effective agency in changing behavior, or alternatively to generalize about the limits of effective legal action (Ladinsky, 1970, pp. 11)."

On the other hand, many reform groups have sought tangible

benefits, thought that they acquired such benefits through the enactment of laws and regulatory programs, and have wound up with symbolic victories only. As Murray Edelman (1964) has pointed out, the
politics of regulatory reform serves to provide tangible benefits to elites
and symbolic benefits to mass publics, to quiet potential unrest, to
deflect potential demands, and to blur the true allocation of rewards
(see also Alford, 1975, Chap. 1). Edelman quotes Chester Barnard in a
statement that has special meaning for law reformers: "Most laws, executive orders, decisions, etc., are in effect formal notice that all is
well—there is agreement, authority is not questioned (Quoted in
Edelman, 1964, p. 33)." According to Edelman, large, dispersed groups
(the kind that press for reform) are not in a position to evaluate the
situation and thus seize upon the symbolic reassurances that the situation is well in hand.

In addition to evaluating success at obtaining tangible benefits
directly from law-reform activity, it will also be necessary to evaluate
more indirect effects. In many situations, social-reform groups and law
reformers use law-reform activity as only one aspect of a campaign
that includes nonlitigation strategies. Litigation, for example, is used to
remove or lessen threats of criminal prosecutions for leaders or
members who are engaging in direct action. Law reform may also be
used for leverage to increase the bargaining power of the social-reform
group, or for publicity, fund raising, and consciousness-raising. An important benefit claimed by law reformers is that the goals and aspirations of social-reform groups are legitimized by successful litigation.
Legitimacy is one of the criteria that Gamson (1975) uses to measure
success; he defines legitimacy as whether a challenging group is accepted by antagonists as speaking for its constituency. By acceptance,
Gamson means consultation, negotiation, formal recognition, or inclu-
sion in the antagonists' organizational structure. This measure is one of
the stated goals of the new public interest lawyers. They seek to open
up the decision-making process so that the interests of their clients will
not only be heard, but listened to.

In theory, acceptance, or the conferring of legitimacy, is a
reasonable measure of success. However, empirically, it is too minimal.
For example, one of the measures of acceptance that Gamson
uses—consultation—is whether the social-reform group is invited to
testify before a legislative body. Perhaps during the time periods that
he was studying, such an invitation would have been an important conferring of status, but today, one would not attach a great deal of importance to this alone.[30] The more serious objection, though, to this

---

[30] In fact, only slightly more than half of Gamson's groups ever achieved even minimal acceptance. This is clearly not the situation for the groups used in this study.

measure of success is that it fails to come to grips with either Edelman's concerns or the issue of staying power. Consultation, negotiation, and recognition may merely be methods used to assuage social-reform groups and to mask the reality of the actual distribution of values. Also, as we shall see, negotiations are often a favorite tactic to cool dissident groups. There have been many instances where social-reform groups and law reformers have entered into negotiations only to realize that their antagonists have been merely buying time and have not been bargaining in good faith. On the other hand, there have been instances where objectives have been accomplished through bargaining. The point is that access to the decision-making process by itself is not a sufficient indicator of success. Access should make a difference in decision-making outcomes.

Evaluating success in terms of these more indirect effects presents even more problems than attempting to evaluate whether litigation has produced tangible benefits for the social-reform groups. Nevertheless, the use of law-reform activity for these nontraditional purposes is widespread and important, and judgments will have to be made based on what theory and empirical evidence exists.

A third level of evaluation deals with the claim of the law reformers that the law-reform activity of social-reform groups is a strategy to revitalize pluralism by opening up the decision-making processes to groups previously underrepresented. To what extent have social-reform groups gained entry and are they listened to? For those who gain access, are they co-opted, or do they participate as others do in institutionalized pluralism, or do they represent autonomous citizen groups changing basic decision-making structures and outcomes? The theory and case studies will shed light on these questions as well.

A final point about "success": Social-reform groups rarely achieve results in isolation from other events, or by themselves. Wilson emphasizes the limited role that social-reform groups have in effectuating social change. He argues that major new policies of government come about through broad changes in public opinion usually caused by dramatic events (wars, depressions, etc.), extraordinary leadership, or the accumulation of ideas filtered through the media. Changes are also accomplished by political entrepreneurs who engineer a program. Once established, a program gets a client association, and it is very difficult, if not impossible, to abandon the program. Organizations can aid the process of social change by putting ideas on the national agenda, but organizations cannot bring about such change on their own. The mobilization of public opinion and professional resources, publicity, and legitimacy can be important contributors to the work of other agents and factors producing social change or preserving gains previously won. Claims differ in their potential for political mobilization and in their ability to attract allies. Because social-reform groups have to work with other forces in society, the goals and issues that they select have to be in tune with goals and interests of other actors for social change. Social-reform groups and law reformers are only one set of actors in the complex process of social change; their precise role is often impossible to ascertain with any degree of precision.

The difficulty in defining and measuring success, yet the necessity for doing so, requires caution. Success will be discussed in terms of type and degree, bearing in mind that while the primary interest is with lasting change, the discussion, of necessity, is limited to contemporary examples, often still in the midst of campaigns. My goal is to shed light on whether certain combinations of characteristics of the variables will more likely lead to certain kinds of success than other combinations, whether groups interested in achieving certain kinds of results are more likely to do so if they can alter some of the characteristics of the variables.

Up to now I have tried to establish a framework for a systematic analysis of legal activity by social-reform groups. The next four chapters deal with some illustrations. I have selected over 35 case studies from 4 principal areas of law-reform activity—environmental litigation, consumer issues, civil rights, and social welfare, which includes welfare reform, health and mental health, and occupational health and safety issues. Within the principal areas, each case study is designed to illustrate a different type of social-reform legal activity. Thus, the analytic framework can be examined in terms of a broad range of actual law-reform cases. Although the cases have not been selected on the basis of a sample, and are thus not representative in quantifiable terms, those familiar with the law-reform activity of social-reform groups will recognize that the cases are by no means aberrational.[31] Each in itself represents an important type of law-reform action by social-reform groups.

The concluding chapter assesses the validity of the theory in terms of the case examples. That chapter is divided into three parts that parallel the three criteria for evaluating success. The first part addresses the question of under what circumstances can social-reform groups accomplish tangible benefits through law reformers and the legal system. The second will examine the nontraditional uses of the legal system—for example, using the legal system for political leverage, publicity, fund raising, and legitimacy. The chapter then turns to whether the use of law reformers is a viable method of revitalizing

---

[31] For a justification of the case study methodology, see Horowitz (1977, pp. 62–64).

pluralism so that underrepresented groups have a meaningful voice in American political life. What are the prospects for accomplishing access, and do the groups have the staying power to make their voices heard? What are the costs of using law reformers in terms of social change or co-optation? And, finally, there is the issue of organizational maintenance for groups who make it. Does successful law-reform activity by social-reform groups represent a revitalization of pluralism or another variant of institutionalized pluralism? Is it a step toward democratizing social structure or toward corporatism?

2

Environmental Litigation

Concern for the preservation of natural resources and the environment has had a long history in this country, but for the purposes of this analysis, we begin in the early 1960s when various social-reform groups began attacking government agencies for failure to take account of environmental considerations in approving projects. One of the most significant early battles centered on the efforts of Consolidated Edison of New York to build the Storm King pumped storage facility on the Hudson River. The utility applied to the Federal Power Commission for the necessary permits and licenses, which were granted routinely. However, an environmental group contested that decision, and in one of the first important environmental cases, *Scenic Hudson Preservation Commission* v. *Federal Power Commission* (1965),[1] the court held that the agency must take into account environmental and aesthetic considerations in decisions on power plant sites. To implement this principle, the agency must grant those who have a special interest in these matters (i.e., the environmental groups) an opportunity to be heard.[2]

[1] 354 F.2d 608(2d. Cir. 1965), *cert. denied.* 384 U.S. 941 (1966).
[2] Much has been written about this particular environmental controversy. For an especially illuminating account, see Trubek (1978).

In that case, the court did not say which way the agency must decide on the merits; as long as the agency considered all points of view fairly, the agency was free to abide by its original position. The conservation group, of course, hoped ultimately to prevail on the merits, but in the meantime it won an important principle. They viewed the Federal Power Commission (and similar agencies) as "captives" of the industry that they were supposed to regulate. Litigation was necessary to open up the decision-making process and to gain a hearing for the environmentalist or consumer point of view. Regulatory agencies would then be more likely to reach decisions that reflected environment or consumer interests if those interests could be heard.

The modern environmental movement started in the years immediately following the *Scenic Hudson* decision.[3] The Environmental Defense Fund was organized in 1967 and began attacking the use of the pesticide DDT. That litigation was used to launch a nationwide campaign that was able to attract large sums of money through contributions, membership drives, and from foundations. Law-reform organizations devoted to environmental causes grew. For example, the Sierra Club organized the Sierra Club Legal Defense Fund, patterned after the NAACP–LDF, with a central staff office coordinating and lending technical assistance to the legal activities of the various Sierra Club chapters throughout the country. In 1970, a group of lawyers and environmental scientists who had been engaged in the *Scenic Hudson* litigation (which was to continue for many more years) formed the Natural Resources Defense Counsel (NRDC). Many other law-reform organizations pursued several different causes, but included environmental issues as major areas of concern.

During this period, the late 1960s, there was also ferment in the Congress. Several congressional hearings and reports expressed concern about the way that federal agencies handled natural resources and the environment. The impact of the federal government on the environment was significant, but individual agencies were either unconcerned about the environment or were relatively insensitive to broader environmental concerns. What emerged from Congress's concern was the National Environmental Policy Act of 1969 (NEPA).

Breathing Life into NEPA

There are three parts to NEPA: (a.) the establishment of the Council on Environmental Quality (CEQ); (b.) a statement of national en-

---

[3] Literature on the growth of the modern environmental movement is vast. See, generally, Liroff (1976) and Anderson (1973). My account is based largely on Trubek (1978).

vironmental policy; and (c.) the "action-forcing mechanism," which was a directive to all federal agencies to add environmental concerns to their other statutory mandates. The model for the CEQ was the Council of Economic Advisors established by the Full Employment Act of 1946, which, over the years, collected basic economic data and established economic criteria to evaluate government activity. There was a conflict, however, about the structure and functions of the CEQ. The Nixon administration wanted a small advisory office in the Executive Office whereas key legislators wanted an agency with sufficient stature and staff to monitor federal activity and general environmental matters (Dreyfus and Ingram, 1976).

The National Environmental Policy Act announced the policy of the federal government to create and maintain conditions of "productive harmony" between man and nature by assuring "safe, healthful, productive and aesthetically and culturally pleasing surroundings."[4] To back up this pledge, the act required that all major federal projects significantly affecting the environment be accompanied by a statement detailing the environmental impact of the proposed action. The requirement for an environmental impact statement (EIS) reflected the general belief by Congress that the decision-making processes of the federal government were not adequately taking into account environmental considerations.

A great many questions were left unanswered by the impact-statement requirement. Did the requirement apply to all federal agencies? Some agencies that dealt with natural resources (for example, the Soil Conservation Service) thought that they already adequately considered environmental matters and that NEPA did not require any changes in procedures (Andrews, 1976). How detailed and specific were the statements to be? Did the licensing or granting agency have to prepare the statement, or could it rely on the developer? What use was the agency supposed to make of the environmental information? None of these questions were answered by the legislative history.[5] To some extent, some of the ambiguities were intended to be resolved by the CEQ, but in its early years, that agency took a low profile. It had limited powers and there were conflicts both within and outside the agency as to its role.

Given an ambiguous statute, a hesitant and somewhat impotent agency, and a hostile administration, one would have predicted that NEPA would have quickly faded from the political consciousness and

---

[4] 42 U.S.C. §4331(a), (6), (2), (3), (1970), Pub. L. No. 91–190, Tit. I, §101 (January 1, 1970) 83 Stat. 852.

[5] See Dreyfus and Ingram (1976) for an inside view of the legislative history of NEPA.

become a dead letter. Instead, it was transformed into a highly visible, active force causing, if not ultimately great change, at least great controversy and anguish among government agencies and developers. What breathed life into NEPA was the explosion of the environmental movement and the emergence of vigorous environmental law reformers litigating a great many successful NEPA cases, which, in turn, bolstered and encouraged a more active role of the CEQ and the Environmental Protection Agency (Wickelman, 1976; Dreyfus and Ingram, 1976).

Earth Day was celebrated four months after the passage of NEPA, and that event signaled the emergence of the environmental movement as a mass political force. As noted by James Q. Wilson, ambitious legislators were quick to see the appeal of environmental concerns. President Nixon, once indifferent, if not hostile, embraced NEPA and appointed conservationists to the CEQ (Dreyfus and Ingram, 1976, p. 257). But it was the environmental lawyers and sympathetic courts that filled the holes in NEPA and added teeth to the vague language. Literally hundreds of lawsuits were brought testing the application of NEPA to various federal agencies and projects. Through a body of case law, the courts began to demand strict enforcement of the EIS requirement. .At first, many agencies claimed that NEPA did not apply to their actions; others did not take the act seriously and filed superficial impact statements. These agencies ran into trouble, and the environmentalists won many cases in court (Trubek, 1978). Highways, urban renewal projects, and various projects that affected wilderness areas and conservation (e.g., dams, roads, exploitation of mineral and lumber rights) were stopped for failure to comply with NEPA. One of the most famous early cases involved the proposed construction of the Trans-Alaskan Pipeline, which was halted for failure to file a proper impact statement. These decisions came as shocks to government and business. Environmental groups and their lawyers were using litigation apparently to great advantage.

Moreover, it is claimed that there were spillover effects from these court victories. Other agencies, not involved in litigation, began to respond on their own either because they were sympathetic to environmental considerations or because they wanted to avoid lawsuits (Wickelman, 1976).[6] Agency response to NEPA was encouraged by emerging changes in the CEQ. Armed with oversight powers granted by an Executive Order, CEQ began to issue more elaborate guidelines for agency implementation of NEPA, which closely followed the sympathetic judicial interpretation of the NEPA requirements. Thus,

---

[6] In a study, the United States Council on Environmental Quality (1976) concluded that court action contributed toward agencies taking NEPA seriously.

scholars have argued that because the guidelines drew their content and strength from the cases and applied to a larger number of federal agencies, court decisions had a great impact beyond merely affecting the litigating parties.[7]

In sum, while there is debate over the ultimate effects of NEPA (a discussion of which I will take up shortly) there is general agreement that the environmental groups and their lawyers and the courts were the key actors in activating NEPA. The courts in hundreds of cases gave expansive interpretations to the application of the statute, ordered agencies to produce more environmental information about their projects, as well as alternatives, and called for the integration of environmental considerations into specific decisions. The courts did this during the time when the CEQ, as well as the Environmental Protection Agency, were unwilling to press for full enforcement, and Congress was only willing to play a limited oversight role (Trubek, 1978, p. 46).

The initial judicial decisions established that NEPA applied to federal agencies and that the agencies had to prepare adequate environmental impact statements. But did judicial review stop there, or would the courts review the "substance" of the agency decision, that is, whether appropriate weight was given to environmental considerations. There was a hint in some of the early cases that the reviewing courts would inquire into the merits of the decision, and for a time, environmental groups vigorously pressed this view. Ultimately, however, the courts shrank back from getting so closely involved in agency decision making. If an agency produced an adequate impact statement demonstrating that it had touched all of the bases, then the court would, in effect, assume that it acted in good faith in weighing environmental considerations and would allow the project to proceed (Trubek, 1977). In taking this limited approach, the appellate courts were following longstanding traditions in which substantive decisions have been delegated by the Congress to the agencies and not the reviewing courts.[8]

The social-reform groups and the law reformers were successful in changing agency procedure with regard to NEPA, but was this all there was to show for the campaigns and the litigation? It is clear that the environmentalists wanted more; they wanted to stop, or significantly

[7] See, for example, Wickelman (1976, pp. 274–279). In contrast, see Cortner (1976) who concedes that the courts were very aggressive in interpreting NEPA but that CEQ remained ineffective and other agencies also defaulted in their NEPA obligations.

[8] See Trubek and Gillen (1978, ch. 8), Cortner (1976, p. 332), and Sive (1977). Sive says courts are returning to the traditional role because agencies have become more responsive to environmental concerns. See also Stewart (1977) for an argument on how the reviewing court can depart from the traditional role in limited circumstances.

modify, water resources development projects, pipelines, power plants, highways, dams, and reservoirs. Were they able to do this? This is a very difficult question to answer both conceptually and empirically, and to date, neither effort has been made in any kind of systematic fashion.[9] The Corps of Engineers, for example, has issued hundreds of impact statements, and has claimed that a great many projects have either been modified or dropped for environmental reasons; yet, it is claimed that only 6% of Corps projects were changed substantively.[10] Others claim that NEPA has been turned into a sterile bureaucratic exercise. This, too, is disputed by those who argue that the EIS requirement has resulted in subtle but significant changes in many government agencies. Offices have been created, staff has been hired, and gradually and imperceptibly improved methods of environmental data-gathering have resulted in changes in administrative decision making (Wickelman, 1976). Partisans and detractors can point to contradictory examples. There has not been a single instance where a nuclear license application has been denied on environmental or safety grounds; but construction has been modified.[11] The Environmental Defense Fund was forced to abandon as fruitless a 5-year litigation campaign against the Corps of Engineers, the Soil Conservation Service, and the Bureau of Reclamation;[12] however, these agencies claim that many projects have been modified or abandoned for environmental considerations.

The Long-Term Complex Case

Environmental law-reform activity has been varied and complex. While there has been no systematic attempt to evaluate the efforts of environmentalists and law reformers, the theory of law-reform activity by social-reform groups provides a framework for such an analysis.

In discussing examples of specific environmental litigation, it is important to keep in mind the basic nature of environmental conflict and the relative position of the parties. In most environmental controversies, the substantive dispute is extraordinarily complex. Not only are there questions of scientific and technical intricacy, but, in addition, there is usually a lack of complete information on the questions involved. There are substantial but often indeterminate risks for the

---

[9] For a recent review of empirical studies of environmental litigation see DiMento (1977).

[10] Compare Wickelman (1976) and Liroff (1976, p. 211) with Andrews (1976, p. 313) and Cortner (1976, pp. 334–335).

[11] See Davis (1976). In 1978, President Carter halted construction of the Clinch River fast breeder reactor project. This was not the direct result of any environmental litigation, but was probably affected by the environmental movement.

[12] The history of this effort is the subject of Trubek and Gillen (1978).

future; there are usually numerous parties involved in the dispute; there may be a number of different outcomes or choices that can be made; there may be more than one decision-making authority; and there will be variations in the distribution of benefits and costs depending on which decisions are made.[13] In most environmental litigation, the odds are particularly weighted against social-reform groups. The economic and political stakes are usually substantial; the projects themselves often involve several millions of dollars in direct costs, and local communities and their political leaders press for what they believe to be increases in employment and tax revenues. The developers and the government agencies enter these disputes with powerful technical and financial resources and strong selective incentives to win. The social-reform groups, on the other hand, like the Sierra Club, the Wilderness Society, and the Friends of the Earth, are purposive organizations pursuing collective goods. Often they have to rely on volunteers for their scientific and technical help. Members who are engineers and scientists donate a few evenings a week, or a day or two on a weekend. In short, while environmental groups have large memberships and have attracted much publicity and political support, the disparity between their resources and those of their adversaries is great.[14]

The first example that will be used is the Trans-Alaskan Pipeline (TAP) dispute. The TAP group applied for and was routinely granted a license to construct the pipeline. In a classic early NEPA suit, the plaintiff environmental organization (the Wilderness Society), without much difficulty, was able to obtain a temporary injunction halting construction completely until a more adequate environmental impact statement was drafted. After a protracted struggle, the Department of the Interior and the industry then took NEPA seriously and drafted a comprehensive impact statement. Many design features of the pipeline were altered to lessen environmental damage and risks. There was further litigation but construction was finally authorized by Congress. The new construction plans were more sound from an environmental standpoint than were the original plans. For example, the initial proposal for the pipeline called for the entire line to be buried underground regardless of permafrost conditions. This would have posed serious stress problems because of differential settlement during thaws.[15] Not only was

---

[13] See Trubek (1977) for an elaboration of the characteristics of complex environmental disputes.

[14] See United States Senate (1977, pp. 7–22) for a comparison of resources between citizen groups and industry in contests before selected federal regulatory agencies.

[15] In March 1973, Atlantic Richfield's president Bradshaw, stated, "Early in the game, environmentalists blocked us for very good reasons indeed. I think, early in the game, we did not know how to make an environmentally safe line. They helped us. We learned a great deal from them [Zemansky, 1976, p. 12]."

the design of the pipeline changed, but the oil companies also agreed to a series of stipulations designed to minimize environmental damage. The stipulations covered construction and long-term maintenance that might cause environmental degradation. In addition to specific environmental provisions, it was clearly established that the environmental protection laws of the United States and Alaska were to apply.[16] The Alyeska Pipeline Service Company, representing the oil companies, and all of the subcontractors, had the responsibility for abiding by the stipulations and instituting an effective quality-control system. Primary responsibility for federal supervision rested with the Department of Interior and its newly created Alaska Pipeline Office (APO). The State of Alaska Department of Environmental Conservation also had a major supervisory responsibility. Other federal agencies also played an enforcement role, for example, the EPA and the United States Geological Survey. The basic administrative scheme was designed to ensure compliance. Specific work projects could not proceed without the issuance of specific permits that would only be granted after the public agencies were satisfied that the applicable environmental protection stipulations would be met.

At least on paper the environmentalists had a substantial impact on the proceedings. Even though some of the groups had hoped that the pipeline would not be built, it was clear that their efforts had resulted in the design of a much safer pipeline, from an environmental standpoint, and the creation of enforcement machinery. But whether this victory proved hollow depended on how the construction proceeded and whether the administrative officials carried out their responsibilities. The environmental impact statement, including the stipulations, was only the first step in achieving social change.

The agreements were violated from the very beginning and continued to be throughout construction.[17] Aside from conflicts over cost, the most important conflict was between the stated need for rapid construction and quality control. Even during the first year of construction, major deficiencies appeared in the administrative machinery. Construction often proceeded without prior approval and in violation of

---

[16] Zemansky (1976, Appendix A) summarizes the stipulations.

[17] The discussion of the implementation is based on Zemansky (1976), which appears to be the most authoritative, documented report available. It was prepared by environmentalists but supported by independent sources. (For example telephone interview with Michael F. Barrett, Jr., counsel, House Subcommittee on Energy and Power, May 1977). The General Accounting Office report (1976), while not as detailed as Zemansky, generally reaches the same conclusions, particularly with regard to the lack of soil erosion control, occurrence of oil spills, and the failure to meet standards for sewage treatment, which the GAO considers to be the most serious environmental problems. There is, of course, another side of the story and reports will continue to be made public that qualify or refute the assertions made in text. For an overview, see Myers (1975).

the environmental stipulations. The violations covered all aspects of pipeline construction. There were violations of ambient air quality standards and an almost total lack of measurement of emissions. Pesticide regulation was haphazard at best, and numerous uses of unauthorized pesticides occurred. Incinerators were faulty and the open burning of trash, garbage, and solid wastes continued in direct violation of the regulations. There was extensive water degradation primarily due to silt caused by construction (there were 900 stream crossings), erosion, improper pumping, and the introduction of wastewater and oil spills. Regulations dealing with solid waste disposal were not complied with; several camps illegally used the most convenient sites. The disposal of wastewater was a particularly persistent problem; either regulations were ignored or equipment broke down causing inadequate sewage treatment and the dumping of raw sewage and wastewater directly on the tundra. The outstanding environmental failure concerned soil erosion: Plans were not approved before construction, which often resulted in inadequate measures, drainage was faulty, the number and treatment of cuts were inadequate, and revegetation did not proceed as proposed. Inadequate measures were taken to protect fish and wildlife, especially passage through stream crossings and under the pipeline itself. Many of the crossings did not meet specifications. The developers were supposed to report all oil spills and ensure prompt cleaning but the reporting system was almost totally ignored and clean-up was sporadic. Most of the major sensational oil spills were either discovered by accident or were too large not to be noticed.

Why was there such a breakdown in enforcement? The developers employed an inadequate quality-control system and were far more concerned with the integrity of the pipeline itself than adherence to the environmental stipulations (Zemansky, 1976, p. 16a). The developers quickly learned how to manipulate the system. A chief tactic was to delay requests for permits until the last minute, then plead great urgency, and promise to provide complete evidence of compliance with environmental protection stipulations at a later date. This pressured lower-level government officials who would agree "this one time only" on the promise of the company to get its plans in earlier next time.

The developers also had control over access to information. They filed the reports of compliance, which the public agencies either had to accept or had to verify on their own. Federal and state inspection was inadequate. A General Accounting Office report estimated that two-thirds of the construction activity was not seen by federal monitors; in one spot check, there was an 18% noncompliance rate with the environmental stipulations (Zemansky, 1976, pp. 14–15). Furthermore, many defects remained uncorrected even after they were reported. The issue of poor quality control intensified when a large number of faulty welds was discovered and it was learned that records had been falsified. But even this showed that attention was mostly concerned with the integrity of the pipeline's construction rather than with environmental concerns.[18]

In addition to the antienvironmental position of the developers, which could be anticipated, the federal agencies also proved to be inadequate. The criticism of the General Accounting Office has already been noted. The Department of Interior's Alaska Pipeline Office (APO) was headed by a retired Corps of Engineers officer who took a prodevelopment position. The APO approved an inadequate quality-control plan and never effectively supervised its implementation (Zemansky, 1976, p. 31). The monitoring system developed by APO was ineffective, and according to the counsel for the House Oversight Committee, government inspectors developed a community of interests with the developers. Environmental considerations were invariably subordinated to engineering considerations; the attitude of the government inspectors was that "we have to get this pipeline built."[19] There were allegations of bribery and malfeasance on the part of the federal inspectors. In the case of the faulty welding and the weld inspections, the Department of the Interior had to override the APO and take matters into its own hands (Zemansky, 1976, p. 16). APO was hostile to the environmental organizations that tried to monitor the environmental stipulations and refused them access to reports and other information, forcing the organizations to file Freedom of Information requests and lawsuits. The EPA wavered in its attitude toward the environmental organizations. Sometimes it honored requests, and at other times it refused. The Alaska Department of Environmental Conservation had a broad range of responsibilities but failed to establish an independent monitoring team. State legislation required the developers to fund the monitoring positions, but they stalled and for months no positions were filled. Finally only two out of more than 20 positions were filled, but these two inspectors left during the early phases of construction.

What was the enforcement role of the social-reform groups and the law reformers? After the environmentalists lost in Congress, the principal law reformers turned to other matters and left supervision to the social-reform groups. Two attempts were made, and both failed. An

---

[18] See *Energy Report* (1976, p. 1080), particularly the developer's admission concerning the falsification of records. See also United States Congress (1976).

[19] Telephone interview with Michael F. Barret, Jr., May 1977.

Arctic Environmental Council was formed, which conducted site visits once a year, but this group was funded and hosted by the developers, and had difficulty obtaining information and publishing its reports. The reports, when published, were short, bland, and undocumented.[20] Friends of the Earth, the Wilderness Society, the Fairbanks Environmental Center, and the Alaska Center for the Environment sought to create their own independent monitoring team, but these organizations were severely hampered by lack of money. They were unsuccessful in raising funds from foundations and lacked sufficient resources (Zemansky, 1976, pp. 79–81).[21] And, they were hamstrung by the developers and the government agencies. The developers refused on-site access to the environmentalists without orders from the APO, which refused to issue them. The group did manage one flight over the pipeline, financed out of personal resources. In addition, as previously noted, the government agencies, and particularly the APO, refused to turn over documents to the environmentalists, forcing them to file suit under the Freedom of Information Act. By their own admission, the social-reform groups failed to ensure compliance with the environmental stipulations.

How does the theory apply to this environmental dispute? In the pipeline situation, the *characteristics of the social-reform groups* did not favor successful action. The groups were large with either a mass or a nonexistent membership. Presumably, as with some environmental matters, incentives could be considered selective because benefits would be enjoyed only by an elite few. This would be true, for example, of certain parts of the Alaskan wilderness. But generally speaking, environmental amenities are collective goods and the small amount of selective goods would not be sufficient to overcome the free-rider problem. Environmental groups are largely purposive organizations. The leaders would not be able to furnish the resources to provide the collective goods for their members and the society at large.

The *distribution of costs and benefits* did not favor successful activity by social-reform groups. The benefits, environmental amenities, were distributed, and the costs were concentrated on the oil companies and contractors. In environmental suits against utilities or industries that have monopoly-like characteristics, environmentally imposed costs will eventually be passed on to the consumer, and thus, costs will

[20] Three reports have been published dated October 1974, April 1976, and July 1976. The contrast between those reports and the Zemansky report is striking. For example, the third and final report contains only 12 pages of observations without any supporting data.

[21] See also Appleton (1974): "In fact, the environmental movement has been unable to provide any sort of effective monitoring of construction activity and is currently without the resources to do so [p. 6]."

be distributed. However, in the short run, the costs are concentrated on the industry. Development is delayed, and there are transaction costs in the mechanics of obtaining price increases and passing them along. There are also the bureaucratic or internal costs to the organizations, which perceive themselves as being forced to do something that they disagree with. They disagree with the value positions of their opponents, and they regard the attacks as infringements on management judgment. These, too, are costs that are concentrated.

The *bureaucratic contingency* is not favorable to successful action. Although an environmental impact statement is made at the top and specifies how development is to proceed, these long-term construction plans are technically complex and require careful monitoring at the field level. In addition to technical complexity and longevity, decisions are made at lower levels of the bureaucracy. Although every step in the construction plan is specified, there can be waivers. For example, the caribou crossings were supposed to be 10 feet high. Could a particular crossing be 8 feet, or could the construction pad be excavated 2 feet if the pipe clearance were only 8 feet? Could the diameter of a culvert be reduced? Could the grade of a particular cut be modified? Could a waste-disposal system be relocated? These discretionary decisions came up all the time, and usually had to be made on the basis of incomplete information while the developers pressed for a speedy decision.

The problem with the *judicial remedies* sought was the court's reluctance to substitute its judgment for that of the agency on the substantive issue. Courts can repeatedly send back an environmental impact statement because it does not pay enough attention to certain points of view. However, it will be the rare court, indeed, that will decide the substantive issue. These are matters the law has handed over to agency discretion. In the Trans-Alaskan Pipeline situation, the court clearly would not get involved in deciding construction and environmental decisions. Rather, the most it did was to see if there was a sensible administrative enforcement system on paper.

The fact that in most situations social-reform groups ultimately will find themselves returning to agencies for these discretionary long-term decisions means that the administrative or bureaucratic contingencies become critical. As this example showed, a recalcitrant agency is hard to cope with; if the courts are only willing to grant an ineffective remedy, the odds for reform groups' success don't improve. Sometimes delay is itself a great victory. Procedural victories and the ability to return to court repeatedly may give reform groups leverage, and may even kill a project altogether. This leverage was present in the

Trans-Alaskan Pipeline litigation and produced a better impact state-ment. But for procedural tactics to have much effect, courts have to order preliminary injunctions, and they are not always willing to do this.

Characteristics of the law reformers did not favor successful ac-tion. There were two great weaknesses in the Trans-Alaskan Pipeline case. The case ultimately went to Congress where on a vice-presidential tie-breaking vote, the oil companies won. The first weakness was that when the case entered the political arena, the law reformers lacked suf-ficient political resources because they are prohibited from lobbying. This is an important, but not a crucial, limitation. The second weakness was that the law reformers lacked the technical, profes-sional, and financial resources to follow-up and see that the impact statement was being implemented by the oil companies. A continuous input of technical resources was needed over a long period of time. The principal law reformers did not stay with the case during the monitor-ing phase. They may have considered monitoring hopeless or inconsis-tent with their organizational needs. After the litigation was over, which was the phase that best fit the training and professional needs and orientations of the law reformers, the grubby, low-visibility, but crucially important enforcement phase, was left to underfinanced social-reform groups.

Another example similar to the Trans-Alaskan Pipeline case con-cerns maritime pollution caused by oil tankers. On behalf of three en-vironmental organizations, a public interest law firm filed suit to en-join the Secretary of Commerce and the Maritime Subsidy Board from awarding construction subsidies for oil tankers; petitioners charged failure to comply with NEPA. Shipyards, ship purchasers, shipbuilding and operating unions, and the shipbuilders' trade association in-tervened.

A settlement was quickly reached, which stipulated that the government would provide a comprehensive environmental impact statement that would cover the following matters: the tanker construc-tion program as a whole, tankers under construction, present and future pollution abatement specifications, oil pollution effects of tankers, alternatives to the tanker construction program, alternative mixes of oil-carrying vessels and their relative environmental effects, alternative design and equipment requirements for oil-carrying vessels, such as double bottoms and fully segregated ballast systems, alter-native energy strategies such as reducing the demand for oil, and the environmental impact of the deep water port development necessary to accommodate supertankers.

The settlement was signed, and at that time was considered an important victory for the environmentalists. The government seemed genuinely cooperative. The immediate problem, though, was whether the environmentalists could take advantage of the opportunity they had won. There were enormous financial stakes involved. Although the industry had marshalled its experts, the environmental groups had a very difficult time. They needed experts willing to devote substantial blocks of time on short notice, if the groups were going to have any sort of effect on the impact statement. Furthermore, as with the pipeline case, the impact statement would function as a kind of blueprint for construction of future vessels and ports. There would always be changes in construction plans as technical and economic contingencies materialized. Changes to meet environmental considerations would be costly; as construction proceeded, the industry would seek modifications of the original impact statement. The environmentalists would have to be ready to consider proposed construction changes from their perspective and be prepared to press their point of view with the government agency. Otherwise, in time, the agency would again fall captive to the industry, which would be the agency's primary source of information.

In fact, the worst fears of the environmentalists proved true. The agency responsible for the tanker regulations, the Coast Guard, never adopted the environmental perspective. The agency kept delaying promulgation of regulations despite repeated pressure from the groups. After the filing of a lawsuit, the Coast Guard, without public notice, formed an advisory committee composed of three government members and eight members associated with the oil and shipping industry; there were no environmental or consumer representatives. The final impact statement and regulations, not unexpectedly, were a substantial retreat from the earlier agreement. The regulations failed to deal with several important issues, such as steps to improve vessel maneuvering and stopping ability, to provide for adequate crew training and qualification, and to implement various construction changes, and ordered only minor changes in other areas.[22] Another lawsuit was filed challenging the final impact statement and regulations.

As of early 1978, the maritime tanker pollution controversy was in flux. The law reformers had always considered going to court as the least desirable alternative; the most the court would do would be to order the production of an impact statement or the issuance of regula-

---

[22] *Natural Resources Defense Counsel* v. *Coleman*, United States District Court for the District of Columbia, Civil Action No. 76–0181, Complaint for Declaratory Judgement, Feb. 2, 1976.

tions; it would not disturb the discretionary powers of the agency. The social-reform groups and the lawyers would continually have to fight the bureaucracy, and they knew that ultimately when the agency had finally learned to touch all of the procedural bases, it would prevail on the substance, because the reviewing court would not substitute its judgment on matters entrusted to agency discretion.

The environmentalists had pinned their hopes on the negotiated settlement, and when that looked unlikely, they tried publicity and lobbying. It may be, however, that external events will change the situation. A change in the market has halted tanker construction, so that part of the controversy is moot for the present, and the recent oil spills due to faulty tankers may have so aroused public and political opinion that the Coast Guard will be forced to issue improved regulations somewhat closer to the environmental position.

If, as a result of presidential and congressional pressure, laws governing the marine transportation of oil are strengthened, the environmentalists and the law reformers can claim some of the credit; at the minimum, they worked hard at creating a favorable media and enlisting the support of other government agencies (for example, CEQ, EPA). On the other hand, it looked like all of these efforts had been in vain until oil spills on the East Coast occurred and the political climate changed. Had these events not happened, it is probable that the environmentalist effort would have failed.

In these two examples, the Trans-Alaskan Pipeline and the tanker regulation, all of the characteristics of the variables were unfavorable to successful law-reform activity by social-reform groups. The availability of the subsidized lawyers allowed the groups to overcome the free-rider problem, but the groups still lacked the resources to modify the industry and government activity.

Can Environmentalists Win?

Although these two cases are representative of the difficulties that social-reform groups face in environmental litigation, there are important examples where the characteristics of the variables have been changed and law-reform activity by social-reform groups has been successful.

In the Trans-Alaskan Pipeline case, the social-reform groups initially tried to stop the pipeline altogether; had they been successful, then, of course, bureaucratic discretion or the limitations of judicial

remedies would not have mattered. Courts can order prohibitory injunctions without resort to administrative agencies, and such orders
are relatively easy to monitor. As it turned out, the conservation groups
were not able to stop the pipeline, and thus confronted administrative
discretion and severe monitoring problems. Sometimes, however, environmentalists are successful in stopping projects. In 1975, the group
that was planning to construct a $3.5 billion power plant at
Kaiparowits, Utah announced cancellation of the project.[23] The project, in the planning and negotiation stages since 1963, was bitterly
opposed from the start by the Sierra Club and the Environmental
Defense Fund. As with the pipeline, enormous stakes were involved. In
addition to the cost of the project, large economic benefits were to
accrue to the area—a permanent community of 15,000 residents, a
payroll for the county of $100 million a year, eventual tax revenues of
$28 million a year. Officials of the group said that the cancellation was
due to delays in the regulatory process, pending litigation, anticipation
of more litigation, and federal and state (California) opposition. There
were probably other reasons as well—there was a drop-off in the
growth of electricity consumption, construction costs had increased,
there were difficulties in raising capital. But, as noted in Chapter 1, it is
not expected that social-reform groups and law reformers can bring
about major social change on their own. In this controversy, they were
key opponents of the project, even though they also had important
allies in government.

The Kaiparowits power plant example illustrates that a particular
kind of result—cancellation—avoids the difficult problems of staying
power through monitoring and follow-up. The advantages of cancellation for the social-reform groups are, of course, obvious. Substantive
goals are achieved and unfavorable characteristics are avoided. But
cancellations are relatively rare. By the time the environmental groups
lock horns with an agency or a developer over a large scale project,
that project has usually been in the planning stage for many years, and
the agency and the developer are fully committed. For example, in the
area of nuclear power, by the time the hearing is convened on the
license application, the agency has already resolved the safety and environmental issues. It is then up to the social-reform group to refute
that judgment and this is unlikely to occur. The group must hire
lawyers and scientific experts for a battle that can last years; it is
estimated that an effective opposition to a nuclear power plant can require expenditures of well over $100,000. And what are the chances of
success? As one scholar (Davis, 1976) put it:

[23] For the story of this episode, see *The New York Times* (1976).

> In every proceeding, the weight of influence, scientific expertise, money, and decisionmaking power lies with the utility and the agency. . . . [I]nsofar as this author knows, the [agencies] have never declined to license a project, nor has a court of last resort ever reversed an agency decision that a permit or license for a nuclear plant should be issued [pp. 650–651].

Even though cancellation may be difficult, similar strategic advantages can be achieved through major modifications that do not require extensive field-level discretion. In the *Scenic Hudson* case, the crucial decision was about what kind of cooling system would be employed: the open-cycle system, which is cheaper and was favored by the utility, or the closed-cycle system, which is more costly and was favored by the environmentalists. Significant stakes were involved; the struggle is already more than 10-years old, but the decision is essentially a one-time decision. In this case, the environmentalists appear to have prevailed (again, not without significant help) and, if the decision sticks, it will not involve serious discretionary or monitoring issues.[24]

Another example is the Calvert Cliffs Park case.[25] In that case, Columbia Liquid Gas Company purchased land on Chesapeake Bay that had been designated, but not yet purchased by the state of Maryland, as an addition to the Calvert Cliffs State Park. Columbia obtained a license from the FPC to build a mile-long pier for unloading liquefied natural gas from tankers and a plant to regasify it for pipeline transport. After threats of litigation by environmental groups, Columbia and other participants in the transaction agreed to substitute a more expensive tunnel for the obtrusive pier, move its plant back away from the shoreline and a fresh-water marsh, and dedicate a large part of its site to the state in the form of scenic easements and parkland. In sum, the adverse effects of this facility upon the adjacent park and shoreline were drastically reduced. Calvert Cliffs stands in sharp contrast to the Trans-Alaskan Pipeline. The Calvert Cliffs case was technically complex, but it was not long and drawn out. Essentially, there was to be one crucial decision: a tunnel for a pier, a different site, and the dedication of part of the site.

There are, of course, many environmental problems that will not lend themselves to one-time decisions made at the top. Instead, continuous field-level decisions have to be made to enforce standards or rules. Pollution abatement measures fall into this category. Enforcement officers have the responsibility to see that potential polluters are

[24] The agency finally decided on the closed-cycle cooling system but Consolidated Edison has until 1980 to complete the project and the option to introduce new data at any time. See Trubek (1978).

[25] Discussion of this case is based on information supplied to the author by the Sierra Club Legal Defense Fund.

not violating the law, and this enforcement machinery has to be monitored.

It will not be argued again why one cannot assume the faithful enforcement of laws of this type. The task of monitoring widespread regulatory enforcement is one of the most serious facing social-reform groups not only in the environmental field, but in all of the other areas that they work in, such as consumer protection, civil rights, employment, health and welfare. As discussed in Chapter 1, all too often the war is really lost in the stage after the rules are changed, where the group can no longer sustain its influence when enforcement problems take over.

One method of considerably easing (although not solving) the enforcement problem is the use of quantified standards of measurement. Theoretically, this allows for simplified statistical measures of performance as opposed to examining individual discretionary decisions. An example of quantified performance standards may be found in the regulation of nontransportation noise which is produced from a wide variety of sources, such as factories, foundries, dogs, and children, to name a few.[26] The Federal Noise Control Act vests extensive jurisdiction with the EPA, but most regulation dealing with nontransportation noise has been reserved for state and local governments. Under most jurisdictions, such noise is regulated by civil and criminal laws of nuisance, disorderly conduct, and disturbing the peace, or by local zoning laws. Most of the law is municipal although there is state regulation. Under the nuisance, disorderly conduct or disturbing the peace statutes, a person or a group is affected by noise and complains to the government either by filing a civil complaint or requesting the police or prosecutors to take action. If it is a criminal matter, the police will usually give a warning and, even if not heeded, may still not proceed; it depends upon their own law enforcement priorities. The same discretionary decision would be made by the prosecutor.

Whichever route is taken, the case is decided by a court that will balance the extent and nature of the harm caused by the noise against the effects of stopping or abating the noise. The economic or social utility of the defendant's activity, who was there first, as well as other factors, will be considered. Since the defendant would be liable only if the conduct is "unreasonable" or "unnecessary," the court, in weighing these factors, would be making a highly discretionary decision. Furthermore, even if the conduct was found unreasonable or unnecessary, the court might still not grant an injunction; this, too, is a discretionary decision. Although empirical evidence is hard to come by, the consen-

[26] The discussion of nontransportation noise regulation is based on Findley and Plager (1974).

sus is that these noise control statutes are rarely invoked. It is obvious that under traditional civil or criminal law, no environmental group could monitor the enforcement of nontransportation noise statutes in any sizable jurisdiction.

In recognition of the problems of enforcement, a few states have set up detailed statutes or administrative regulations specifying objective performance criteria. The rules are complicated; they define levels of noise, classify types of property and space in which different levels will be permitted, specify measuring distances and time periods, and provide exceptions. Nevertheless, the technology has been developed sufficiently so that specific criteria can be used and measured inexpensively in terms of expertise and equipment. Although these statutes and regulations are relatively new, it would seem that enforcement monitoring problems are greatly lessened. There is little room for discretion; either the noise source has exceeded the specified limits or it has not, and if it has, then the remedy is clear. Discretion is at a minimum.

The approach taken by these few nontransportation noise statutes should greatly ease problems of enforcement. This is one reason polluters stoutly resist such efforts to create simplified enforcement mechanisms. The history of the Clean Air Act provides a useful example. As with noise, air pollution can be defined in general or specific terms and precise performance standards can be imposed at sources of emission (for example, coal-burning stacks) or specific pollution-control alterations can be imposed for particular sources. Supporters of Clean Air legislation and the EPA have been locked in a protracted battle with industry over efforts to implement clear-cut performance standards. The industry has sought to maintain discretionary individualized standards knowing full well its advantages when field-level enforcement is discretionary.[27]

Sometimes social-reform groups do not have to fight alone. In the *Scenic Hudson* case, very early in the proceeding, the Atomic Energy Commission (AEC) staff, after extensive study, adopted the same position as the environmental groups. As noted the factual issues were exceedingly complex; the administrative trial consumed 25 full days of hearings lasting over 9 months and producing 20,000 pages of expert testimony. However, most of the testimony on the environmental side came from the AEC staff. This is unusual since in most environmental cases, the agency is on the side of the developer. In the *Scenic Hudson* case, the agency's activity was, in effect, similar to the contribution of the law reformers, and was a valuable resource that lessened the ef-

[27] For a discussion of this controversy see R.E. Ayres (1975).

fects of the free-rider problem for the social-reform group. This would be analogous to the situation in the Trans-Alaskan Pipeline case if the federal and state governments, in fact, decided to monitor the construction process. Such government monitoring would be a resource on the environmental side that the group would not have to supply. To the extent that a social-reform group can attract outside support, whether from the government or elsewhere, it overcomes some of the unfavorable characteristics that arise when a large, dispersed group pursues collective goods.

Alliances can also serve to overcome other unfavorable characteristics of variables. An example of an alliance between environmentalists and a nongovernment group with vested interests involves a Corps of Engineers project to reconstruct Locks and Dam 26 on the Mississippi River at Alton, Illinois.[28] Locks and Dam 26 is at a pivotal crossroads of the Upper Mississippi and Illinois Waterway; it is a key intersection that affects the total inland waterway of the Midwest, extending east on the Ohio River and south on the Lower Mississippi River. The particular project, although large in its own right, is only the start of Corps plans to reconstruct the entire Upper Mississippi River Navigation System, with estimated costs, in 1974, in excess of $3.2 billion. The project was opposed by the Sierra Club and the Illinois Branch of the Isaak Walton League, but, joining them as plaintiffs were 20 Midwestern railroads who fear competition from improved navigation. It was, interestingly, an alliance between environmentalists and vested interests.

From what has been said so far, the cost of litigating this suit need not be elaborated. The railroads, however, are paying that cost. The presence of the railroads not only supplies the resources to overcome the free-rider problem, but also alters the distribution of benefits and costs of the social-reform groups' action. Without the presence of the railroads, the benefit–cost distribution would not be favorable to successful action by social-reform groups: The costs would be concentrated on the Corps and the benefits would be distributed. With the presence of the railroads, benefits are now concentrated as well; it is to the railroads' self-interest to supply the collective goods to the environmentalists.[29]

Another way of avoiding unfavorable characteristics of some of the variables is to use law-reform activity for extrajudicial purposes; by extrajudicial I mean for purposes of delay, publicity, harassment, em-

[28] This case is discussed in *Atchison, Topeka & Santa Fe Ry. Co.* v. *Callaway*, 382 F. Supp. 610 (D.C. 1974).

[29] Of course private parties such as individual landowners may use environmental statutes to protect their own property from the adverse effects of development, but, here, selective goods are being sought. See Sax and DiMento (1974).

barrassment, increasing costs, and mobilizing political opposition, as distinguished from relying on the court decision itself to produce social change. There were suggestions that this occurred in the Kaiparowits Utah Power Plant case; the costs due to the delays caused by pending and anticipated litigation were one of the reasons cited by the builders' group for abandoning the project. There are occasions when social-reform groups have used courts successfully for extrajudicial purposes. The failure to file an adequate environmental impact statement allows the group to obtain a temporary injunction, which gives it time to try to mobilize resources. Sometimes, delays can be political resources. There have been instances where Corps projects have been delayed, and then local political support has been turned against the projects forcing the Corps to cancel. Sometimes there are situations where more than one agency's approval is necessary for a project, and environmentalists have been able to use the impact statement to persuade one of the agencies to deny permission.[30]

In cases of this type, it is immaterial that if the matter proceeded in court, judicial remedies would be unfavorable to successful action by a social-reform group; the group is not going to court for a final decision on the merits. By limiting the use of the courts for extrajudicial purposes, the groups are changing the characteristics of the judicial remedy from unfavorable to favorable. The publicity and delay created by the temporary injunction and the order for a more adequate impact statement are all that is needed from the court. Similarly, since the goal of the group is to force cancellation of the project through political resources, unfavorable bureaucratic contingencies are also avoided. The use of the courts for extrajudicial purposes has been important to environmentalists. As we shall see in subsequent chapters, this use has also been important to other social-reform groups in other contexts.

In fact, it could be argued that extrajudicial uses of the courts have been the most important accomplishment of the environmentalists to date.[31] As noted in the beginning of the chapter, all commentators concede that it was the law-reform activity of social-reform groups and the courts that breathed life into NEPA. Whatever the subsequent impact of NEPA, it most likely would have been a dead letter without this legal activity. The courts were used for consciousness-raising, for dramatizing the issues, and for arousing political and social concern for environmental issues. Although systematic evaluations have not been done, and opinions differ, several commentators believe that this consciousness-raising has been effective, that environmental concerns

[30] Examples of both situations are give in Friesema and Culhane (1976).
[31] Compare Sax and DiMento (1974): "I (Sax) have always viewed the (Environmental Protection Act] largely as a tool for educational and institution-building at the local level [p. 5]."

are now part of the political culture, that ambitious politicians are taking up these issues, and that there have been concrete changes in behavior. It was noted that the Corps of Engineers, for example, has adopted the practice of issuing impact statements and claims to have modified or cancelled many projects, that systems for developing environmental information have been improved at the administrative level in other agencies, that this information is working its way into the decision-making processes, and that there is much more of an environmental awareness throughout government. Other manifestations are the support for environmental concerns given by prestigious, blue-ribbon bodies not previously identified with the activists and social-reform groups. For example, a recent report by the Miter Corporation study commission on nuclear power recommended a halt to the fast-breeder-reactor program (Nuclear Energy Policy Study Group, 1977). It seems unlikely that such a body would have reached similar conclusions 4 or 5 years ago. And recently, President Carter has halted construction of a major fast-breeder-reactor plant, citing the uncertainty of safety and environmental effects, a position long argued by the social-reform groups. While one could not claim that the change in outlook is due solely to the law-reform litigation involving NEPA, it would be equally in error to claim that the extraordinary amount of litigation and its attendant publicity had no substantial effect on the climate of public opinion. Environmental groups and the law reformers helped place these concerns on the national agenda.

One can adopt this view of the contribution of the environmental law reformers but still have doubts as to how much will be changed. The activities of the Corps of Engineers chillingly sound like the regulatory situations that Edelman (1964) described, and that were discussed in Chapter 1. Historically, regulatory reform is launched with great symbolic meaning, but rarely does it serve to perform as promised. Yet, Edelman notes, the supposed beneficiary groups became apathetic to the actual failures, but continue to support the regulatory programs and laws. Why this discrepancy? Edelman's thesis is that regulatory programs are designed to stimulate symbolic satisfaction while masking reality. The symbols, and especially legal ones, are designed to promote quiescence, which is especially successful with large, dispersed groups that are not in a position to analyze reality, whereas small, vested interest groups are able to learn what in fact is happening and to press their interests for tangible rewards. The Corps of Engineers is now telling the country that all is well, that they are taking NEPA seriously, and that many tangible changes have resulted. The agency can point to its ever-increasing number of fully prepared, lengthy, complex impact statements as evidence of its concern. It is extremely difficult to evaluate the Corps' position. It has hundreds of projects under way, or on the drawing boards, all over the country, extending far into the future. Who knows whether the cancelled projects were dropped for environmental reasons or because the Corps just decided they were of low priority for other reasons? Who can check all of the environmental impact statements (EIS) that are now being routinely filed?

The activity of the Corps is apparently not unique. A recent survey by the Council on Environment Quality showed that in the 5½ years since the enactment of NEPA, over 7000 EIS drafts have been prepared and made available for comment and the CEQ (as well as environmental groups) is seriously concerned that the flood of paper serves to mask what is really going on. Such fears are only increased by the strong endorsement given to NEPA by its former enemies in business, labor, and government. Conservative congressmen cite support from their constituents (Kirschten, 1977, p. 1119). Developers, perhaps, have learned to cope and the public is being reassured (Edelman, 1975, pp. 309, 313).

The leaders of the principal environmental groups are not likely to accept the Corps' statement of compliance at face value. After all, they have met the Corps in a number of battles, and to a great extent have been beaten badly.[32] But the knowledge and perception of the environmental leadership is not what is at stake. Environmental organizations rely on purposive incentives and the ability to attract outside support from elites. The leaders, members, potential outside contributors, and probably most important of all, the public at large and the politicians have to believe not only that the cause is just but, in addition, that there are enemies to vanquish. The activities of the Corps, as well as other public and private developers, viewed most cynically, are classic in their efforts to undermine the mobilization needs of the environmental groups. To the extent that government agencies can persuade the public that all is well, that they are enforcing the law, and that in allowing development to proceed they are safeguarding our natural resources and environment, then purposive incentives should weaken and outside contributors will seek out what they perceive are more pressing social problems.[33]

Summary and Conclusions

In Table 2.1, the characteristics of the variables of the theory are summarized for each of the examples. A plus (+) check means that in

---

[32] The Environmental Defense Fund, for example, was virtually totally defeated in its 5-year campaign against the Corps' water resource development program. See Trubek and Gillen (1978).

[33] Compare Liroff (1976, pp. 214–216).

Table 2.1 *Environmental Litigation: Summary of Theory Variables*

Variables	TAPS	Tankers	Kaiparowits	Scenic Hudson	Calvert Cliffs	Noise	Locks and Dam 26	Political Decisions
Groups								
Small size						+	+	
Outside funding	±	±	±	+	±	±	+	±
Selective benefits						+	+	−
Large size	−	−	−	−	−	−	−	
No outside resources	−	−	−	−	−	−	−	
Collective goods only	−	−	−	−	−	−	−	−
Distribution								
Benefits concentrated; costs distributed								
Benefits distributed; costs distributed								
Benefits concentrated; costs concentrated						+	+	
Benefits distributed; costs concentrated								

66

Bureaucratic					
One time	+	+	+	+	+
Top solution	+	+	+	+	+
Technically simple	+	+	+	+	+
Discretion reduced					
Long term	−				
Field-level implementation	−				
Technically complex	−			−	
Discretion required	−	−	−		−
Judicial					
Preventive injunction	+				+
Court solution	+				+
Order can be monitored					
Regulation injunction					
Remand to agency	−	−			
Order complex					
Law Reformers					
Affiliated					
Technical resources					
Political resources					+
Independent	−	−	−	−	−
No technical resources	−	−	−	−	−
No political resources	−	−	−	−	−

that particular example the characteristic was favorable to successful social-reform-group, law-reform action; a minus (-) check means the opposite.

For the Trans-Alaskan Pipeline case there was some outside funding to the social-reform groups, but not a great deal in comparison to the job that had to be done. All the other characteristics of this example were unfavorable to successful action. Although all the evidence is by no means available, it looks like the construction of the pipeline was a defeat for the environmental cause. In two of the examples, nontransportation noise and Locks and Dam 26 on the Mississippi River, it is still too early to make any prediction as to how environmental considerations will fare. In both of these situations, however, there are favorable characteristics. With nontransportation noise, discretion has been reduced and performance measurement is technically simple. With the Locks and Dam 26, there are small groups, strong selective incentives, and a more favorable distribution of benefits and costs.

In the last column, I have lumped under "political decisions" those cases where environmental groups were able to persuade the local community and political leaders to oppose a project (in the actual cases, usually Corps of Engineers projects) which was then cancelled.

The political decisions and three other cases—Kaiparowits Power Plant, *Scenic Hudson*, and Calvert Cliffs—can be judged as successes from the environmental standpoint. All of these cases had many characteristics, such as collective goods only and an unfavorable distribution of benefits and costs, that were not favorable to successful action. On the other hand, the groups in *Scenic Hudson* had very important outside resources in the form of AEC staff support, and in the "political decisions" cases, I assume, the groups and the law reformers did have available political resources. However, what distinguishes these cases is the bureaucratic contingency. All of these cases could be solved at the top, they were one-time decisions, and there was little or no discretion. Even though they were also technically complex, these favorable characteristics are unique among the examples and greatly facilitate the chances of success. The other distinguishing characteristic is the limited use of the courts. In the Alaska pipeline and tanker pollution cases, the courts will not impose a solution; that will be left to the agency, which throws the groups back into the unfavorable bureaucratic problems. *Scenic Hudson* was also a remand to the agency but the bureaucratic characteristics were not unfavorable. In Kaiparowitz and the political decisions cases the courts were only used for limited, if not extrajudicial purposes; hence, the judicial remedies were favorable.

To the extent, then, that the cases in this chapter represent important types of environmental litigation, the conclusion is that the most important determinant of successful law-reform activity for social reform will be what kind of solution is required of the administrative agency. The groups have a better chance of success if what they want is one-time, can be decided at the top, and can minimize discretion. A cancellation satisfies all three criteria, but major modifications can also succeed. If a group cannot reasonably obtain this kind of remedy, then it will need staying power for the long haul. In this situation, it should seek alliances, as in the Locks and Dam 26 example, to lessen the unfavorable characteristics of group size and incentives and the distribution of benefits and costs.

In environmental litigation, the courts can only be used for limited purposes. The basic problem is that the courts will not substitute their judgment on the merits for that of the agency. This means that ultimately the groups will have to return to the agency and the bureaucratic contingency becomes crucial. On the other hand, courts have been used successfully for limited and extrajudicial purposes, such as gaining time and publicity, which can allow the groups to employ means other than litigation to pursue their goals.

3

Consumer Protection

Origins of Consumerism

Although the origins of consumer protection can be traced to the beginning of the country, the consumer movement, as an explicit political force, is generally dated from the late nineteenth century.[1] At that time, the concern was primarily economic: Consumers sought protection from monopolistic pricing. The Interstate Commerce Commission was established, at least in part, to protect small farmers from the pricing practices of the railroads. At the beginning of the twentieth century, consumer concern turned to the safety and wholesomeness of products. In 1906, the Meat Inspection Act and the Pure Food and Drug Act were enacted. These were not only explicit, modern consumer-protection statutes, but the events which lead to their enactment shed light on some of the political conditions for present day activity by social-reform groups.

[1] Government efforts, for example, to standardize weights and measures benefit consumers as well as producers. See Nadel (1971, chap. 1) for a brief historical account of consumer protection. The first part of this chapter dealing with the history and politics of consumer protection draws extensively on Nadel. See also Snow and Weisbrod (1978).

71

Concern about adulterated and synthetic products had been in existence for some time prior to the enactment of the legislation. Moreover, this concern was not only expressed by consumer groups but also by producers; farmers, for example, felt threatened by the advent of synthetic products such as oleomargarine. Consumers and farmers were disparate groups seeking collective goods, but they were joined by more powerful vested interests. The domestic meat-packing industry supported the Meat Inspection Act as a way of curtailing imports, and the American Medical Association supported the Pure Food and Drug Act as part of its campaign against patent medicines. In both cases, these organizations were important in the passage of the legislation.

Other factors also helped promote the proposed legislation. Behind the Pure Food and Drug Act was Dr. Harvey W. Wiley, then chief chemist for the United States Department of Agriculture. Dr. Wiley had long been a crusader for a pure food and drug law, and was skillful in publicizing his cause with Congress and the general public. In addition, dramatic events helped push through the final legislation. At a critical moment in the legislative battles, Upton Sinclair's The Jungle was published dramatizing the filth and corruption in the meat-packing industry. President Theodore Roosevelt, shocked as the rest of the nation, ordered his own investigation, which was even more damaging than the book. At the appropriate time, Roosevelt released the government report and gained passage of both pieces of legislation.

Another important aspect of this early legislation was that it reflected a widespread current of public opinion. This was the era of muckraking and Progressivism in American politics. The Progressive politicians used consumerism as a way of broadening their appeal. The purity and safety of food and drugs were part of a more general concern about political and corporate corruption.

The consumer movement lapsed during World War I and revived during the New Deal period. In 1938, the Federal Food, Drug and Cosmetic Act was passed, which focused mainly on false advertising and which strengthened considerably the 1906 act. As with the earlier legislation, there was a great struggle over the 1938 act, and its passage was also helped by dramatic events. In one case, over 100 deaths occurred from a toxic drug the FDA could not prevent from entering the market under its existing authority.

Although these legislative enactments were considered to be key victories for consumer protection groups, enforcement was undermined by subsequent administration. The transformation of the Interstate Commerce Commission from protection of consumers to protection of railroads is a well-known story. The same happened with the two most important consumer protection agencies, the Federal Drug Administration and the Federal Trade Commission. Neither of these agencies was ever adequately funded to fulfill its enforcement obligations and both quickly lapsed into relying on cooperative arrangements with the regulated industries. Within a short time industry was able to assert its dominance over the Congress and the agencies. Consumer protection interest during both periods turned out to be temporary, or, in the case of special interest groups (e.g., the AMA), secondary to other, more important goals. Subsequent administration invariably turned out different from what the reformers expected. The consumer groups lacked the ability to counter industry pressure in the administrative agencies.

Size and Strength

The 1960s witnessed an unprecedented burst of consumer protection legislation (Nadel, 1971, chap. 2). In 1962, Senator Kefauver, aided by the thalidomide crisis, was able to push through amendments strengthening drug safety. The real outpouring of legislation was between 1966 and 1968 when 11 major pieces of legislation were enacted. Why did consumerism come of age during this period? According to Mark Nadel (1971), most knowledgeable participants agreed that the political timing was right for consumerism. By 1965, President Johnson realized that he could not prosecute the Vietnam war and fulfill his domestic promises. After initial success with Congress, he began to suffer domestic defeats, and rising inflation precluded proposals that would be costly. Consumerism, as in the Progressive days, was a consensus issue that Johnson sorely needed. In addition, consumer protection programs impose practically no demands on the federal budget. For the same reasons, consumerism was also of great benefit to Congress in general and to ambitious liberal key congressmen in particular.

The importance of Ralph Nader to the consumer movement in the 1960s cannot be overestimated. There had been some concern with auto safety prior to 1965, which was when Nader published *Unsafe At Any Speed;* shortly thereafter he catapulted into national prominence when it was revealed during congressional hearings that General Motors was trying to harass and intimidate him.[2] There was great outcry at this corporate misbehavior and auto safety legislation was

[2] In the 1950s various universities conducted studies of auto safety and in 1956 Representative Roberts began an investigation of the need for seatbelts. See Welles (1966).

enacted shortly thereafter.[3] This legislation was considered a breakthrough for the consumer movement. It was the first time that the
automobile industry had been subjected to regulation, and it showed
Congress that it had the power to do it.

Nader had great appeal during this period. In the summer of 1968,
Nader brought together a team of young law students who subsequently produced a scathing report on the FTC. This was the start of
"Nader's Raiders," large numbers of student and young professional
(mostly lawyer) volunteers or staffers working for low pay who organized into teams and investigated various government agencies, corporations, and law firms. A number of organizations were spawned out of
Nader's activities, such as the Center for Responsive Law, the Center
for Auto Safety, and the Project for Corporate Responsibility. In addition to organizations more or less directly under Nader, some organizations were financially independent, and, in some instances, former
Nader workers started their own organizations. By 1974, Nader or
Nader-type organizations had emerged in the areas of auto safety, aviation, health research, corporate responsibility, land use, water quality,
food safety, women's issues, and science and technology.[4]

The appeal of Nader groups, especially for young lawyer activists,
was also due to the fact that they were part of a larger movement. At
the time that Nader moved center stage, the civil rights movement was
already a decade old; it grew during the late 1950s and early 1960s,
but, by 1965, had begun to lose some of its appeal, especially for white
students. The War On Poverty was getting under way, but some young
lawyers were also seeking alternatives to OEO Legal Services or were
antigovernment. Nader was for the consumer, the victim of giant public
and private bureaucracies. Nader's movement represented a facet of
participatory democracy: Consumers could get together and with a
skilled, sympathetic lawyer make their voices heard. Working for
Ralph Nader combined missionary zeal and camaraderie, self-sacrifice,
independence from government or business or private law practice,
and, for most, an exciting professional life in Washington, D.C. By the
late 1960s, the appeal of Nader organizations to law graduates rivaled
the drawing power of Legal Services (Handler, Hollingsworth, and
Erlanger, 1978, chap. 2).

As of 1973, there were approximately 21 Nader organizations
based in Washington, D.C., with all but 4 fully funded by Nader. The

---

[3] On the effects of *Unsafe At Any Speed* and the disclosure of the GM investigation, see Sanford
(1976), De Toledano (1975, p. 40), Gorey (1975, pp. 16–17) and *Automotive News* (1970).

[4] In addition to Nadel (1971) and Snow and Weisbrod (1978), see Wark (1971) on the growth of
such organizations.

budget for the total operation was $1.6 million. Five hundred thousand dollars came from Nader's personal funds raised through writing and lecturing; $300,000 came from foundation grants; and $800,000 was the net received from private contributions. In addition, there are Nader-type Public Interest Research Groups (PIRG) in 22 states with more than 50 full-time personnel and 500,000 student members whose donations to these organizations total $1.4 million (Snow and Weisbrod, 1978).

Although Nader groups became the dominant force in the consumer movement, there are other organizations, some with long histories of involvement. In 1973, it was estimated (Snow and Weisbrod, 1978) that there were approximately 80 national, state, and local organizations; however, less than half a dozen have sufficient resources to maintain even a small permanent Washington staff. Next to Nader, the most important organization is the Consumer Federation of America (CFA), the largest consumer organization in the country. CFA was organized in 1967 with 56 participating organizations; it rapidly expanded to almost 200 organizations within 5 years. But during that period, it experienced considerable growing pains and financial instability. One source of internal difficulty, which is important for the analysis of this monograph, stems from the fact that the CFA membership is composed of consumer groups and what are called "supporting" groups, organizations that are not primarily concerned with consumer issues, such as labor unions, rural electric cooperatives, and public power groups. Although the supporting groups pay most of the cost of CFA, they have restricted voting rights; nevertheless, it is still charged that the supporting groups dominate the policies of CFA and cause conflicts with the consumer group members. The most visible and serious conflict is over trade protection; the trade unions and the consumer groups are split, forcing CFA to avoid taking a public stand (Swanston, 1972). Nevertheless, the organization seemed to thrive on the adversity of the Nixon years, and by 1976 appeared strengthened internally and financially. It has a full-time staff of 10 and a budget of $300,000 (Demkovich, 1976).

Probably the next most important consumer organization is Congress Watch, a Nader spin-off, which, in 1976, had a full-time staff of seven lobbyists, a small number of researchers, and a budget of about $120,000. Consumers Union, perhaps the best-known organization, opened a Washington office in 1972, with two full-time lawyers to represent consumers in courts and before agencies, but budgetary cutbacks have forced the resignation of Ralph Nader from the board of directors (Demkovich, 1976, p. 1740). Two other organizations that specialize in children's television advertising and diet have some lobbying efforts. The Council on Children, Merchandising and the Media is a one-person organization acting as a full-time lobbyist (CCMM) and the other organization, Action for Children's Television, through a series of foundation grants, benefits, and contributions and membership fees, now has a staff of six full-time, and four part-time employes. However, the organization cannot afford to hire a full-time lawyer.[5] In addition, there are some other groups, the National Consumer Congress, Health Research Group, and Tax Reform Group, which have small staffs and slender budgets.

Unions also take an active interest in consumer matters. The AFL-CIO, for example, has an effective lobbying capability when it decides to support a particular consumer measure. However, consumerism is only a by-product for the union; it is careful what measures it will support, it tends to wait until a particular piece of legislation is well along in the legislative mill, and, as noted, it will be in conflict with consumer measures when it thinks that those measures will threaten jobs (Nadel, 1971, pp. 163–170; Vogel and Nadel, 1977).

There have also been changes in the public sector concerning consumer protection. In addition to the outpouring of consumer protection legislation since 1970, many state and local governments have enacted their own consumer protection laws. As of 1973, 43 states had laws similar to the Federal Trade Commission Act to prevent unfair and deceptive practices in commerce. In 1973, there were some 20 federal and 200 state and local agencies engaged in providing consumers with information and other kinds of protection. The federal government alone spent at least $1.2 billion on consumer protection programs in 1973 (Snow and Weisbrod, 1978). Consumer protection continues to enjoy presidential favor. As with the Johnson administration, the Carter administration, concerned about inflation, opted for consumer protection—a cheap domestic program as far as the federal budget is concerned. Carter announced his support for the proposed Agency for Consumer Advocacy, for which consumer groups fought for 10 years. He has made a significant number of consumer-oriented appointments; perhaps the most noteworthy is Joan Claybrook, Ralph Nader's chief lobbyist, as head of the National Highway Traffic Safety Administration. But others as well have been appointed to important positions. The new chairman of the Federal Trade Commission has an activist consumer background and that agency will continue its revitalization course. Harrison Wellford, former executive director of Nader's Center

---

[5] The work of these two organizations is the topic of Thain (1978).

for the Study of Responsive Law, is now with the Office of Management and Budget as executive director for reorganization and management. Carol Tucker Foreman, past executive director of CFA, is an assistant secretary of agriculture for consumer services (Demkovich, 1977b, p. 394).

On the other hand, the FDA, one of the most important consumer protection agencies, continues to flounder. The troubles of the FDA illustrate the difficulties that social-reform groups encounter. The regulatory task of this agency is immense. It must supervise for safety and efficacy a $10-billion-a-year market in prescription and over-the-counter drugs manufactured by 2500 companies. And this is less than half of the agency's regulatory responsibilities. It also must oversee the products of 50,000 food companies that market $130 billion worth of goods, in addition to cosmetics, medical devices, some veterinary medicines, and such diverse products as microwave ovens and aerosol sprays. Although the agency has always been underfunded and understaffed, that has not been the major problem. Since 1962 the agency's budget has increased tenfold and its staff has tripled. Rather, because the agency is constantly buffeted by industry and consumers, it has suffered serious demoralization, it cannot fill many important staff positions, and it has become fractionalized. The most that the agency has been able to do is lurch from crisis to crisis. In the last 3 years, it has been subjected to more than 100 congressional hearings and 50 highly critical reports by the General Accounting Office. Senator Kennedy summarized the results of the hearings of his two subcommittees, as follows:

> These accounts included serious allegations of undue industry influence, improper transfers, details or removals, alteration of files and forced withdrawal of memoranda, bias toward drug approvals, improper manipulative use of advisory committees, disappearance of critical agency action memoranda into what the F.D.A. Commissioner termed "a mysterious bottomless pit," and incredibly slow-moving ineffective enforcement and compliance programs with years elapsing between the discovery of a problem and the initiation of a solution, and inappropriate use of medical officer recommendations [Quoted in *The New York Times*, 1977a, col. 1].

The results, then, of government activity in consumer protection are mixed. The FDA, now, and probably in the foreseeable future, will continue to present a formidable challenge to consumer groups. The agency deals with massive numbers of decisions, often of low visibility. It is constantly pressured by knowledgeable, well-financed vested interest groups staffed with skilled lobbyists, and it is an agency that is pressured to take the easy way out. It is hard to conceive of social-reform groups mounting the strength to keep abreast of this agency on a day-to-day basis. On the other hand, the FTC, under its new chairman, and the National Highway Traffic Safety Administration, should be supportive of consumer interests. The Consumer Product Safety Commission, with authority to act against hazardous products, covers anywhere from 10,000 to 100,000 products that have been associated with at least 30 million consumer injuries yearly. It got off to a slow start, but promised some new directions (Gardner, 1973).

The difficulty of assessing the impact of other government activity is that unless one is able to examine empirically the work of the agencies, there is always the danger of symbolic reassurance. The government announces its support for consumer protection, laws and regulations are enacted, agency budgets are increased somewhat, and the country is assured that consumers are being protected. As with the Corps of Engineers in environmental matters, the pattern is what Edelman describes as the principal effects of government regulatory activity. Consumer protection is good politics, but if the past is any guide, the realities of administration undermine the promises made in laws and speeches.

Can consumer groups strengthen the resolve of government agencies to regulate? All agree that as compared with 10 or even 5 years ago, these organizations are considerably stronger. The political timing continues favorably; a great deal of consumer protection legislation has been enacted into law, and politicians and business adversaries attest to the importance and effectiveness of some consumer groups.[6] The mass membership organizations, such as CFA and Consumers Union, are effective in notifying their members about the current state of consumer problems and stimulating mail to Congress. Nader, through his contacts with the press, Congress, and especially the bureaucracy, is not only able to generate publicity and advise his constituency, but also is able to lobby both the Congress and the agencies. A great deal of Nader's information is through leaks from lower-level workers in both corporations and agencies, although most of his information does in fact come from readily available public documents.

On the other hand, the resources of all of these consumer groups, when compared with those of their adversaries, are severely limited. With the possible exception of Nader, the consumer organizations are weak when it comes to the all-important task of lobbying, especially lobbying the federal bureaucracy.[7] As a result, their only constant con-

[6] See statements quoted in Demkovich (1976).

[7] The United States Senate Study on Federal Regulation (1977) lists a number of examples of the disparity in resources between consumer groups and the regulated industry. For example, 11 major airlines spent $2.8 million in legal representation before the CAB in 1976 as compared with $20,000 spent by Aviation Consumer Action, the major consumer organization.

tact with Congress is usually testimony at hearings, whereas most lobbyists work from their offices (M. V. Nadel, 1971, pp. 164–165). How
the Carter administration will change the balance of power is uncertain. The appointments, mentioned above, are promising but several
important agencies, such as the FDA, remain untouched. Judging from
the past, consumerism will probably continue to be good politics for
the President and many ambitious members of Congress. But this also
could have costs as well as gains for consumer groups. These organizations rely on purposive incentives. Symbolic support from national
leaders combined with some highly visible proconsumer appointments
could weaken the incentives of the supporting elites; they could be led
to believe that consumer protection no longer needs their scarce charity
resources. There already are reports that recruitment into consumer
groups is slackening, that the groups are not well funded, and that they
have to spend considerable time, energy, and resources just to survive
(Demkovich, 1976, p. 1744).

Consumer Litigation

In efforts to increase their power, consumer groups have turned to
the legal system. In some instances, such as Consumers Union, the
organization has created its own legal capability. Consumer Federation
of America, on the other hand, has a private, public interest law firm
on a small retainer. Then, there are foundation-supported public-
interest law firms that take consumer protection cases. Under what circumstances can consumer groups hope to accomplish their goals
through law-reform activity? As with Chapter 2 on environmental protection, the theory of this book will be examined in light of selected
consumer litigation. The cases are real and while not representative
quantitatively, are within the range of important consumer protection
litigation.[8]

The first illustration involves a case in Wisconsin that successfully
challenged the rate of interest charged by major retailers on revolving
charge accounts as a violation of the state usury laws.[9] The court order
had two parts: One section ordered the stores to lower their finance
charges to what the court held was allowed under the Wisconsin usury
law; the other ordered the stores to refund the excess charges to

[8] Several of the examples are taken from Snow and Weisbrod (1978) where an effort was made to
select a representative sample of reported cases. While this methodology does not guarantee quantitative representation, it does give confidence that the cases are not exotic examples.

[9] This case is slightly altered for purposes of analysis. The litigation was, in fact, brought by the
state's attorney general, an elected official who was trying to establish consumer support. The case
and subsequent legislative activity is discussed in Davis (1973).

customers who could prove that they had been overcharged. The major retail stores then sought an amendment to the usury laws, but as the price of this change, the consumers were able to extract from the legislature a consumer protection statute. Prior to the court decision, the consumer groups had lacked the strength to push their bill through the legislature, but they did have enough strength to prevent the amendment to the usury laws. The court decision gave them the necessary leverage.[10] I will analyze three aspects of law-reform activity in this particular case: the two separate parts of the court order, and the use of the litigation as a bargaining device in the political arena.

Characteristics of the social-reform groups do not favor successful activity. Consumer organizations are either mass membership or paper organizations. Incentives are primarily purposive; material incentives are present, but usually of a minimal nature. For example, in the Wisconsin usury case, the leaders of the consumer groups knew about the availability of refunds; their interest in informing all other consumers would not benefit the leaders. Rather, their interest was purposive in the hope that consumers who were informed would be grateful and join the organization. Lowering the finance charges was probably even more remotely related to strengthening the organization; the vast majority of consumers would simply notice (presumably) the lower charge and have no idea what caused it. We have a situation, then, of leaders operating under purposive incentives for mass or nonexistent membership organizations.

The *distribution of benefits and costs* did not favor successful activity. The benefits are widely dispersed and the costs are concentrated. The goods are collective; they can be enjoyed by anyone without making any contribution to the production of the goods. This applies to lowered finance charges, knowledge about the availability of a refund, and increased consumer protection in the form of legislation. Thus, the groups face the free-rider problem. At least in the short run, costs are concentrated on the manufacturers and the retail stores; they have strong economic incentives to resist.

The effects of the *bureaucratic contingency* are more variable. One part of the court order instructed the stores to lower their finance charges to comply with Wisconsin law. The bureaucratic contingency here was favorable to successful action. The decision would be made at

---

[10] The politics became very complicated. The governor joined the consumer groups and vetoed the first attempt pushed by consumer finance companies. Later, splits began to develop between various segments of the credit community and eventually a comprehensive consumer act was passed. In the final result, it was clear that the consumer groups could not have done it alone; the governor played a crucial role, but he, too, could not have succeeded without the consumer groups and the leverage provided by the court decision.

the top level of management. There would be no discretion at any level of the bureaucracy—decisions would be routine, field-level personnel would play no role, and monitoring would be simple.

Another part of the order authorized customer refunds. This presented great problems for the consumer groups; they had to notify and explain the court decision to a widely dispersed group of people. Then, each individual had to decide whether it was worth the bother to try to get the refund. Each application for a refund involved field-level decision making, and although the decisions were capable of speedy solution (documentary evidence and arithmetic calculations), there was the potential for field-level delays and other forms of obstruction. Thus, consumer groups confronted masses of citizen and lower-level bureaucrats over a long period of time, and (unless closely monitored) discretionary decisions.[11]

The usury lawsuit was also used, as noted, as a strategic weapon to increase leverage in a political struggle for a consumer protection bill. In large part, because of the lawsuit, the credit community agreed to a consumer protection law as the price for favorable amendments to the usury law. When lawsuits are used for leverage, there is, of course, no problem of implementation as such.

Judicial remedies yield to a similar analysis. The judicial remedies were, in one regard, effective, that is, ordering the lowering of the finance charges, and thus capable of being monitored. These successful enforcement prospects also increased the value of the order as leverage for favorable legislation.

With regard to refunds, the remedy was less effective. The order was to pay money damages and was susceptible to quantification. Some large class action refund suits were filed, but generally speaking, refund orders require field-level decisions and consumer initiative in quantity. For reasons already stated, judicial remedies of this type are not usually effective.

The *characteristics of the law reformers* were suitable for the Wisconsin usury litigation. This was an ordinary litigation. The amount of technical skill required was within the grasp of competent lawyers. It was high-visibility litigation admirably serving the publicity needs of the lawyers. The lawyers themselves could monitor that aspect of enforcement that related to future interest charges. Implementing the refund part was an entirely different matter. Enforcement is not

---

[11] Several lawsuits were filed, including some class actions, which included statutory punitive damages. The suits never went to trial, and when the final legislation was passed, the legislature retroactively repealed the legislation authorizing the suits. If the class action suits had been successfully prosecuted, then perhaps some of the problems of consumer refunds could have been solved.

technically complex, but law reformers would find a multitude of refund cases boring and wasteful of their professional time.

Implementing the leverage function of the order requires political
resources. Whether the law reformers could do this would depend on
the applicability of the lobbying prohibition, the kind of lobbying
called for, and how many resources were needed. If the lawyers could
legally lobby (or otherwise avoid the prohibition), the lobbying activity
required was open and relatively short term, and a great many
resources were not required, the characteristics of law reformers would
not be unfavorable. Many lawyers by training have adequate lobbying
skills. On the other hand, if a hard, long fight was still called for, requiring extensive political mobilization, then the burden would fall on
the consumer groups, or if long-term, patient, behind-the-scenes lobbying were required, then the characteristics of the law reformers would
not be that helpful; they would have performed their role in getting the
favorable court ruling.

Aspects of the Wisconsin usury case can be found in different
kinds of law-reform activities by consumer groups. Where the goal is
the promulgation of clear rules, such as specifying the maximum rate
of interest, the unfavorable characteristics of the bureaucracy and
judicial remedies may be avoided. One example is where consumer
groups seek judicial orders outlawing restraints of trade. In 1974, the
Virginia Consumer Council, a consumer group, successfully sued the
Virginia State Board of Pharmacy to overthrow a state statute banning
the advertising of prescription drugs (see Snow and Weisbrod, 1978).
The law was aimed at preventing the expansion of discount drug
chains into Virginia. Although the characteristics of the social-reform
group and the distribution of benefits and costs were unfavorable to
successful activity by social-reform groups, the characteristics of all of
the other variables were favorable. There was no bureaucratic contingency in that no implementation of a rule was required. Presumably,
after the decision was announced, discount drugstores now operating
under normal market conditions would enter the Virginia market and
begin advertising lower-priced drugs. The state's pharmacy board
would be powerless; it would not be able to seek enforcement of an unconstitutional statute. Similarly, the judicial order, a prohibitory
declaration, would be favorable to successful action. And, as in the
Wisconsin usury case, the characteristics of the law reformers also
favor successful action because this was a straight law-reform case emphasizing strictly legal issues.

The Virginia decision had even greater benefits for consumers. As
a result of that decision, the Consumer Federation of America began

encouraging consumer groups in other states (35 states had similar laws) to work for the repeal of these laws. State attorneys general, as well as the United States Justice Department, also seized the issue, and finally, even the FDA and the FTC began questioning advertising bans and proposing alternatives.

On the other hand, although the rules were changed, in several states there were reports that in fact very little prescription drug advertising occurred, and more significantly, no impact on prices had been noted. The consumer groups assumed that market forces, released from the restraints, would result in tangible benefits to the general consuming public. Why this development has not occurred is unclear. It may be that it is still too soon after the decision, or it may be that there are informal agreements among pharmacists that still restrain advertising. The different reasons have different implications for the social-reform groups. If it is the first reason, then the groups can anticipate successful action. If it is the second reason, additional resources will have to be expended to track down informal agreements in restraint of trade. This, as we know from antitrust litigation, is a difficult and time-consuming process with uncertain results.

Sometimes removing a restraint on trade accomplishes the market result for the social-reform group, but follow-up activity is still required depending on the regulatory scheme. For example, in California, law reformers succeeded in persuading a milk price-fixing board to suspend the minimum retail price for milk. As distinguished from the Virginia case, effects were immediate and substantial. For example, in the Los Angeles area, milk prices dropped 6 and 7 cents a half gallon. On the other hand, large milk retailers, intent on trying to reestablish minimum prices, are trying to get the agency to invoke a fall-back part of the statute which prohibits retailers from selling milk "below cost." This effort requires more work on behalf of the social-reform groups and the law reformers who have to protest through occasional letters, testimony at hearings, and so forth. But so far, the bureaucratic contingency is not very severe, and certainly within the capability and staying power of the groups and the lawyers.

The Virginia pharmacy case illustrates an important aspect of much of law-reform activity by consumers. There is an assumption that behavior will change as a result of a rule change, and that consumers will receive tangible benefits in the form of lower prices. Much advertising litigation is predicated on similar assumptions. Social-reform groups have, on occasion, been effective in prohibiting certain kinds of advertising or in forcing corrective advertising. With children's television, host-selling has been banned, and the amount of commercial time sold on children's programs has been reduced.[12] Again, as with the pharmacy case, bureaucratic, judicial, and law-reformer character-istics are favorable to successful action. The key assumption is that the changes in advertising will lead to changes in consumption which will benefit consumers. Whether this is true is an open question.

There are instances where only obtaining the provision of informa-tion clearly has not been of tangible benefit to the consumer. Perhaps the most dramatic failure of an information-producing rule occurred when, as a result of a petition filed by consumer groups, the FTC in-stituted a procedure requiring all major companies to provide the agency with documented substantiation for claims made in their adver-tisements (Snow and Weisbrod, 1978). The commission started by ask-ing for substantiation from manufacturers of automobiles, electric razors, air conditioners, toothpaste, and head cold remedies. The FTC required documentation "to support claims regarding the safety, per-formance, efficacy, quality, or comparative price of the product adver-tised," and evidence that the material would be "made available to the public [Snow and Weisbrod, 1978, p. 312]."

The program had two purposes: One was to provide information to consumers and the other was to deter advertisers from making claims that lacked substantiating evidence. There is no way of knowing whether the second purpose was ever achieved, but it is clear that the first purpose was a failure. Massive amounts of highly technical data were submitted to the agency. Neither the agency nor the consumer groups had the resources to make much use of the data, and after two years, the FTC deemphasized the disclosure aspect of the campaign.[13] Thus, although the order looked clear-cut and easy to monitor, in fact this was not the case. The advertisers could have submitted adequate, inadequate, irrelevant, or even false evidence for all that the agency or the consumer groups knew. Whether the order was complied with re-quired extensive day-to-day monitoring of field-level decisions. The agency would not do this, and the social-reform group lacked the capacity to force them to.

Similar results can occur when the action seeks to force release of information held by government agencies. Several consumer groups, including Consumers Union, sought to publicize the fact that interest rates charged by banks on consumer installment loans varied from bank to bank (Snow and Weisbrod, 1978). The Federal Reserve System collected this information, but refused to release it to consumer groups. A lawsuit was filed, and a federal court ordered the release of the data.

---

[12] As Thain (1978) points out, these efforts were due to agency lobbying rather than litigation by lawyers.

[13] In addition to Snow and Weisbrod (1978), see Leone (1972, p. 46) on the FTC procedure.

An appeal is pending. Assuming that the decision will be sustained, what results will be accomplished? There are two questions. The first, which is similar to the FTC advertising-substantiation case, is how will the information be disseminated once it is released to the plaintiff organizations, which is all that the court order provided. The information has to be updated on a monthly basis, and all that Consumers Union planned to do was to publish the data once as part of its series on banking. Another plaintiff organization had plans to publish a shoppers' guide, but it was not clear whether this would be updated. In other words, unless the order required periodic publication by the government or by the banks, which it did not, the social-reform groups would have to invest substantial follow-up in gathering and disseminating the information on a periodic basis. In this case, more attention should have been paid to the remedy sought to obviate the follow-up problems. An order could have provided for banks to display their interest charges, in the manner of retail merchants, or disclose that rates are negotiable, which is usually true.

In addition, there is the question of what the consumers would do with this information even if disseminated. It is clear that comparative shopping for bank loans could result in substantial savings, but the evidence from Truth-in-Lending laws is not very promising. Despite disclosure of interest rates, consumers tend to do little comparison shopping for credit terms and tend to consider only downpayment and monthly payment requirements.

The problem of dissemination of information has, of course, been recognized in some instances. Consumers Union brought an antitrust suit against American Express, the credit card company, and a local Bank Americard bank, seeking to force the companies to abandon their requirements that merchants could not offer customers cash discounts in lieu of using the credit card. As part of the settlement, the defendants, plus other credit card companies, agreed to change the rule. The issue was taken up in Congress and a statute passed, and eventually the Federal Reserve Board was forced into issuing implementing regulations. The theory of the consumer organization was that merchants, freed of this restraint, would offer a discount that would be lower than the regular retail price but higher than the net left after the merchant deducted the percentage that went to the credit card company. It was assumed that major retailers, such as oil companies, would disseminate the information to their retail outlets and would experiment with offering cash discounts as a way of increasing sales. In fact, this has happened at least in some parts of the country. However, reliance was not to be placed solely on market forces. Instead, as part of its overall strategy, Consumers Union planned a massive education campaign so that both merchants and customers would be aware of the discount possibility. Packets of information explaining the change in the law were distributed to consumer organizations throughout the country.

The Consumers Union case will be successful only to the extent that vast numbers of retail merchants decide to take advantage of their new freedom to make extra money; once merchants and customers are educated, the decision will be whether the anticipated profit is worth the extra cost. The social-reform group is thus relying on education and market forces to change massive numbers of field-level discretionary decisions.

In other types of situations, however, massive numbers of field-level decisions have to be changed through force of law. This presents a much more serious challenge to social-reform groups. One of the most severe challenges concerns the Equal Credit Opportunity Act, which bars discrimination in lending on the basis of sex, marital status, race, color, national origin, age, or religion.[14] One problem of enforcement is that 12 different federal agencies share the responsibility for enforcing the law. Banks are under the jurisdiction of the Comptroller of the Currency, the Federal Reserve Board, and the Federal Deposit Insurance Corporation; the Federal Home Loan Bank Board supervises most savings and loans. The SEC regulates stockbrokers and dealers, and the Small Business Administration regulates small business investment companies. The FTC is in charge of nonbank credit card companies, finance companies, mortgage bankers, retail stores, plus other types of creditors. Since the enactment of the law in 1975, more than 2000 complaints have been filed with the FTC alone. The Federal Reserve Board has the sole authority to interpret the law, and has issued regulations, which don't seem to please anybody. Creditors complain about the "overkill" of federal regulation, and consumers argue that the regulations are not stringent enough.

Other problems are disseminating the necessary information through the vast number of creditor bureaucracies that vary so much in size and complexity, and educating lower-level officials in the standards and procedures of the law and the regulations. Spokesmen for major lending institutions claim that the essence of credit decisions is discrimination. In the words of an official of the American Bankers Association, "It's based primarily on how good you feel someone's chances to repay the debt will be." Field-level loan officers have to learn about the new law and regulations and be persuaded to follow new procedures that require them to change their ways and that cause them more work, which they feel is unnecessary. And, they no doubt

[14] The discussion of the Equal Credit Opportunity Act draws heavily on Demkovich (1977c, p. 354).

resent the implication that the effects of their present ways of doing business have been prejudiced. Consumer organizations claim that these officers have been turning down blacks and women for years based merely on their own biases and prejudices.

Another serious problem with enforcement concerns the customer. The customer has to be aware that his or her credit was denied illegally, that there is a remedy, and that there is a chance of success. According to the executive director of a consumer group, this kind of consumer education will be difficult to accomplish because

> Unlike other areas of consumer protection, people do not complain about the lack of available credit, either because they're ashamed and think there's something wrong with them, or because they've been turned down all their lives and are conditioned to it, almost expect it. That kind of cultural conditioning will take years to dissipate, if ever [Demkovich, 1977c, p. 354].

Assuming, then, that credit is denied and the consumer complains, the next problem is what constitutes a valid determination of lack of creditworthiness and what constitutes illegal discrimination. Credit agencies traditionally have used a number of criteria that have the effect of excluding minorities and women. Consumer groups claim such criteria have no relevance to the creditworthiness of the particular applicant. Some of these criteria include the age of a neighborhood, age of the applicant, whether an applicant has a high school diploma, or has previously owned a home, or has a prior police record regardless of the final disposition of the charges. Recognizing that the average credit applicant might have great difficulty in proving intent to discriminate when a credit agency used various criteria, Congress specified that the "effects test" should be applied to credit transactions. The *effects test* refers to a 1971 Supreme Court decision which held that in employment discrimination cases, an employer may not administer a qualifying test even if neutral on its face, which has the practical effect of excluding large numbers of minorities, unless it can be proved that the test is job related.[15] The importance of the ruling is that once the practical effects are shown, the burden of justification rests on the employer; as applied to credit, it would fall on the creditor to prove the relevance of the criteria to creditworthiness. The effects rule, consumers hoped, would greatly ease problems of enforcement.

Two problems arose, however, with the use of the effects test. One is that in recent decisions the Supreme Court has retreated from its previous rulings, and the current status of the rule is very much in

---

[15] *Griggs v. Duke Power Co.*, 401 US 424 (1971); *Albermarle Paper Co. v. Moody*, 422 US 405 (1975).

doubt.[16] The other is that the Federal Reserve Board, in its interpretive rulings, has declined to clarify how the effects test can apply to credit transactions. What constitutes discrimination and who has the burden of proving discrimination in credit transactions is also very much in doubt.

In the meantime, consumer groups are complaining that with the exception of the FTC, the various federal agencies responsible are neither enforcing the law nor educating the industry or the public about the requirements of the law. The Federal Reserve Board, for example, has failed to update examiner manuals or required participation in training seminars; it delayed in establishing an office to monitor compliance; and it has not been sufficiently aggressive in collecting or disseminating data on rejection rates.

It is easy to see why the Equal Credit Opportunity Act represents a type of situation that is one of the most difficult for social-reform groups to confront. All of the characteristics of the variables of the theory are unfavorable to successful law-reform activity by social-reform groups. The consumer groups are mass organizations pursuing collective goods; enforcement of the law can be enjoyed by any credit applicant. The credit agencies, although numerous and diverse, are represented by powerful trade associations. The benefits are dispersed among all credit applicants, and the costs are concentrated on the industry. But the most serious problem concerns the bureaucratic contingency. The basic standard or rule is vague and requires close examination of field-level discretionary decisions and proof of discrimination. Moreover, these countless credit decisions are made daily in offices nationwide by banks, major credit-card companies, savings and loan associations, retail stores, mortgage companies, finance companies—in short, virtually every kind of credit institution. How can these agencies possibly be monitored? The people most likely to suffer from discrimination are the least likely to have knowledge of the law and the ability to complain. Social-reform groups and law reformers lack the capacity to learn about these people's grievances and take their claims on any systematic basis. As we shall see, the problems raised by the Equal Credit Opportunity Act, controlling massive numbers of discretionary field-level decisions, are not unique. They apply in civil rights and social welfare, the subjects of the next two chapters.

Law-reform activity by consumers encounters serious bureaucratic contingencies in other kinds of situations. The description of the cur-

[16] See *Washington* v. *Davis* 96 S.Ct. 2040 (1976); *General Electric Co.* v. *Gilbert*, 97 S.Ct. 401 (1976).

rent state of affairs in the FDA is not very encouraging given the slender resources of most consumer groups and law reformers. On a particular issue, especially with an appropriate dramatic event, groups and law reformers can mobilize and may even succeed in a prohibitory order on the part of the agency, but in the long run, the disorganization, fractionalization, and demoralization of the agency make it peculiarly vulnerable to industry pressure. Industry has the resources to keep abreast of the myriad discretionary decisions made in that agency; the consumer groups and the law reformers do not.

Rate regulation also poses peculiarly difficult problems for consumers. Consumer groups have been trying to cope with a variety of problems of utility regulation. Foremost are the issues of cost and reliability of service; others include service shut-offs, security deposit requirements, late payment charges, and estimate billings. But the most important issue is cost (Leflar and Rogol, 1976). Setting the rates is a discretionary decision for the various utility commissions. The public utilities have a duty to provide "adequate service" at "reasonable rates," in exchange for a "fair rate of return" on their investment. In rate proceedings, one of the most serious problems is analysis of a vast amount of highly complex and technical data to determine what reasonable rate will bring a fair return on the investment. Commission staffs are usually underfinanced and undermanned. Consequently, the industry holds a distinct advantage at the proceedings, especially since its costs of preparation are passed onto the consumer. Over the years, most utilities' arguments in rate proceedings were usually accepted without challenge. Public utility commissions came to be recognized as classic cases of agencies captured by the regulated industry.

Through a series of judicial decisions, statutes and administrative rule changes, standing has been liberalized and consumer groups have been given an opportunity to intervene and participate in agency rate-making proceedings. However, the groups lack the capacity to take advantage of this opportunity. There are many reasons why the ordinary consumer group cannot participate effectively, but without doubt, cost is the most important. It is estimated that the cost of contesting a major rate case could be as much as $100,000. Consumers Union, the largest and most financially secure consumer group, can only contest an occasional proceeding (Leflar and Rogol, 1976, p. 246).

Consumer groups, of course, have recognized the difficult bureaucratic problems they encounter when dealing with government. This is one of the important reasons why they have fought so hard for a consumer protection agency; they feel that a separate government agency, devoted to their cause, will relieve them of some of the burden

(Demkovich, 1977a, p. 1744; Vogel and Nader, 1977, pp. 30–33). They also favor the concept of an agency funding the participation of consumers in their proceedings. The FTC, which has the largest program to date, has allocated more than $1,000,000 to pay the legal fees of groups that have appeared before it to crossexamine industry witnesses, agency staff, and to present their own evidence (see Trubek and Trubek, 1978). The Product Safety Commission and the FDA are currently considering petitions to institute similar programs (Demkovich, 1977c, p. 1743). Nader organizations are seeking to meet the challenge of utility regulation by establishing Residential Utility Consumer Action Groups (RUCAG) in the various states. RUCAGs would be statewide citizen groups financed by voluntary check-off contributions on utility bills. The idea is to establish a continuous, securely financed consumer group that would have the resources and that would develop the expertise to represent consumers in utility regulatory proceedings. Thus far, legislative proposals to establish RUCAGs have been introduced in about a dozen states, but none has been enacted. Such bills are bitterly opposed by utilities (Leflar and Vogel, 1976). By these reforms, consumer groups seek to institutionalize the consumer perspective in government decision making.

Consumer groups, like environmental groups, also use the legal system for extralegal purposes. Litigation creates publicity and raises public consciousness. Another tactic is to use a court decision for political or leverage purposes only, similar to the way that consumer groups used the Wisconsin usury judicial decision to bargain for a consumer protection statute. In a famous case, Ralph Nader was bumped from a flight by Allegheny Airlines; he sued and was awarded $50,000 damages in a case that received a great deal of publicity. The decision was reversed on appeal and remanded for a new trial, but Nader accomplished his objective: Through the adverse publicity, the Civil Aeronautics Board was pressured to look into the bumping rules and is in the process of devising new rules, presumably more in line with Nader's views. In this case, Nader was not interested in enforcing the judicial decision (Snow and Weisbrod, 1978).

The Center for Auto Safety

Consumer groups also seek allies. I mentioned earlier the alliance on many consumer issues with the AFL-CIO. Another famous alliance concerns Nader's spin-off, the Center for Auto Safety. The history of the center's efforts ties together a number of strands in this chapter.

The center has confronted, probably with a fair degree of success, one of the most powerful manufacturing interests in the country. It has done this during a period when there was substantial consumer satisfaction with the product. In addition, it has had to fight the government agency that was created to enforce safety requirements.

The seed money for the Center for Auto Safety came from the settlement of Nader's privacy suit against General Motors and the royalties from his book *Unsafe At Any Speed*. Nader recruited Lowell Dodge in 1969 to monitor the National Highway Traffic Safety Administration, out of which grew the Center. In 1970 the center was incorporated with an independent board of directors. Nader's influence was strong in the early years. According to Dodge, "About 90 percent of our actions were independent . . . but the 10 percent that he [Nader] had a say in were the critical 10 percent. Anything that was going to have major impact he shared in the shaping, shared in the initial strategizing, in the approach [from Sanford, 1976, p. 45]."

In addition to Nader's seed money, the center also was financed by the Consumers Union. At the present time, the State Farm Companies Foundation is the largest single contributor, but money also comes from: the Allstate Foundation; from royalties from *What To Do With Your Bad Car*[17] and *Small on Safety: The Designed-In Dangers of the Volkswagen;* from special grants, such as one from the Massachusetts Institute of Technology for a study on the installation of seatbelts in taxis; from serving as a back-up center for attorneys who litigate liability claims; from private contributions (although the amount obtained in this manner was described as a "trickle"); and from the American Trial Lawyers Association (ATLA). When the center started, its budget was about $15,000; today it is about $200,000.[18]

Over the years, the center has developed a number of strategies. First, there was need for publicity among both the general public and the auto industry. The "Lemon Book," for example, was written to be read by the auto industry; it got the center "on the map with the auto industry," although it achieved considerable public success as well. The center has always tried to create and maintain good relations with the press. Great care was taken to cultivate *The New York Times, The Washington Post, Automotive News,* and *The Wall Street Journal.* The center also shaped its work product so as to make it newsworthy. There was a conscious effort to issue substantive information rather than mere press releases or cosmetic data. A special arrangement was

[17] The so-called "Lemon Book" by Nader, Dodge, and Ralph Hotchkiss.

[18] See De Toledano (1975, p. 153) and Sanford (1976, p. 22). Information also from interview with Lowell Dodge, March 25, 1976.

cultivated with columnist Jack Anderson whereby he received the center's important stories first. In all cases, however, the center was careful to select issues that had the "highest outrage quotient" with the public, for example, flammable school buses.[19]

Nader and the center also encouraged employees to leak information of improper corporate practices. In one case, the center contacted a General Motors employee who gave the center 2500 documents from the company's internal reporting system on auto defects. The center then asked the Justice Department to bring criminal charges against the company for concealing defects. In addition, the center gave copies of these documents to the American Trial Lawyers Association for use by its auto liability attorneys.[20] In another effort to get information on the auto industry's attitude toward safety, Nader went to the U.S. Patent Office, looked up the names of all scientists and engineers who had invented safety devices that were not being used, and contacted these people (Mueller, 1969).

A third strategy is lobbying.

> Until Nader . . . the common pattern on the Hill with consumer legislation was for the sponsor to introduce the strongest bill they could . . . and then hold on while it got whittled away. . . . The auto-safety law reversed that pattern—it reached Congress . . . in minimal form and became *strengthened* during its progress through Congress [Lowell Dodge, personal communication].

According to one Nader associate, Nader has attempted to maintain close relationships with the products liability bar. This alliance caused considerable controversy when the ATLA pledged $10,000 to the center for the compilation of an index of auto defects. At about the same time, the no-fault auto insurance bill was pending in the Senate. It was defeated, in part, because of the opposition of the ATLA and, some said, because Nader did not speak out in favor of no-fault.[21]

Despite the center's urging others to litigate, that tactic was "fourth or fifth" on the center's own list of available strategies, partly because of the personal proclivities of its director and partly because of the high cost of such litigation.[22] When litigation was necessary, the center sought out prestigious Washington law firms to handle the cases on a *pro bono* basis, with the center usually limiting itself to the role of friend of the court. In recent years, however, the center has developed a greater in-house litigation strategy.[23]

[19] Interview with Lowell Dodge.
[20] Interview with Lowell Dodge.
[21] On this controversy, see Sanford (1976, pp. 33–38), De Toledano (1975, p. 129), Young (1972, p. 11).
[22] Interview with Lowell Dodge.
[23] Interview with Lowell Dodge, March 25, 1977; interview with Michael Sohn, March 26, 1976.

Finally, Nader and the center have established important relationships in Congress. In addition to his early alliance with Senator Ribicoff, Nader has working relationships with such important legislators as Senator Gaylord Nelson, the chairman of the Senate Small Business and Monopoly Subcommittee, who was also a member of the center's board. Senators George McGovern, Edward Muskie, and Warren Magnusson are also friendly with Nader, the center, and generally favor consumer safety issues.[24]

Because of these ties, the center has been able to influence the nature and type of hearings held on auto safety, and often, to testify at the hearings. And because Nader and the center always used detailed facts and figures rather than mere rhetoric, they received an enthusiastic welcome and were listened to carefully.

Another important alliance, in terms of money, publicity, and political leverage is that between the center and the auto insurance companies. In addition to financial contributions, the Allstate Insurance Company, for example, announced a 20% discount on collision insurance for cars that could sustain, without damage, front and rear crashes at speeds of up to 5 miles an hour (*Automotive News*, 1970). It is thought that such incentives put additional pressure on the auto industry to make better bumpers, but also they alerted the public about the need for auto safety.[25]

As stated above, the center has never placed a high priority on litigation but there have been some crucial cases, most notably *Nader v. Volpe* (1969). This suit began when the center learned that General Motors' engineers had found that wheels made by Kelsey–Hayes were defective. Nader then approached a Washington law firm asking it to bring a Freedom of Information Act suit to obtain the GM reports. The litigation was successful, and the reports did show defects. Ultimately, the government sued GM, and the definition of the term "defect" was established by the case.[26]

Another case, which was an effort to examine White House involvement in delaying the installation of air bags during 1972–1973, was lost. However, the center viewed the case in terms of publicizing the air-bag controversy, and serving notice on the administration that it was willing to fight against enormous odds.[27]

The center's litigation strategy, then, served at least two functions. One, of course, was to win on the merits, but the other, considered equally important, was the publicity. As one attorney stated, "The

[24] See De Toledano (1975, p. 126); *Automotive News* (Jan. 8, 1968, p. 6; March 18, 1968, p. 6).
[25] See *Automotive News* (1970). Information also from interview with Lowell Dodge.
[26] Interview with Michael Sohn.
[27] Interview with Michael Sohn.

litigation addressed more than the case before it. There is a publicity function, but we don't go to court without a strong case."[28]

The center's relationship to the National Highway Traffic Safety Agency (NHTSA), organized in 1966, started out well but then quickly declined. William Haddon, Jr., the first head of the agency, was applauded by Nader. Joan Claybrook, now head of NHTSA, was an early speechwriter and special assistant to Haddon, and went on to become one of Nader's most valuable assistants.[29] At this time, according to one agency staff member, there was a groundswell of public agitation and "everyone was running toward auto safety." There was a good but "prickly" alliance between the two groups, with the center always trying to prod the agency into doing more.[30]

However, shortly after the NHTSA issued its first safety standards, Nader accused it of "having sold out to Detroit [De Toledano, 1975, p. 122]." Then, in December 1968, Nader wrote to Senator Nelson, the author of the tire safety law, charging that

> The bureau's leadership has shown a singularly inadequate ability to recognize the necessity to carry out the statutory missions and to enforce the law. . . . This has been the case since enactment of the law in 1966. . . . Dr. William Haddon simply does not take the law seriously enough; he is survey-and-research oriented. . . [*Automotive News*, 1968, p. 6].

Part of the difficulty may have been the budgetary and organizational problems that the agency faced. Its total budget between 1966 and 1969 was only $57.5 million, and in 1968 its staff was frozen at 382, only 86% of the level authorized by Congress in 1966. More importantly, the NHTSA had only 10 employees engaged in defect review, and had no independent, in-house research capability. Thus, the agency was largely dependent on the center or, more realistically, on the auto makers themselves, for data on safety and defects. In addition, the agency was under the control of the Federal Highway Administration which, according to Senator Ribicoff, was dominated by highway interests. Finally, in 1968, President Nixon placed his aide Egil Krogh in a high post at the Department of Transportation, and "everything came to a crashing halt." After a brief respite under Claude Brinnegar as Secretary of the Department of Transportation, the tone of the agency

---

[28] Interview with Michael Sohn.

[29] See De Toledano (1975, p. 122). Information also from an interview with lobbyist for GM, March 24, 1976.

[30] Interview with NHTSA staff member, March 25, 1976.

under President Ford, who had strong ties with Detroit, again "changed toward big-business types."[31]

As effective as the center was, according to one NHTSA staff member, it did not fully utilize its potential vis-à-vis the agency. First, the center did not fully grasp the process and organization of the agency; nor was it sufficiently aware of who held decision-making authority or of agency–industry relationships. In addition, the center never milked the agency for all available information, and did not use the agency to fight the auto makers in Detroit. For example, if the agency did not receive data or information from the center, "It would bow to Detroit because that was easiest to do."[32]

Despite its limitations, the Center for Auto Safety is an example, at least in theory, of one of the most promising consumer organizations. It is backed by or at least identified with Nader, surely the most powerful and well-publicized consumerist of the day. It has strong allies in Congress and it has the financial backing of vested interest groups, the auto insurance companies. It can call on public interest lawyers, and although it cannot lobby, Nader can lobby for it. As far as consumer organizations are concerned, it is probably one of the most powerful. On the other hand, it is fighting an enormous adversary, and, on a comparative basis, the resources of the Center are minute. And, until the recent appointment of Joan Claybrook as head of NHTSA, it had to fight the principal government enforcement agency as well.

Most observers agree that the center's greatest success is its sheer survival. And, by surviving, it has served an important gadfly function. The center considers among its achievements the establishment of safe bumper and tire standards, and it is proud of its role in demanding recalls of defective autos and in participating in general education and publicity work. Among its failures, however, are its inability to stop repeal of the seat-belt interlock system and its ongoing battle over air bags.[33]

The future of the center is not at all clear. First, is the ever-present problem of money, although the insurance company foundations provide a relatively secure base on which to build. Second, is the need for

---

[31] See *Automotive News* (1969, p. 22; 1970, pp. 1, 26). Information also from an interview with an NHTSA staff member.

[32] Interview with NHTSA staff member. The industry takes a very different view of the ties between the center and the agency. According to one industry representative, William Haddon was "rabid" on the auto safety, and this "colored some policymaking" at the agency. The DOT was also perceived as being antiautomobile, although many on the staff "didn't know anything about auto safety." The auto industry as a whole saw itself as being at a distinct disadvantage in the bureaucratic arena.

[33] Interview with former center director.

a strong, energetic director, which is crucial in small organizations like the center. Third, is the problem of future issues. The safety of passenger autos is still important, but attention has shifted, with the exception of the air-bag question, to highway and nonpassenger car issues like truck and bus safety. These issues tend to have a lower publicity value with the general public than do, for example, safe bumpers. However, the safety of recreational and all-terrain vehicles is becoming increasingly important, and the center may be able to capitalize on this issue.[34] Finally, the center has achieved some success in provoking procedural reforms within the NHTSA on questions such as what constitutes standing and what goes into a defect notice. But, according to one observer, there has been a lack of sufficient follow-through on auto safety, particularly on monitoring the NHTSA. The reason for this is lack of funds to hire sufficient numbers of people with technical expertise.[35]

Summary and Conclusions

Table 3.1 summarizes the characteristics of the variables for each of the examples. In four cases, the social-reform groups sought and accomplished the promulgation of clear rules involving essentially one-time decisions—the ordering of lower interest rates on bank loans, outlawing the bans on advertising prescription drugs and the minimum price of milk, and changes in children's television advertising. Subject to the caveat about the meaning of success, these actions can be counted as successful. Regardless of whether the rule changes in the drug and children's advertising cases will result in tangible benefits to consumers, the changes are what the social-reform groups sought. If in fact discount drug companies do not decide to expand their markets, or children still demand junk food, then perhaps social-reform groups ought to reconsider their basic strategies, but it would be unreasonable to label their law-reform actions as failures. No group can foresee or control events so far in the future or so little understood. In the California case on the retail price of milk, some follow-up is necessary, but it does not appear to be overwhelming.

In these four cases, the only variable characteristic that was favorable to activity by social-reform groups was the *bureaucratic contingency*. All the others were unfavorable. What, then, accounts for success? The answer is that when all that is required is a rule change

---

[34] Interview with former center director and interview with NHTSA staff member.

[35] Interview with center-associated attorney.

without long-term, technically complex, or field-level discretion, then the normally unfavorable characteristics of the law reformers can accomplish the task, which is usually a straight law case. The subsidized law firm supplies the resources and overcomes, for the limited purposes, the free-rider problem, the unfavorable characteristics of group size and the *distribution of benefits and costs*.

In two other cases, legal activity was used for political leverage purposes only. Those were the Wisconsin usury case and Nader's suit against Allegheny Airlines. These two actions were successful in terms of the limited goals of the groups: a statute was enacted, and the CAB was prodded into reconsidering the bumping rules. It may be that subsequently the groups will lose. The consumer protection statute may be ineffective if implemented, or the CAB may reject an improved bumping rule, but these were not the immediate object of the litigation, which was primarily for political leverage. In these two cases, most of the characteristics of the variables were unfavorable, but because of the limited purposes of the litigation, the judicial remedies and the characteristics of the law reformers were sufficient for the action to succeed. What was involved were straight law cases; the court decision by itself triggered the other agency or political action and there was no need for enforcement of a court order. The law reformers could use their traditional legal skills, although in both examples, the law reformers also had some political resources as well.

Six of the examples indicate failures in the law-reform activity. They all involve bureaucratic contingencies with unfavorable characteristics (long-term, field-level implementation, discretion) and no other favorable characteristics in any of the other variables. These examples are the refund part of the Wisconsin usury case order, the FTC advertising substantiation order, the Federal Reserve Board information on bank loan rate charges, the Equal Credit Act, and utility rate regulation. I have also included in this category FDA enforcement. Although a specific FDA case example was not discussed, the general characteristics of that agency indicate that social-reform groups will continue to have great difficulty in monitoring enforcement. The examples in this group illustrate one of the most important conclusions of the theory, namely, the great difficulties that social-reform groups face when confronted with long-term, field-level discretionary decisions.

There are two other examples that involve unfavorable bureaucratic contingencies but where the chances of success are considerably improved. These are the credit card discount cases and the auto safety campaign. In both cases, there were important changes in the other variables that account for the (possible) success. In the credit card case,

Table 3.1 Consumer Protection, Summary of Variables

Variables	Wisconsin Lower interest rates	Refunds	Leverage	Drug advertising ban	Milk price-fixing	Children advertising	FTC ad substantiation	FRB bank loan rates	Credit card Cash discounts	Equal Credit Act	FDA enforcement	Utility rate regulation	Allegheny Airlines	Auto safety
Groups														
Small size														+
Outside funding														+
Selective benefits														+
Large size	−	−	−	−	−	−	−	−	−	−	−	−	−	
No outside resources	−	−	−	−	−	−	−	−	−	−	−	−	−	
Collective goods only	−	−	−	−	−	−	−	−	−	−	−	−	−	
Distribution														
Benefits concentrated; costs distributed														
Benefits distributed; costs distributed														
Benefits concentrated; costs concentrated														+
Benefits distributed; costs concentrated	−	−	−	−	−	−	−	−	−	−	−	−	−	−

	1	2	3	4	5	6	7	8	9
Bureaucratic									
One time	+	+	+	+	?	+		−	
Top solution	+	+	+	+	+	+			
Technically simple	+	+	+	+	+	+			
Discretion reduced	+	+	+	+	?	+			
Long-term					−		−		−
Field-level implementation					−		−		−
Technically complex					−		−		
Discretion required	−		−		−		−		−
Judicial									
Previous injunction	+		+						
Court solution	+	+	+						+
Order can be monitored	+	+	+					+	
Regular injunction	−								−
Remand to agency	−								−
Order complex							−		−
Law reformers									
Affiliated	−				+		+		+
Technical resources	−				+		+		+
Political resources	−	+			+		+	+	+
Independent	−	−	−	−	−	−	−	−	−
No technical resources	−	−	−	−	−	−	−	−	−
No political resources	−	−	−	−	−	−	−	−	−

the law firm made an alliance with Consumers Union, which conducted the implementation campaign. This changed the characteristics of the law reformers from unfavorable to favorable; for the purposes of this legal action, the law reformers were affiliated and had technical resources.

The auto safety campaign is a complex example. There could be argument about whether the activity of social-reform groups can be counted as successful. Certainly, we have not attained the goal of safe automobiles, and there were many factors that produced the auto safety legislation and regulations that were probably not causally related to the activity of the Center for Auto Safety. Nevertheless, I think a persuasive argument can be made that thus far this has been successful social-reform activity. The center has taken on one of the most powerful adversaries in the country, and has also had to fight an unsympathetic regulatory agency. The center has kept the public aware of auto safety problems, has forged and maintained powerful political allies in Congress (and perhaps even in the White House), and, although it has suffered some substantive defeats, it has also had a significant hand in most of the major changes imposed on the industry. In Chapter 1, it was pointed out that it is unrealistic to expect a social-reform group to accomplish major social change on its own. Furthermore, social-change victories are rarely complete; there are generally compromises and partial solutions, particularly in hard-fought areas. Given the circumstances under which the Center for Auto Safety labors, its record seems pretty good.

In the auto safety campaign, the bureaucratic contingencies are mixed. Auto safety rules are made at the top, are one-time, usually involve a minimum of discretion, and monitoring is fairly easy. An example of such a rule is the one requiring installation of seat belts on all new cars. On the other hand, there is continual controversy within the Department of Transportation about whether to adopt safety requirements. These controversies are long-term, technically complex, and ultimately are discretionary decisions for the agency. These characteristics are unfavorable to law-reform activity by social-reform groups. To overcome these unfavorable characteristics, the characteristics of three other variables are favorable. The center has alliances with vested interest groups (automobile insurance companies) that change the characteristics of the group from unfavorable to favorable: There is small size, outside resources, and selective benefits. The distribution of the benefits and costs is also not as unfavorable as in other actions, since benefits are concentrated with the insurance companies. The characteristics of the law reformers are also favorable.

Although the center is formally independent of Ralph Nader, it is publicly identified with him and thus has powerful political resources, and can call on the Nader organizations for technical and lobbying resources.

Predictions would also change if the Nader RUCAGs were adopted to deal with utility rate regulation. The characteristics of the social-reform groups would become favorable because of a stable source of funds and selective incentives for the leadership. The organizations would be similar to political parties. The characteristics of the law reformers would also change. Presumably such consumer groups would have a law firm on a more or less continuing relationship to deal systematically with agency and industry problems. The law reformers would be affiliated, and have technical and political resources to aid them in their legal work.

4

Civil Rights

As shown in Chapters 2 and 3, social-reform groups faced great difficulties when change depended on long-term, field-level discretionary decisions. While this bureaucratic contingency was present in several of the environmental and consumer actions, it becomes of crucial importance in civil rights and in social welfare (the topic of Chapter 5). In these two areas, the ultimate test is how the poor and minorities, as individuals, are treated by public and private officials exercising discretionary authority—police, teachers, social workers, doctors, hospital personnel, landlords, and employers, to name only a few of the powerful people the disadvantaged face in their daily lives.

Discretionary, field-level decisions posit a bargaining relationship; the official has choices, and, at least in theory, the client has the opportunity to present facts and reasons why the official should make certain decisions. In fact, the clients who are the concerns of this chapter and the next—the poor and minorities—are often not in a position to present their case or assert their rights. They lack knowledge of the substantive law and procedural remedies available to them; they often lack help necessary to prosecute their claims; and, because they often must continue to deal with their adversaries, they are fearful of retaliation. They are a dependent population. They do not have the educational background, the resources, or the access to information that others in society have.[1]

The basic conditions for social change have been illustrated by the discussion of the Equal Credit Opportunity Act in Chapter 3. Changes in the law can be made at the top, but unless pressure is exerted throughout the bureaucracy, and especially at the field level, it cannot be assumed that lower-level officials will change their ways of doing business. With the Equal Credit Opportunity Act it could not be assumed that credit officers would recognize and agree that their previous behavior was prejudiced, and that they would become familiar with and agree to abide by the new law and regulations. However, enforcement not only required internal, bureaucratic efforts at education and supervision, it also required an extensive amount of consumer education. People had to be made aware of the existence of their rights, the means to pursue those rights, and the resources. When change is required for large numbers of field-level decisions, information and pressure have to come from two sources, the administrative supervisors and the clients.

As we shall see, in the areas of civil rights and social welfare, social-reform groups have been active in getting laws changed and regulations issued. In many areas, the substantive and procedural laws, on paper, guarantee basic rights; in practice, these rights are not fulfilled because enforcement relies too much on the *complaining client,* which is the basic model of law enforcement in this country. We assume that if the law grants a right and a procedural remedy, a person sufficiently aggrieved will assert the claim through the procedural remedy. This is the adversary system. If the process works, it serves two functions. It satisfies the individual with the claim, and it also calls attention to how the law is being administered. Presumably, if enough claims are successfully prosecuted, the bureaucracy will be forced to change its procedures.

As in the equal credit example, and as the examples in the next two chapters will show, the adversary system does not work to vindicate client rights or change official behavior when the clients are poor or members of a racial minority. These people cannot cope with intransigient field-level bureaucrats.[2] Social-reform groups and law reformers, for the most part, are aware of the problems of the adver-

---

[1] The constraints that the poor and minorities operate under in dealing with officials is, by now, thoroughly documented. See generally, Rubenstein (1976) and Handler (forthcoming).

[2] In addition to the authorities cited in Note 1, see Handler (1966).

sary system in civil rights and social welfare, and when they can, they try to seek methods to avoid these difficult enforcement problems. In these two chapters, I will discuss some of the devices that are being tried; in some situations, they have been successful, but in others they have failed. Securing justice for those who are discriminated against has proven to be one of the most difficult problems our society faces.

This chapter starts with the most significant social-reform effort in recent history: civil rights for southern blacks. My focus is primarily on school integration and voting rights. The other two examples also are about civil rights issues. They involve the efforts nationwide against discrimination in housing and employment.

School Desegregation

Southern blacks have been struggling for civil rights for 300 years. In this century, with the formation of the NAACP, their struggle took a particularly legalistic form. The NAACP, and its later spin-off, the NAACP Legal Defense Fund (LDF) began to attack segregation laws in the federal courts, and, as previously mentioned, won many important Supreme Court cases.[3] The modern era starts with *Brown* v. *Board of Education* (1954),[4] the Supreme Court decision that declared unconstitutional segregation in the public schools. The importance of this case for black civil rights leaders cannot be overestimated. They considered it "a visible sign . . . that the white establishment and the federal government were supporting the legal road to changing their subordinate position [Oberschall, 1973, p. 206]." According to Louis Lomax (1971, pp. 83–86), many blacks were confident that victory for an integrated society had come. They felt that the white establishment of the South, while not in favor of integration, would insist on law and order, and not be bullied and cowed into submission by poor whites, fanatics, and mobs. It was anticipated that local school boards would voluntarily obey the Supreme Court.

The white supremacists also felt that the decision was of momentous importance. According to Anthony Lewis (1964):

> Any breakdown in school segregation necessarily endangered the perpetuation of the southern myth that the Negro is by nature culturally distinct and inferior. And there was the fear—surely felt deeply by many in the South, however others regarded it—that school integration was a step toward racial intermarriage [p. 5].

[3] On the history of the NAACP and the LDF, see Rabin (1976).

[4] 347 U.S. 483.

Mississippi's Senator James Eastland said, "The people of the South will never accept this monstrous decision. I predict this decision will bring a century of litigation [Quoted in Lomax, 1971, p. 85]."

Desegregation began almost immediately in the border areas of the country, and by 1956, several hundred school districts integrated voluntarily (Lewis, 1964, chap. 3). Then the tide turned. The Southern Manifesto of 1956, signed by 101 United States senators and congressmen, called the *Brown* decision a "clear abuse of judicial power."

Southern states started their campaigns of massive resistance, and violent resistance movements spread rapidly throughout the South. Southern whites were a determined, substantial minority in the nation as a whole, and a militant majority in their home states. Opposition to *Brown* took two forms: (a) Social and economic pressure, violence, and mob action to intimidate blacks and moderate whites; (b) massive legal battles to challenge the ruling. Every school district would litigate. Every other move toward desegregation would be resisted in court. The Southerners hoped that eventually public opinion would turn against the Court, and the decision either would be reversed or would lapse for lack of enforcement. At this time, the North was relatively indifferent to civil rights, and the federal government, under President Eisenhower, was equivocating in its support of the Supreme Court (Bickel, 1962, pp. 255–266).

The legislative parts of the massive resistance strategy took a variety of forms. Initially, laws provided for withdrawing state funds from any school district that adopted desegregation plans, closing such schools, repealing compulsory education laws, providing tuition grants for private schools, cutting off salaries of teachers in desegregated schools, and preventing school boards from borrowing from their usual commercial sources. As these laws were declared invalid, more subtle techniques were adopted, such as pupil placement laws. These laws, which did not mention race, allowed local officials to assign pupils to schools on the basis of various criteria. In fact, the assignments were used to perpetuate segregation. Black students who objected faced a maze of administrative hurdles, followed by difficult court battles. School boards also adopted plans assigning students to schools on the basis of geographic zones. Determining whether the lines of any particular plan were gerrymandered to preserve segregation presented questions difficult to litigate, especially if blacks had the burden of proof. Where desegregation plans were adopted, school boards fought in court as long as possible (United States Civil Rights Commission, 1963, pp. 1–57).

By 1961, the United States Civil Rights Commission (1961, pp.

177–178) reported that desegregation was proceeding only when ordered by courts. Moreover, the cases were hard fought, long, and complicated. In the typical public school case, 7 years would elapse between the start of the litigation and actual admission of black children to white schools. Charles Silberman (1964, p. 289) reported that 10 years after the *Brown* decision two of the four school districts in the original case had still not admitted a single black student. In 10 states in the Deep South, less than six-tenths of 1 % of all black students were in desegregated schools. Writing in 1963, Louis Lomax (p. 125) reported that it took 7 years of effort to get only 7 % of the black children in the South into desegregated schools.

Segregation in public schools was not the only issue. The federal courts invalidated segregation laws for many other public facilities; the follow-up here also required litigation when communities refused to comply voluntarily. The NAACP and other civil rights organizations did not have the resources to challenge this kind of massive resistance on a comprehensive basis. Even after years of struggle, some communities did not have a single desegregated facility, and in others, desegregation was minimal (for example, a few lunch counters only) (Oberschall, 1973, p. 223).

Although the dominant black social-reform group, the NAACP, concentrated on attacking desegregation through the courts, other alternatives, especially direct action, also developed. The first dramatic instance of direct action was probably the Montgomery bus boycott (1955–1956).[5] On Dec. 1, 1955, Mrs. Rosa Parks, boarded a bus in Montgomery, Alabama, and, weary after a day's work, refused to give up her seat to a white. She was arrested. Although Mrs. Parks was a civil rights activist, her refusal to move was apparently not planned nor part of a campaign. Nevertheless, news of the arrest spread rapidly throughout the black community and over the weekend a boycott of the bus system was organized. The boycott was conducted by the newly formed Montgomery Improvement Association (MIA), composed mainly of church and community groups, and its newly elected president, Dr. Martin Luther King, Jr., a young Baptist minister.

On the Monday morning following the arrest, the buses passed through the black neighborhoods empty. White reaction was bitter at the revolt. Gangs terrorized blacks and committed acts of violence. King and other leaders were arrested and jailed on various charges. The bus company was intransigient. Nevertheless the boycott continued. The boycott tactic had a number of advantages for blacks. It

[5] For accounts of the Montgomery bus boycott and the birth of the Southern Christian Leadership Conference, see Lomax (1971, chap. 8) and Oberschall (1973, pp. 126, 223–224, 267–268).

was not illegal; thus, the leaders and participants could not be legally arrested. It avoided confrontation, which was important because any confrontation in the deep South at this time would have meant brutal repression. At the same time, the black leaders displayed moderation and self-discipline, which was helpful in attracting outside support. The disadvantage of the boycott was that the city council was under no real pressure to yield until the city began to feel the economic impact of the loss of revenue. For a long time there was a stalemate. The matter was finally resolved by a lawsuit in which the court declared the ordinance unconstitutional. The leaders used litigation to sidetrack more militant members of the group. The court decision legitimated the position of Reverend King and was valuable publicity in the North. The city lost, but it could save face by blaming the courts. The litigation allowed both sides to avoid escalating the conflict.

The buses, for a time, became desegregated in Montgomery, and black groups in other cities were encouraged to make similar moves. Perhaps even more significant is the fact that the Montgomery bus boycott launched Martin Luther King, Jr. on his road to national and, eventually, international prominence. He, along with other black clergymen, formed the Southern Christian Leadership Conference (SCLC), which quickly became one of the most important black social-reform groups, rivaling, and, for a time, eclipsing the NAACP.

Despite the great fame of King and the SCLC, the work remained undone, even in Montgomery. After the boycott was over, white violence increased, juries refused to convict whites for acts of violence against blacks, and the city passed several new segregation ordinances. Schools, parks, playgrounds, and every other public facility remained segregated. Martin Luther King's organization lacked the resources to challenge these laws (Oberschall, 1973, p. 223). Silberman (1964) reports that 7 years after the court ordered integration of the buses, most blacks "had returned to the old custom of riding in the back of the bus [p. 142]."

Why did the segregation campaigns in the South run into such difficulty? One obvious answer has already been stressed; white resistance was fierce and resourceful. Moreover, the black organizations had to fight alone; they received virtually no support from the moderate white South, and only belated, grudging support from the federal government. But an additional important reason was the social condition of the beneficiaries of the campaign, the southern rural and urban blacks. Even by the early 1960s, in the rural and small towns of the South, the vast majority of families were at poverty or near-poverty income levels. Most were sharecroppers, agricultural wage earners, laborers, and domestic servants. Black voter registration never exceeded 15% of the electorate; blacks had no political power. Their leaders were totally dependent on whites and were not in any position to help the black community. In short, blacks in the rural and small towns were almost totally dependent on whites for jobs, income, credit, and supplies. Economic dependency not only applied to the working class but also to schoolteachers, small businessmen, professionals, and ministers.

In the southern cities, blacks had some political power, but the dominant pattern was a "bourbon-black" alliance designed to keep down working-class whites. Black leaders tended to be older and accommodationists; they were unwilling or unable to challenge segregation, and were content to derive personal benefits from the status quo. (Oberschall, 1973, pp. 209–213).

In time, the older accommodationist black leaders were challenged by militants. But during the early years of the desegregation campaigns, the social-reform groups failed to mobilize the lower-class black community. It was difficult to expect black families to send their children to white schools in view of the hostility, harassment, and social and economic sanctions that almost surely followed. Integration of buses and public facilities not only required the striking down of laws, but the continued use of the facilities by the ordinary working black. Although rarely discussed, the NAACP had trouble persuading parents to start integration suits. According to Lomax (1971), in 1962, "Parents, on the whole, don't seem to be interested in doing so; some of them fear reprisals, but the major explanations for this lethargy seem to be that school integration simply isn't something that large numbers of Negroes get excited about [p. 125]." In addition, southern teachers feared losing their jobs if schools were integrated. The NAACP was organized, and led by the black middle class. It drew its financial support from white, middle-class liberals. It could be, as Lomax claims, that although segregation constituted a continuing and serious indignity to blacks, desegregation was not a high priority among lower-class blacks.[6]

The NAACP and other black leaders have insisted, however, that desegregation, especially in education, is one of the keys to the social, political, and economic emancipation of blacks. But whatever the case, the early desegregation campaigns illustrate the same point that was made in the discussion of the equal credit law: A massive education campaign was needed to inform and persuade large numbers of people

---

[6] Needless to say, the charge that the NAACP was not really in touch with the average southern black is a hotly debated point. In addition to Lomax (1971), see Oberschall (1973, p. 213) and Bell (1976b).

to learn about and pursue their rights. Only then would lower-level officials change their behavior and enforce the law.

   The characteristics of the social-reform groups in the desegregation campaigns, therefore, did not favor successful activity by social-
reform groups. Although there is debate as to whether the NAACP and
other black groups were in touch with lower-class blacks, and how
much membership support came from the ordinary black, it is clear
that the leadership was drawn from the middle class. Even more important is that financial support came from northern white liberals·
(Oberschall, 1973, p. 217). These organizations fit within the definition
of the funded social movement organization of McCarthy and Zald
(1977). They are led by full-time staff that works hard to keep up the
flow of outside funds from the "conscience" constituency, that is individuals who will not benefit from the collective goods supplied by the
organization. These contributors are motivated by purposive incentives. The legitimacy conferred on the blacks' demands by the Supreme
Court and the lower federal courts, the vision of an integrated society,
and the love, peace, and nonviolence of Martin Luther King, Jr., all
served to increase this support. The basis of this support was
dramatically illustrated when another important group, the Students
Nonviolent Coordinating Committee (SNCC), turned militant and
separatist; its strong white liberal support immediately dried up.

   There were other incentives operating among the black groups.
Clearly selective incentives were important for recruiting leaders. The
NAACP was not only challenged by SCLC, but SNCC and the Congress
of Racial Equality (CORE) also rose to prominence. Moreover, within
each organization, there were rivalries among local leaders and aspiring leaders. In addition, there were loners, such as James Meredith, and
clergymen with their own churches. Again, there is a diversity of opinion as to whether the proliferation and competition among black
social-reform groups was a benefit or a loss to the movement as a
whole, but no one denies that selective incentives were powerful in
motivating people who wanted to be leaders (Oberschall, 1973,
pp. 222–223).

   What were the incentives for lower-class blacks, those vast
numbers that the groups sought to help through the desegregation
drives? According to Wilson, lower-class membership is primarily interested in material incentives, and these are hard to supply, especially
on a continuing basis. Did desegregation of schools and public facilities
supply these incentives? Were they immediate and material enough to
induce the ordinary black in the South to make the necessary sacrifice?
Again, there is a difference of opinion. Lomax, as mentioned, was

clearly of the view that desegregation was not a salient issue for the ordinary black. School integration suits, especially in the early years, took years to complete; the final orders were not of much relevance to the children of the original plaintiffs. The NAACP recognized the problem of the lack of immediate tangible benefits to the ordinary black family, and sought to overcome this hurdle through education campaigns. However, rewards were remote and intangible.

In any event, desegregation of schools and facilities are collective goods, goods that any black could enjoy without making any contribution to the cost of obtaining the goods. The organizations had to appeal to purposive incentives of elites, who were the white liberals, and highly motivated, dedicated blacks. In sum, the social-reform groups were large with a mass or paper membership; their goals were collective goods; they faced the free-rider problem; they were basically funded social movements relying heavily on infusions of support from elites and contributing beneficiaries.

In regard to the *distribution of benefits and costs,* in the civil rights examples, benefits were widely distributed. Analysis of the distribution of costs is more complicated. In the long run, the costs of these efforts are widely distributed since whites must share facilities with blacks, but the short-run costs were concentrated in that local politicians lost office if they did not resist black demands. The political importance of unflinching resistance to black demands is well illustrated by the rapid growth of the White Citizens Councils. These councils, which were the principal and most effective organizations of resistance, spread through the local service clubs (Rotary, Kiwanis, Lions, etc.). Often members would join as a block as soon as a council was formed. The councils spread through networks of friendship and politics; as they multiplied and became a political force, moderate white strength faded. The councils soon were supported publicly by the local press and the entire political establishment—senators, congressmen, state legislators, and local officials (Oberschall, 1973, p. 216; Rodgers and Bullock, 1972, pp. 71–73).

The desegregation campaigns present the *bureaucratic contingency* in its most acute form. Implementation of desegregation required behavior changes in hundreds of school boards, bus companies, park districts, municipal services, and so forth, throughout the South. The bureaucracies were decentralized. Implementation required field-level penetration to monitor and regulate discretionary decisions extending over long periods of time. It required enormous staying power on the part of the social-reform groups. The history of school desegregation has been told elsewhere and will not be repeated here (see Rodgers and

Bullock, 1972, chap. 4). What is important, though, for our purposes, is a discussion of a number of methods that were used to cope with the bureaucratic contingency of discretionary field-level decisions. The existence and continued persistence of field-level discretionary authority was one of the most important weapons in the hands of those who opposed desegregation, and there has been a continuing struggle to search for ways to limit that discretion to ease the otherwise insuperable burden of monitoring compliance.

Discretion exists in a decentralized system. There are over 6000 school districts in the 17 southern and border states alone, and, of course, thousands more as desegregation issues turned to the northern states in the 1960s. Most of the decision-making authority rests with the school boards, although from time to time, state legislatures have intervened. By the early 1960s, most southern states had pupil placement laws under which school officials had the authority to assign individual students to various schools. Under these laws, various criteria were used including discretionary criteria—the "pupil's personal qualifications, such as health, morals, and home environment" and the "effects of the admission of the particular pupil on the other pupils and the community." It is easy to see how such laws, without ever mentioning race, would be administered by southern officials to invariably assign black students to black schools and white students to white schools. In addition, if a black student wished to challenge the assignment, there were administrative roadblocks (for example, petitions were denied for failure to use the official form when forms were in fact not available), the pupil had the burden of proof, and the court relief was of questionable value. Although the court could order relief for a particular plaintiff, each new case would have to start afresh. Or, if the school board feared a broader order, it could grant relief administratively and thus make the proceeding moot. Not unexpectedly, the United States Civil Rights Commission (1963) found that after 9 years of operation, pupil placement laws perpetuated segregation.[7]

Accordingly, civil rights activists began to press for desegregation plans that would achieve a racial balance of students determined by quantitative measures (an "effects" test) and that would switch the burden of proof from the pupils to the school boards. The early plans called for desegregation of one grade a year, but then the courts began to decide that this pace was too slow.[8] However, the question remained as to what comprised a "desegregation plan." Basically, two types of

[7] See *Green* v. *County School Board*, 391 U.S. 430 (1968) invalidating a "freedom-of-choice" plan on the grounds that it did not, in fact, result in a constitutionally satisfactory racial balance. The Court relied on the statistical results of the plan.

[8] See *Swann* v. *Charlotte-Mecklinburg Board of Education*, 402 U.S. 1 (1971).

plans were approved. One was geographic zoning, but the stumbling block with that involved who had the burden of proving that the redrawn district lines were essentially gerrymandered to preserve segregation. The courts went both ways on the issue. But regardless of the burden-of-proof issue, the geographic plan did result in at least some reduction of field-level discretion. The test of the validity of the plan was no longer decided by individual cases, that is, whether a particular student should be in a particular school. Rather, at least part of the test looked to quantifiable effects of the plan, that is what proportion of the races attended what schools. A geographic plan could be outlawed if it did not produce enough mixing of the races, regardless of the motives of the school district drawing the lines. The naked statistical results would be the measure of legality.

In such a situation, although an agency still has discretion in selecting the various options, that discretion is sharply reduced because the plaintiff's burden of challenging it is greatly eased. If the statistics, which are fairly easy to gather, show discrimination, then even though the plaintiff has the burden of proof, that burden has been satisfied and the agency has to come up with a new plan that will produce better results.

The other desegregation plan that was used was "freedom-of-choice" under which, as the name implies, every student, regardless of race, had the free choice of attending whatever school he or she desired. Free choice plans, in practice, did little if anything to achieve desegregation. It would be the rare white who would opt for a black school. The reverse was probably also true. There were many social and economic pressures discouraging blacks from taking advantage of the free choice. In addition, the United States Civil Rights Commission found active discouragement by school officials either by informal methods or by difficult administrative procedures. In the freedom-of-choice plans, the issue of the measure of enforcement is squarely posed. If, in fact, blacks do not appear in formerly all-white schools, or vice versa, will that alone invalidate the plan, or will those seeking to challenge the plan have the burden of showing that discriminatory administration has occurred? The Supreme Court held that such a plan is invalid if it does not actually produce an acceptable racial balance, although mathematical ratios are to be considered a "starting point" rather than an "inflexible requirement." But in any event, school district plans are to be judged by effectiveness, that is, quantifiable racial balances, rather than intent to discriminate.[9] Otherwise field-

---

[9] 391 U.S. 430 (1968); *United States* v. *Montgomery County Board of Education,* 395 U.S. 225 (1969) upheld a district court order fixing a specific hiring ratio of black teachers to white teachers.

level discretion would be maximized since the burden of proof becomes too difficult to handle on a case-by-case basis.[10]

There were other methods in addition to the numbers of blacks attending formerly all-white schools by which school boards perpetuated segregation. It was found, for example, that even in newly integrated schools, there could be segregated classrooms, lunchrooms, recreational facilities, buses, athletic and extracurricular activities. Also, black teachers, principals, and administrators lost their jobs.

During the first 10 years of desegregation efforts, then, the battle was over how much discretionary authority school boards would retain in implementing the *Brown* decision. Southern segregationists were well aware of how important the existence of discretionary authority was. Legally, or extralegally, through political and social pressure, they could count on their local officials, often with the approval of the federal district court judges, to devise an array of strategems to thwart integration. Social-reform groups and law reformers could not cope with this strategy as long as the substantive criteria conferred discretionary authority on the school districts and cases had to be litigated on a case-by-case basis, with the burden of proof on the plaintiff. The groups simply lacked the strength to challenge the large numbers of decisions, and the lack of a creditable threat to challenge served to increase further field-level discretionary authority. The principal method of meeting this challenge was to impose a quantifiable measure of effects: If a particular plan did not in fact produce a desired level of integration, then it would be presumed invalid unless the school district could show nondiscriminatory reasons for the persistence of segregated patterns (Fiss, 1971). There was nothing secret about the practical importance of a quantifiable test in trying to overcome the bureaucratic contingency in other activity by social-reform groups dealing with civil rights and social welfare, and the use of such a standard of performance becomes a principal issue.

In the mid-1960s, additional developments occurred in school desegregation that have importance for social-reform groups. The Civil Rights Act of 1964 was enacted, which recognized that the courts and social-reform groups could not fight desegregation battles alone. Under that act, executive enforcement was placed in HEW and under Title VI of the act, HEW had authority to cut off federal funding for school districts that failed to implement suitable integration plans. In addi-

---

[10] *Swann v. Charlotte-Mecklinburg Board of Education*, 402 U.S. 1 (1971); *Davis v. Board of School Commissioners*, 402 U.S. 33, 37 (1971), "The measure of any desegregation plan is its effectiveness." For a critical account of this approach, see Glazer (1975, chap. 3), which is critically reviewed in Bell (1976a).

tion, the Justice Department was given authority to initiate desegregation suits on behalf of private plaintiffs. The federal government, which had passively tolerated southern resistance under the Eisenhower administration, would, it was hoped, pursue a more active role and thus relieve some of the burden on the civil-rights organizations (Kirp and Yudof, 1974; Orfield, 1969).

Federal executive intervention quickened the pace of integration, but progress was still slow. The HEW guidelines, to the disappointment of civil rights groups, took a gradualist approach, allowed "good faith" efforts to excuse school districts, and had time-consuming procedures for financial cut-offs. On the other hand, Congress made sure that HEW lacked the staff and resources for vigorous implementation. The Justice Department filed over 100 suits during the first year and a half of the new law, and some of the district courts stiffened their requirements for school boards. During this period, attention turned to segregation in the North, and HEW concluded that the primary cause of the persistence of widespread segregation was segregated living patterns. In 1967, HEW began to order busing to achieve integration, and this started the present controversy. When the Nixon administration took over, federal executive enforcement sagged. One of the major approaches of the administration was to deemphasize HEW's enforcement role, increase the Justice Department's litigation role, and sanction freedom-of-choice plans. Thus, while claiming adherence to the principles of the *Brown* decision, Nixon fulfilled his promise to his southern supporters by emphasizing discretionary authority at the field level. Local school boards could continue to seek ways of evading the law through sympathetic federal judges or a Justice Department more under the control of the President than HEW (Rodgers and Bullock, 1972, pp. 81–102).

The role of the federal government, then, remained ambiguous at best. During the early years of the desegregation campaigns, the social-reform groups had to go it alone. They had some northern liberal support, but they faced a passive, hands-off federal administration. With enactment of Title VI of the Civil Rights Act (1964), presumably HEW and the Justice Department would join the battle and help the social-reform groups overcome the bureaucratic contingency; funds could be cut off and the Justice Department could assume more of a role in litigation. To the extent, though, that the federal government faltered in its obligations, it created even more difficulties for the social-reform groups. An incompetent, inefficient, or recalcitrant federal enforcement agency only makes matters worse for the plaintiffs because they have to view the federal government as an enemy along with the defendant school district.[11] Not unexpectedly, federal courts are normally reluctant to make judgments against the Executive and issue sweeping, strong orders. But unless the courts do, the federal enforcement agency, by failing to investigate promptly, make strong factual findings, and recommend or take decisive action, can only serve to delay and frustrate the social-reform group. In many instances of discrimination in education, the federal government has exacerbated the bureaucratic contingency.

In the school desegregation campaign, customary *judicial remedies* proved unsatisfactory. Initially, the court orders required affirmative behavior on the part of officials and relied on complaining clients to monitor enforcement. If a particular student felt that he or she was unjustifiably denied admission to a particular school, the student's representative would file a complaint with the administrative agency (the school board), and if the claim were still denied, there would be judicial review. As stated in the beginning of the chapter, initially students and families could not cope with the administrative delays and continually fight the discretionary decisions; the social-reform groups could not persuade families to start suits.

In parts of the country where district court judges were eager to uphold the law, some developed strategies designed to make judicial remedies more effective. By now the test was quantified effects: Regardless of motive, were the schools still segregated? If so, then whites and blacks would be bused to different schools to achieve acceptable levels of integration. Needless to say, busing orders produced great controversy, and several courts soon realized that they could not rely on individual plaintiffs and civil-rights organizations to shoulder the burden of devising and supervising implementation of the plans.[12] Instead, these courts employed various techniques for administering orders. In Boston, the district court used the Community Relations Service of the Justice Department to help with the desegregation plan. In Detroit, the judge formed a committee of experts to work out the details of pupil and faculty reassignments and to supervise enforcement. In these instances and others, the courts changed the normally unfavorable characteristics of the judicial remedy to potentially more favorable ones by the extraordinary use of administrative machinery.

The Montgomery bus boycott was a different situation. Martin Luther King, Jr. never had any illusions concerning the ability of court

[11] See *Adams* v. *Richardson*, 356 F. Supp. 92 (D.D.C. 1973) aff'd per curiam (D.C. Cir. June 12, 1973).

[12] For a collection of materials dealing with the busing controversy, see Kirp and Yudof (1974, pp. 354–390) and Glazer (1975, chap. 3).

orders to bring about desegregation; his tactic was direct action. The court order was used for other, limited purposes, that is, to save face and provide an out for both sides, to cool militants, to gain publicity and legitimacy. For these goals, the court decision served its purposes. The court order by itself was sufficient for leverage and fund-raising purposes (Oberschall, 1973).

In school desegregation, the characteristics of the *law reformers* would ordinarily be considered favorable. They were not independent free-floating, foundation-supported lawyers that could pick and choose their cases. Rather, they grew out of and were intimately tied to the social-reform groups and could draw on what political and technical resources the groups had. The litigation involved traditional legal skills. The problem, though, in the desegregation campaigns was that the social-reform groups and their legal resources were simply overwhelmed by the opposition. During the period of the desegregation campaigns, social change through law-reform litigation simply required too many individual lawsuits in too many places. The social-reform groups required the active intervention of the federal government. When this happened the pace of desegregation quickened. When the federal government backed off, the pace slackened.[13] In the Montgomery bus boycott, the characteristics of the law reformers were also favorable. This was a straight law case not calling for special political or technical resources.

The desegregation fight was, and still is, probably the most ambitious undertaking of law-reform activity by social-reform groups. It was initiated as pure law reform through Supreme Court litigation but the course of its tortured history illustrates some of the major issues confronting law-reform activity in civil rights and social welfare. It is clear that the civil rights organizations, even with their outside contributors, could not achieve the integration of a major American institution, such as the public school system, on their own. At the very minimum, they needed vigorous help from the federal executive, and this they never got, although when HEW and the Justice Department were active, the importance of their efforts was apparent. It was only with federal help that there was any hope of coping with the intransigency of the white communities both in the North and the South. The segregation controversy, thus, illustrates a cardinal point of this book: Social-reform groups cannot accomplish major social change alone. In addition, this battle also illustrates other points of importance. One is the idea of limiting the all-important bureaucratic contingency of field-

[13] Compare the findings of Jenkins and Perrow (1976) that the United Farm Workers succeeded only after the government and the liberal community came to their aid.

level discretion by using a quantifiable measure of performance. The
other is the willingness of certain federal judges to employ innovative
administrative machinery to overcome the normally unfavorable
characteristic of the judicial remedy.

Voting Rights

In many respects, the history of voting rights for blacks is a mirror
image of the school desegregation controversy. The voting rights struggle represents eventual triumph over field-level discretion and significant results for social-reform groups were accomplished. It is perhaps
the most dramatic and significant example of success discussed in this
book. The active participation of the federal government was crucial.
On the other hand, positive results were most pronounced in those
areas of the country where the social-reform groups were active and
spurred the federal intervention. Thus, both were necessary to implement legal changes.

Blacks were legally granted the right to vote in both federal and
state elections through the ratification of the Fifteenth Amendment to
the Constitution in 1870. For the next 20 years, the franchise was exercised; blacks registered, voted, and were elected to office. Then, starting in the 1890s, southern and border states passed a number of laws
that systematically and effectively disenfranchised blacks. For example, between 1896 and 1904, the number of registered blacks in
Louisiana dropped from 130,334 to 1342 (Rodgers and Bullock, 1972,
p. 17).

Initial civil rights efforts concentrated on Supreme Court litigation
to challenge the disenfranchisement statutes. In 1914, the Court
declared unconstitutional state laws that allowed most illiterate whites
to vote but that required blacks to pass a literacy test.[14] The most
significant legal development involved the challenge to the white
primary, which Southerners claimed was a private, political party matter and not official state action banned by the Fifteenth Amendment.
After a struggle lasting 24 years, the Supreme Court, in the 1940s, held
that in the South, the primary is the election within the meaning of the
Constitution and that blacks could not be barred from voting in
primary elections.[15]

Despite the law-reform litigation effort, the elimination of the laws
that officially disenfranchised blacks did not significantly increase

[14] *Guinn v. United States*, 238 U.S. 347 (1914).
[15] *Smith v. Allwright*, 321 U.S. 649 (1944).

black political participation.[16] Southern whites used two principal methods to discourage blacks from exercising the franchise. One was intimidation and coercion. Blacks who registered to vote were arrested and subjected to harassment by local police and to misdemeanor arrests. In addition, they suffered economic sanctions, such as evictions, denial of credit, and the refusal of white merchants to sell to them. In some communities, local newspapers printed the names of blacks who registered. Although federal law prohibited the intimidation of voters, it was not enforced. In fact, the widespread intimidation could not have succeeded without the help of local law enforcement officials and the neglect of the federal government.

The second method of discouraging black applicants was discretionary administration of the various tests used to qualify applicants. Local registrars interpreted state laws requiring certain standards of literacy, an ability to understand the Constitution, and good character of all voting applicants. Each element of the registration test was administered differentially for each race. In Alabama, six blacks with doctorate degrees were declared illiterate. While whites were given simple clauses of the state constitution to interpret, blacks were required to analyze complex sections dealing with corporate taxation. To attest to their good character, blacks were required to submit vouchers signed by registered voters, which limited registration where no blacks were previously registered and where white voters would not vouch for black applicants. In addition, if any blacks passed these tests, registrars would also limit registration by delaying the processing of their applications, denying applications for trivial mistakes, refusing to help blacks handle the forms, failing to notify applicants that were rejected, and refusing to let rejected applicants see their applications to learn where the error occurred (Rodgers and Bullock, 1972, p. 5).

With the 1957 Civil Rights Act, the legal system began its journey toward a comprehensive solution to the systematic disenfranchisement of black voters. That statute authorized the Justice Department to bring suits on behalf of private citizens who claimed violations of voting rights; the involvement of the federal government would give encouragement to blacks as well as provide the resources for the expensive litigation. The suits could be brought in federal district courts, thus avoiding the maze and dilatory tactics of state administrative and judicial proceedings, and persons accused of discrimination could be tried without juries.[17]

---

[16] See Rodgers and Bullock (1972, p. 18). In 1947, 3 years after the elimination of the white primary, only 600,000 of the 5 million eligible blacks in the South were registered to vote.

[17] 42 U.S.C. § 1971(b)(c).

Unfortunately, very little progress occurred under the 1957 act. By the fall of 1959 only three cases had been filed by the federal government, and two had been decided unfavorably. Until 1960, the constitutionality of the act itself was in doubt. In one successful case the attorney general of the United States filed suit to prevent the discriminatory purge of registration rolls in Louisiana and was successful in restoring 1377 black voters to the rolls.[18] But purge cases were simple, easy to detect, and the remedy was simple and complete, namely, restoration to the rolls. Cases of discrimination in the registration process presented far more difficult problems.

In other suits filed under the 1957 act, the government ended white primaries in Fayette County, Tennessee, and obtained a temporary restraining order to block evictions of registered black voters in Fayette and Haywood counties, Tennessee. Most cases, however, moved very slowly in part because the government was not willing to commit adequate manpower and funds for the enforcement of the new law. For example, more than 25 months passed between the filing of a suit to compel registration of qualified black citizens and the final district court order to a county board of registrars in one southern state to place 64 black applicants on the voting rolls, to register any black applicant who was qualified, and to stop using literacy tests in a discriminatory manner.

The Civil Rights Commission's investigation of black voter registration concluded that low rates of registration were due in part to apathy, but mostly to racial discrimination. The trouble came "not from discriminatory laws, but from the discriminatory application and administration of apparently non-discriminatory laws (United States Civil Rights Commission, 1959, p. 131). " Finding that the remedies under the 1957 act were insufficient, the commission recommended a tougher and more activist role for the federal government. The Civil Rights Act of 1960 was enacted with an important new feature: federal registrars or referees to replace local officials who refused to register blacks.[19] If discretion could not be controlled, then those exercising discretion could be replaced. Though the referee section was an important breakthrough, the implementation machinery doomed it to failure. To appoint a federal referee, the government had to file suit in federal district court and obtain a court finding not only of discriminatory disenfranchisement, but that such activity was a persistent pattern or practice in that particular area. Then, for at least a year after such a

---

[18] *United States* v. *McElveen*, 180 F. Supp. 10 (E.D. La. 1960). See *United States* v. *Raines*, 362 U.S. 17 (1960) and *United States* v. *Alabama*, 362 U.S. 602 (1960) reversing recalcitrant district courts. For lack of progress under the 1957 act, see United States Commission of Civil Rights Report (1959, p. 131).

[19] 42 USC §1971(e) (1964).

finding, a person discriminated against could not apply for an order declaring him qualified to vote. To get such an order required another long process. The court could hear the applicant or could, at its discretion, appoint referees from among qualified voters in the district.

Implementation of the 1960 act moved extremely slowly and its effect on black voter registration was slight.[20] Between 1960 and 1962, the numbers of registered blacks in the South rose by only 17,000. The voter referee provision was hardly used at all. Though the Civil Rights Commission had determined that approximately 100 counties in eight southern states were engaged in substantial discriminatory disenfranchisement, the government refused to send in referees and chose to rely on court orders against local registrars.

In its 1961 report, the Civil Rights Commission statistics showed that for 129 counties in 10 states where blacks constituted a substantial portion of the population, less than 10% of eligible blacks were registered to vote. In 23 counties in 5 states, no blacks were registered at all. The commission also found that a greater concentration of blacks generally meant a smaller proportion of blacks registered. Reasons for lack of black registration had not changed in spite of the 1957 and 1960 voting acts. Local voter registration officials were continuing their practices of discrimination because they had the support of the southern political and judicial systems, which were powerful enough to obstruct the Justice Department.

By the early 1960s, however, the politics of voting registration began to change. Young blacks had grown impatient and frustrated with the strategy of civil rights through case-by-case court order, an approach that was time consuming, costly, and seemed to produce few results. Attention turned to nonviolent, direct action. SNCC began voter registration projects. Not unexpectedly, SNCC workers met with political harassment, violence, arrests, and slowdowns at registrars' offices (Oberschall, pp. 229–231, 1973; Lomax, 1971, p. 318). However, this time the response of the federal government was different. During his first year in office, President Kennedy moved cautiously on civil rights, but did initiate several lawsuits striking down registration procedures. In 1962, the administration turned to stimulating grass-roots efforts to get blacks to register and vote. It brought together the leaders of the major civil rights organizations and urged them to organize voter registration campaigns in the South. In return, the administration provided money from private foundations to finance the projects and the Justice Department provided legal protection. The organizations

---

[20] For deficiencies under the 1960 statute, see *United States* v. *Ward,* 222 F. Supp. 617 (W.D. La. 1963), rev'd., 349 F.2d 795, modified 352 F.2d 329 (5th Cir. 1965).

formed the Voter Education Project, initially funded by a grant from the Taconic Foundation, and began voter registration drives. In the meantime, Justice Department suits continued to attack legal barriers, such as the literacy test, on a case-by-case basis, and the administration sought new legislation (Lomax, 1971, pp. 246–253).

In 1964, Congress passed another civil rights law, which prohibited the rejection of applicants for immaterial errors or omissions. Under the 1964 act, anyone with a sixth-grade education was to be presumed literate and eligible to vote; the burden shifted to the state to prove illiteracy rather than requiring the applicant to prove literacy. Written literacy tests had to be available for inspection by the applicant. The act also contained a broad prohibition against the application of different standards for blacks and whites in testing and processing applicants.

In some parts of the South, progress in black voting registration began to show. The Voter Education Project reported in 1964 that an estimated 43% of voting age blacks were registered in 11 southern states. (United States Commission on Civil Rights, 1961, p. 8). Several factors may have accounted for this increase. The federal government may have made greater use of the provisions of previous civil rights acts and of the 1964 act. Justice Department lawyers may have persuaded southern registrars that they would face prosecution under federal law if they refused to comply. The publicity generated by the Voter Education Project encouraged blacks to register in areas where they had not tried to before. The federal restrictions on discretionary use of literacy tests to bar blacks also had an effect on the increase (Rodgers and Bullock, 1972, p. 26).

In the deep South, however, the civil rights laws were less effective. Georgia, for example, had some counties where only 3–4% of the eligible blacks registered, while 95% of the whites were registered. In Louisiana, the number of registered blacks dropped due to a law permitting local registrars to challenge and remove "improperly registered" voters from the voting rolls. Litigation to enforce voting rights for blacks was slow and tortuous. Some southern judges refused to apply standards established by the Supreme Court. Cases dragged on for months and even years. In Mississippi, the average voting rights case took 18 months for a decision; an appeal took an additional year (Rodgers and Bullock, 1972).

Some civil rights groups tried unsuccessfully to increase black political influence by direct political action rather than the indirect route of voter registration. After the 1964 Democratic Party Convention refused to seat the Mississippi Freedom Democrats, SNCC tried to build its own political party, but this proved difficult. After a year and a half of dangerous grass-roots political activity, the black-organized party in Lowndes County, Alabama, failed to gain the 20% of the electorate needed for legal recognition even though the county was 81% black. Blacks were still intimidated by harassment, violence, and other forms of pressure to register and vote for their own party. Less ambitious voter registration drives also met with bitter resistance. Blacks continued to face intransigent voting registrars, corrupt and brutal law enforcement personnel, and in many instances, prejudiced state judges. These problems led the Civil Rights Commission to conclude, in its 1964 report, that civil rights legislation still failed to compel state officials to apply voting standards fairly.

In August 1965, in the wake of mass beatings of civil rights workers by Alabama law enforcement officials and the murder of civil rights worker Viola Luizzo, Congress passed the Voting Rights Act of 1965.[21] The main purpose of the act was to eliminate the discretionary authority of local registrars by replacing them with federal registrars. Discrimination was presumed to exist in all states or counties in which less than 50% of the voting age public was registered or had voted in the 1964 presidential election. If written complaints from 20 or more residents claiming voting-rights discrimination were received by the Attorney General, and he believed them meritorious, he could appoint federal examiners. Counties with a history of discrimination could also receive federal examiners to register voters and poll watchers to observe the voting and count ballots. Rather than attempt to prosecute individual complaints, the federal government could now by-pass lengthy litigation and operate directly on voter registration. In areas where a poll tax was still in use, the attorney general was directed to initiate suits immediately to challenge the constitutionality of the tax. Literacy tests and other discriminatory devices were completely abolished, and the only requirements allowed were those dealing with age, residence, and criminal record. Finally, the act provided civil and criminal sanctions against anyone who interfered with persons seeking to vote or those who were helping others to vote.

Examiners were sent into some counties almost immediately after the act became law and offices were established in county seats or major towns of the counties of the states covered by the law. By December 31, 1967, examiners had been sent to 58 counties in five southern states. Initially, responses were encouraging. Civil rights workers assisted in organizing and transporting groups of applicants to registra-

---

[21] Oberschall (1973, p. 231) thinks that the murder was perhaps the single most important event leading to the passage of the 1965 Voting Rights Act.

tion offices. In the first 7 1/2 months after the act was passed, 300,000 black voters were registered (Rodgers and Bullock, 1972, p. 30).

More effective enforcement, however, was hampered by administration policy. Partly because of lack of manpower, the Justice Department decided that before a county would be assigned an examiner there should be the potential for registering at least 1000 new black voters. This excluded more than 185 counties and parishes in states in which less than 50% of the black voting age population was registered. These counties and parishes were not assigned examiners because they did not have voter registration drives, nor any active local political organization, and the Justice Department felt that the presence of examiners alone could not aid black political participation.

Many other areas of the deep South did not benefit from the provisions of the act immediately because of Justice Department policy not to support an affirmative program to encourage black voter registration. Examiners were not authorized to notify any residents of the procedures or purposes of the program; they could only post a brief notice in or near their offices. One black citizen told the commission that she was unaware that federal examiners had been appointed to her county until she saw it on television. The Civil Rights Commission repeatedly recommended that the federal government take an activist role in supporting and encouraging black citizens to register and vote. To overcome a history of suppression and resulting apathy, black citizens needed more than passive representatives of the government in their communities. Voter registration drives by private groups had accomplished a great deal along these lines, but there remained many areas in the South that had not been reached.

There were other complaints about the practices and policies of the Justice Department. The attorney general was authorized to appoint federal observers to monitor elections in the states covered by the act. During 1966 and 1967, approximately 1500 observers attended elections in the South. Yet, in several counties in Alabama, Georgia, and Mississippi during the 1966 elections, it was reported to the Justice Department that no black person had been selected to serve as a polling official or observer, and that there were many cases of discrimination against black voters. Black leaders reported that in other counties in South Carolina, Alabama, and Georgia, election officials failed to provide adequate assistance to illiterate and inexperienced black voters, and that voter lists had not been properly purged of persons who had died, moved away, or had been otherwise disqualified. Civil rights organizations and others doubted the effectiveness of the observer program. Representatives of SNCC reported that, while monitoring elections at which federal observers had been assigned, they noted many violations that federal officials chose to ignore. The Law Students Civil Rights Research Council reported that during the 1967 general election in Mississippi, federal observers could not be distinguished from local officials and made no attempt to identify themselves (Rodgers and Bullock, 1972, pp. 23–39).

The Justice Department initiated litigation in three areas under the 1965 Act: (a) securing substantive rights to black voters and candidates; (b) establishing the constitutionality of the act and implementing its administrative provisions; and (c) removing economic burdens from the franchise. The Justice Department seemed to prefer to use informal negotiation and persuasion rather than litigation when possible. For example, department attorneys were assigned to certain counties on election days to deal with complaints and, according to the department, were often successful in persuading election officials to comply with the law. Prior to election days, local officials often entered into negotiations with the Justice Department to avoid the assignment of observers. In some cases the department did not receive complaints until election day, and part of election day would have elapsed before attorneys could secure compliance through negotiation. Then there was no assurance that these same discriminatory practices would not recur in subsequent elections.

The poll tax, one of the remaining legal barriers to black voter registration, was eliminated from federal elections by the Twenty-Fourth Amendment. A Supreme Court decision in 1966 held that the poll tax as applied to state elections violated the Fourteenth Amendment.[22]

Nevertheless, despite the lack of complete vigor on the part of the Justice Department, progress continued. By 1966, the size of the black electorate had increased 11% and increased another 8% 2 years later. The increase in the six states in which federal examiners were present was almost three times that in states not covered by the provisions. Those six states were the ones with the least black registration in 1964 (Rodgers and Bullock, 1972, p. 30). Comparing specific counties in states where examiners were sent, the rate of increase in black registration was more than twice as great in examiner as in nonexaminer counties. Federal examiners were most active in Alabama, Mississippi, and Louisiana, and in those three states more than 90% of the 150,000 blacks were registered. Largest gains in black registration occurred in Mississippi, going from 6.7 to 59.8% after the 1965 Act. In Alabama,

---

[22] *Harper v. Board of Elections*, 303 U.S. 663 (1966).

black registration increased from 19.3 to 51.6% and in Georgia, from 27.4 to 52.5%.

Even in counties where no federal examiners were appointed, black registration rose. Rodgers and Bullock speculate that willingness of registrars to comply with the new law was only part of the explanation for the increases. The work of SNCC, CORE, NAACP, and the Voter Education Project probably had a very important influence. Education in the freedom schools was important in developing black political motivation, a job in which the federal government had very little part (U.S. Civil Rights Commission, 1961, p. 162).

Examiner counties in which there was neither a Voter Education Project nor any other civil rights organization had significantly lower numbers of black applicants. The Civil Rights Commission found that the combination of federal intervention and private civil rights efforts was the most successful. In those examiner counties where civil rights workers had been active, there was a sharp decrease in the number of applicants after Labor Day, when most civil rights workers went back to jobs and school. Counties with the Voter Education Project but without federal examiners had the lowest number of applications, which suggests that discretionary application of rules by local registration officials was still a factor in discouraging black registration.

According to a Voter Education Project survey, the rise in registration was accompanied by a rise in the number of blacks voting. In 1966 the black vote accounted for the winning margin for a United States senator in South Carolina, a governor in Arkansas, and two members of the House of Representatives. Project records show that in Arkansas approximately 85,000 of a total of 115,000 to 120,000 registered blacks voted in the November 1966 elections; in South Carolina, 100,000 of 191,000, and in Georgia, 150,000 of 300,000.

In the 11 southern states, there were 159 black officeholders after the 1966 elections. After the 1967 elections there were more than 200, twice as many as before the 1965 act. In five predominately black counties in Mississippi where there had been great resistance to black voting, blacks won several victories in the 1966 elections. In Holmes County, Mississippi, one of the first to be assigned federal examiners, the number of black voters increased from 20 in 1965 to 5844 in 1967. In the 1967 elections, 12 black candidates ran for state and county offices and 2 won offices, 1 a seat in the Mississippi House of Representatives.

Today, 20% of the people living in the 11 southern states are black, but less than 2% of the 79,000 elective offices in the South are held by blacks. Blacks comprise 12% of the total population, but hold only three-tenths of 1% of all elected offices. Out of a voting age population of 6 million, 3.5 million southern blacks are now registered. Though these figures seem low, they do represent progress made by blacks since the Voting Rights Act of 1965.

Elections in 1974 resulted in considerable gains for blacks in the South. Over 72% of black candidates seeking office were successful. Before the 1974 elections southern legislatures had 6 black senators and 54 black state representatives. As of 1978 there are 10 black senators and 84 black state representatives. In all, there are 97 black legislators from the South in Washington and in southern capitals. Many other southern blacks have been elected to county and city posts in recent years. John Lewis, director of the Voter Education Project, believes that blacks are now "reaping the harvest made possible by the landmark 'one man-one vote' Supreme Court case, the hard-won Voting Rights Act and the citizenship education effort that still goes on."[23]

Many blacks are still not satisfied that progress has been as rapid as it should have been. They point to many instances of discriminatory disfranchisement that still persist in the South. Small towns and rural areas in the Deep South exhibit many of the same problems as in predesegregation days. One such town is Shaw, Mississippi, target of the famous *Hawkins* v. *Shaw* case.[24] In 1972, a United States district court ordered the town of Shaw to equalize municipal services for its 60% black population. After a great deal of publicity and a certain amount of violence, the town has sunk back to its former state and black residents still do not have sewers, paved streets, or street lights.

Voting and political activity in Shaw, Mississippi has not been affected much by the Voting Rights Act. In the 1973 elections, for the first time, a slate of black candidates opposed white officeholders. Despite a majority black voter turnout, the black slate lost by clear margins. Black leaders reported numerous violations of the law and coercive tactics. White poll workers entered booths with black voters, allegedly to make sure they knew how to work the levers properly. Whites also kept track of who was voting and how. Black candidates filed complaints of election irregularities with the Federal Bureau of Investigation but received no answer. A few black leaders in Shaw are now trying to form a community organization to improve their status but they are working against great odds.

In other southern towns these same practices persist. Blacks are often given misleading information concerning elections, ballots are thrown out for minor errors, black poll watchers are banned from

[23] Quoted in B.D. Ayres, Jr., *The New York Times*, November 11, 1974.

[24] The following account is based on Harry Hart, *New Times*, January 10, 1975, p. 42.

observing the vote count, and polling places are often located in white businesses or plantation company stores.

Although the situation in *Shaw* indicates that the voting rights campaign has not been completely successful, it nevertheless has probably been more successful than any other similar contemporary example. The political position of blacks has changed greatly during the last two decades, a remarkable accomplishment considering the odds that social-reform groups initially faced. The problems of discretionary field-level decision making were severe. The system was a decentralized bureaucracy made up of local registrars who had legally been granted discretionary authority to administer vaguely worded tests. This authority was backed by a strong community desire to keep blacks disenfranchised by whatever means were necessary. The local registrars were supported by the white community, corrupt local law enforcement, and both state and federal trial courts. The measures that finally overcame these hurdles were draconian, at least by American traditions. Step by step, legal discretionary authority was reduced and then eliminated; at the end, remedial provisions could be invoked by the use of statistical tests alone. Then, to cope with illegal practices on the part of local officials, even after discretion was removed, the local officials were physically removed from the administration of registration and replaced by federal officials.

Even these strong measures were not sufficient to accomplish the desired social change. In dealing with large numbers of disadvantaged people, it is also necessary to mobilize the clients of the system to participate, to seize, and to utilize the rights that the law and others have given them. Thus, in voting rights, substantial success in the heartland of the South was only accomplished with the continued, active efforts of social-reform groups.

The success of the voting rights campaign, then, depended on the combination of several significant factors. The social-reform groups were seeking collective goods: Any black could register and vote as a result of the groups' work but he or she did not have to contribute anything to the cost of the groups. The groups were able to overcome the free-rider problem through the use of northern white liberal support, aided by the efforts of the Kennedy administration. They relied on purposive incentives for the foundation support, but selective incentives for the support of political leaders. The Kennedys, of course, hoped to strengthen their liberal support in both the North and the South.

It is quite clear that the social-reform groups could not have accomplished their goals alone. They needed and eventually got the active support of the federal Executive, which took a number of forms including encouraging the organizations and promising and delivering financial resources, assuming the burden of litigation, obtaining the necessary legislative changes, and pursuing the all-important administrative remedies.

The legal system also played an important role. Court litigation initially served two purposes. One purpose was to clear away the underbrush, the legal structure of disenfranchisement. As noted, this involved a series of cases, initially undertaken by the social-reform groups, and then by the Justice Department. Part of this effort also involved the legal defense of those arrested and charged who sought to register and vote. The second purpose of the litigation was consciousness-raising. These cases, as in school desegregation, were good press. They highlighted the problems that blacks faced and were important in establishing the legitimacy necessary for purposive incentives for white liberal support. However, for reasons already elaborated, judicial remedies were not sufficient by themselves to accomplish the goals. Legislative and administrative changes were also necessary to attack the problem of field-level discretion.

Housing

One need hardly elaborate on the fact that discrimination in housing is widespread and persistent; in fact, as compared with political, economic, and educational areas, minorities have probably made the least amount of progress in housing integration during the past two decades (Rodgers and Bullock, 1972, pp. 139–140; Danielson, 1976, pp. 2–11). Racial residential segregation is universal; according to Karl and Alma Taeuber, it exists in a "very high degree" regardless of city size or characteristic (for example, industrial, suburban, commercial), the number of black residents in a city, their relative economic status, the character of local laws, or other forms of discrimination or segregation.[25]

The effects of housing segregation are serious. Blacks live in overcrowded conditions, are at the mercy of landlords, and have to pay more for poorer housing. They are forced to live in areas of the city where services are poorer and are denied opportunities to compete for better jobs as plants move out of the central city. Given the realities of school desegregation, their children will continue to be educated in all black schools. They lack access to the more desirable shopping and

[25] Quoted in Rodgers and Bullock (1972, p. 139).

recreational facilities. Parents as well as children will be denied the benefits of an integrated society.

There are many reasons why residential segregation has persisted.[26] Land-use control is exercised by local authorities. Local governments, under state enabling legislation, enact zoning laws that specify the uses of various tracts of land within the local jurisdiction. The administration of the zoning law, including the power to make changes, is vested in local zoning boards. In an earlier day, local zoning laws were forthright in explicitly determining the racial use of land, but these laws were struck down. In recent times, zoning laws have been able to accomplish the same result through a more indirect approach—for example, by prescribing a minimum floor size or lot size for residential dwellings, which has the effect of raising the price of residential housing in a particular area to a point that excludes the vast majority of urban blacks. If blacks still manage to purchase residential property in a white area, local authorities use other weapons. In some instances, public bodies have condemned the land purchased by blacks for public parks, or construction has been stopped by building inspectors who allege deviations from the building codes. As with school desegregation and voting, if local officials are sufficiently determined, they can usually find legal or illegal methods to block black housing development.

The determination of whites to exclude blacks from their neighborhoods is fierce. Again, one need only mention the reasons given—the decline in land values, the deterioration of the neighborhood with the feared increase in crime, the decline in the quality of the schools, miscegenation, and so forth. Whatever the validity of the reasons, they are strongly held by white suburbanites, so much so that when the NAACP turned to housing segregation in the 1960s, it recognized that breaking down these walls would prove much more difficult than its previous campaigns in education, voting, and employment. Not only would the civil rights organizations have to attack public action, but they would also have to fight private discrimination. Even if laws are invalidated, whites still have to be willing to sell to blacks, and blacks have to be willing to live among hostile whites. Prior to 1948, restrictive convenants in deeds were used by whites to prevent subsequent white owners from selling to nonwhites. In 1948, the Supreme Court declared such agreements not enforceable in state or federal courts.[27] But this decision only allowed a willing white to sell to a black; it did

---

[26] In addition to Rodgers and Bullock (1972), see Shields and Spector (1971) and Trubek (1976).

[27] *Shelley* v. *Kraemer*, 334 U.S. 1 (1948).

nothing about whites who refused to sell to blacks, and residential housing segregation has persisted.

Another source of housing discrimination has been the federal government (Rodgers and Bullock, 1972, pp. 142–146; Danielson, 1976, p. 199; Shields and Spector, 1971, pp. 319–322). Federal mortgage guarantors (the Federal Housing Authority and the Veterans Administration) have tolerated private discrimination. These agencies long supported restrictive covenants until outlawed by the Supreme Court, but thereafter continued to finance segregated housing. Over the years, few federal loans went to blacks or even to housing in integrated neighborhoods. The Civil Rights Commission accused the FHA of being "a major factor in the development of segregated housing patterns."[28]

The banks and other lending institutions have also served to maintain segregated housing by denying loans to blacks, or rejecting loan applications from black areas ("redlining"), or imposing more stringent conditions on loans to blacks. When blacks can get loans, the interest rate is usually higher than that paid by whites (Rodgers and Bullock, 1972, p. 141).

The role of realtors and developers is more complex. In some instances, realtors will *block-bust,* a technique of scaring white residents into selling their houses cheaply before the threatened influx of blacks results in an even greater decline in property values, and then selling the property at inflated prices to blacks. Some developers have also been interested in attacking exclusionary zoning in order to build lower-priced single or multidwelling housing. But generally speaking, most realtors and developers are not interested in housing for lower-income urban blacks. Where exclusionary zoning has been eliminated, most new development has, in fact, been for upper-income whites (Danielson, 1976, p. 79; Komesar, 1978).

In sum, when in the 1960s social-reform groups turned their attention to segregated housing, they faced formidable obstacles. White-only housing was maintained by extremely determined white suburbanites backed by local zoning laws and other local governmental powers, a tolerant federal government, private lending institutions, and most developers and real-estate agents.

By the late 1960s, several different social-reform groups began to actively press for the elimination of exclusionary zoning. These organizations, referred to as the Open Suburbs Movement (OSM), included traditional civil rights groups, such as the NAACP, the LDF, the ACLU, and the Lawyers Committee for Civil Rights Under Law, as well as specialized groups, such as the National Housing Committee Against

[28] Quoted in Rodgers and Bullock (1972, p. 140).

Discrimination in Housing and the Suburban Action Institute, an organization created to gain access to the suburbs for low- and moderate-income families.

Although there is diversity among the groups, there are common characteristics. By and large, the OSM is led by activist middle-class white liberals, financed by foundations and other conscience beneficiaries. The groups, on the whole, lack popular support for their program, including from inner-city blacks. The consensus seems to be that for most blacks, living in an integrated neighborhood does not have the urgency of alleviating discrimination in jobs, schools, and public facilities. In addition, it need hardly be mentioned that the OSM also lacks popular support from the suburban neighborhoods. Moreover, the growing power of suburban communities is reflected in the state legislatures and Congress. With rare exceptions, whenever an issue of opening up the suburbs comes before these bodies, they have vigorously turned back the demands of social-reform groups. There is not even much support for the OSM from the cities. On the one hand, leaders in the central city know that the suburbs are refusing to share the metropolitan area's burdens, but on the other hand, these leaders want available resources (e.g., federal money for subsidized housing) to be channeled into rebuilding the central wards. Nor does the OSM command the support of the national liberal coalition of politicians, clergy, and intellectuals, which have supported school desegregation and voting rights. Whether living in an integrated suburb seems less important, or strikes too close to home, opening the suburbs has never really caught on.[29]

This general absence of popular support has meant that the OSM lacks the capacity to obtain its results through the political process, thus forcing the groups to use litigation as their principal strategy. The willingness to use litigation is reinforced by other factors. Many of the groups are prohibited from lobbying because of the tax laws. But in addition, many of the civil rights groups have a longstanding preference for litigation. In the opinion of some, litigation has resulted in some court victories and has had some influence with private industry and government departments. Litigation, it is felt by the group leaders, has good publicity value, has the chance of creating political leverage in local situations, can create new rights for whole classes of citizens, and lends legitimacy to the goals of the movement.

The potential usefulness of a litigation strategy was stimulated by the passage of the Housing Act of 1968, which called for the creation of

[29] For a description of the OSM and its support and lack of support, see Shields and Spector (1971, pp. 301–308, 312–316); Danielson (1976, pp. 107–149).

6-million units of subsidized low- and moderate-income housing units over a 10-year period. What this meant to the OSM was that the supply of subsidized housing would not be the problem; rather, the issue would be whether such housing could be located in the suburbs. To accomplish this, exclusionary zoning laws had to be invalidated. HUD and the building industry, goaded through civil rights pressures, would build the housing in the suburbs once the legal barriers were removed. Litigation, and more particularly, a major Supreme Court decision declaring exclusionary zoning unconstitutional, became one of the major tactics of the OSM (Trubek, 1976, p. 129; Danielson, 1976, p. 114; Sager, 1969).

There were other tactical decisions concerning litigation strategy. In a typical zoning case, a developer would seek to overturn the zoning law as it applied to a particular parcel of land. The OSM lawyers eschewed this approach; it was too time-consuming, and because there was little carry-over from one decision to the next, the reform prospects were minimal. The local government would relitigate each new request for a zoning change. Instead, the groups opted for litigation that potentially had a broad reach. For example, on Long Island, the NAACP and the NCDH challenged a large suburb's entire zoning code on the ground that under the code, it would be impossible for lower-income families to live in that suburb. The Suburban Action Institute brought a lawsuit to set aside all forms of restrictive zoning in New Jersey. A local ACLU and the NCDH brought suit against 23 suburbs in one county (Danielson, 1976, pp. 170–171).

Hopes for the big Supreme Court decision were never realized, and, in the meantime, the litigation strategy ran into other difficulties. The Nixon administration terminated the program of massive block grants for subsidized housing, the only housing that poor urban blacks could afford. That administration also undermined whatever tendencies there were in HUD and the Justice Department to enforce equal housing laws. For example, for a brief period, HUD cut off all grants to municipalities that refused to permit subsidized housing in white suburbs, but Nixon overruled this policy. In the meantime, little federally subsidized housing was in fact built in white suburbs. Under the 1968 Fair Housing Act, the Justice Department has authority to act if it finds a "pattern or practice" of discrimination. But again, under the Nixon administration, it interpreted the law to mean that suits could not be filed merely because there were no minorities in particular suburbs. Instead the department required an "actual display" of discriminatory conduct. Examples of this include condemning land bought by blacks for development and refusing to issue sewer permits (Rodgers and Bullock, 1972, pp. 152–154). The broad-scale litigation also ran into difficulties. The suburbs fought back bitterly and with great skill and resources. In many communities, funds were raised by neighborhood associations to hire high-priced law firms. And, local governments litigated against the social-reform groups. The result was that litigation almost invariably was time-consuming and sapped the slender resources of the groups (Trubek, 1976, pp. 129–130; Danielson, 1972, pp. 83, 168).

As noted, on occasion home builders are on the side of the social-reform groups; they, too, want the elimination of exclusionary zoning laws that limit their ability to make money. Of course, not all builders view exclusionary zoning in this light. In some localities, local builders fear the intrusion of large outside builders and will join with the suburbs to protect their local position. But even the alliance with the OSM is not trouble-free. While large scale developers have joined in seeking to overturn the zoning laws, they have not been especially interested in building the kind of housing that would suit the membership of the social-reform groups. Instead, they are interested in building higher-density high-income housing in the desirable suburban localities. And once the litigation is successful, the social-reform groups have no control over what type of housing their developer allies will choose to build. In Pennsylvania, for example, restrictive zoning laws were overturned as a result of a series of cases but all of the new high-density housing that was built was for owners and tenants in higher-income brackets. Finally, once the litigation is successful, and the suburbs have been opened up, the developers have no incentive to keep supporting the social-reform groups to make sure that subsidized housing is, in fact, built. In most cases, the normal market will not produce housing that minorities can afford and implementation work is required (Danielson, 1976, pp. 130–141; Shields and Spector, 1971, pp. 317–318).

The difficulties that the OSM faced can be illustrated by three cases. In two lawsuits brought against the Chicago Housing Authority and HUD, the court found that since 1950 public housing in Chicago had only been built in segregated neighborhoods, and it ordered no new public housing to be built in predominately black areas, and that new public housing had to be built in integrated areas. But nothing happened. Under state law, all proposals for public housing in Chicago had to be approved by the Chicago Planning Commission and the city council. At first, the housing authority simply refused to submit any proposals for new housing. After further litigation, including a court of appeals decision, the authority did submit and the council did approve a proposal for a small number of units. There was further litigation in the trial court, and this time, an angry judge ordered the withholding of Model City funds from the city until substantially more units of housing were approved. However, this decision went too far, and was reversed on appeal. Then, as a result of further litigation, the court ordered the housing authority to proceed with projects, and suspended the state statute that required city council approval. But still no new public housing was started in Chicago. This time, community groups in opposition to public housing in their localities filed suit, which was eventually dismissed. Ten years after the initial litigation there is still no new public housing in integrated neighborhoods in Chicago.[30]

In the Chicago case, one of the stumbling blocks was the recalcitrance of the developer, the Chicago Housing Authority. However, even where developers want to proceed, litigation has proved fruitless. In *Kennedy Park Homes Association* v. *City of Lackawanna,* a civil rights group formed an association for the purpose of developing federally subsidized housing, and purchased a tract of land in a white area from the Roman Catholic Diocese. Opposition in the area was quickly mobilized and the city adopted a moratorium on all new building until sewer problems were solved, and designated certain areas, including this tract, as park and recreational land. Suit was filed by social-reform groups (with Justice Department intervention on the side of the plaintiffs) and the court ordered the city to stop interfering with the project, including the halting of all other projects that might unduly tax the sewer system.[31]

In this case, one would think that the judicial remedy would have been sufficient. As distinguished from the Chicago housing case, which required affirmative action by a reluctant agency, the principal actors here were willing to go ahead once the legal barriers were removed. Nevertheless, the project was not started. The city was still able to throw up a series of roadblocks, mostly on environmental, health, and safety issues, which required the social-reform groups to engage in expensive and time-consuming studies to refute the allegations. Eventually, the costs of the project exceeded the limits allowed by the federal subsidy program (Danielson, 1976, pp. 31–32, 166–167).

The *Kennedy* case illustrates the difficulty of implementing favorable zoning court orders. Courts may overturn local zoning ordinances and even announce general criteria for new development, but they are not going to enact a new zoning law and police all of the deci-

---

[30] *Gautreaux* v. *Chicago Housing Authority,* 480 F.2d 210 (7th Cir. 1973) and *Gautreaux* v. *Romney,* 457 F.2d 124 (7th Cir. 1973) discussed in Komesar (1978, pp. 21–34).

[31] 436 F.2d 108 (2d Cir. 1970), cert. denied, 401 U.S. 1010 (1971), discussed in Komesar (1978, pp. 34–37).

sions required by local officials for the approval of building projects. Thus far, the courts have been unwilling to take on the supervisory role that they are shouldering in school desegregation. This means, then, that whether goals will be implemented in exclusionary zoning cases depends on the ability of social-reform groups and developers to fight continuous battles with local officials who draw their strength from the aroused, united, and bitter white opponents (Trubek, 1976, p. 145).

A contrasting example in the housing area is the Yerba Buena redevelopment project controversy in San Francisco.[32] This was a proposed urban renewal project that involved 87 downtown acres where a complex of convention center, sports facilities, parking garage, luxury hotel, and offices and stores were to be built; estimates of the cost ran as high as half a billion dollars. The project was a longstanding dream of developers and elites, and planning for it began in 1954 by the San Francisco Redevelopment Authority, aggressively backed by the wealth and power of the city, including the largest corporations, city hall, the hotel owners, the convention and tourist industry, the building, construction, and hotel unions, the two newspapers, and the radio and television stations. The main hurdle was acquisition of land. The redevelopment agency was aided by HUD, whose philosophy at that time was large-scale downtown development and local discretion. In 1965, plans were approved by local government, and the federal government set aside $19.6 million for the project. However, to use its powers of condemnation, the redevelopment agency had to show that the area was "blighted" and that decent, sanitary alternative housing would be made available to the area residents at rents they could afford. About 4000 residents lived in the Yerba Buena project areas. Most were elderly, single, white males who lived in boarding houses and residential and transient hotels. In addition, there were about 700 small businesses in the area.

From the very start, the redevelopment agency never included specific relocation plans for the area residents. As was typical of urban renewal and highway construction projects, the development agencies supplied some referral or finder services and some cash grants and simply dispersed those in the way of the bulldozer. Urban renewal had earned the epithet "Negro removal" since most projects were located in urban ghettos. The intention of the Yerba Buena planners was clear. A key element in the design was the creation of a "protected environment," which meant removing all of the poor residents from close proximity to the project. As one executive of a corporation that was plan-

[32] The Yerba Buena discussion is based on Hartman (1974) and extensive interviews with the principal lawyers for the tenant group, Public Advocates, San Francisco, 1974–1977.

ning to locate its headquarters in the project stated: "You certainly can't expect us to erect a 50 million dollar building in an area where dirty old men will be going around exposing themselves to our secretaries." [33] The redevelopment agency clearly thought that removal of the residents was necessary to attract sufficient private investment.

By the late 1960s, the redevelopment agency started its campaign to rid the area of its residents. It began buying up some of the hotels and canceling leases, pressuring residents to give up their leases, refusing to keep up repairs and provide maintenance, and initiated a public campaign depicting the area as full of bums and winos. The residents were anything but a disorganized, transient community; instead they were for the most part, former working-class people who were settled in the neighborhood. They knew the record of relocation of past urban-renewal projects in the city, and they also knew that comparable housing for them was not available in other parts of the city. At first, the residents began to seek help from the local legal services agency, which unsuccessfully tried to get HUD to intervene to enforce the housing act. Finally, primarily as a result of the stepped-up harassing tactics of the redevelopment agency, the residents formed an organization, Tenants and Owners in Opposition to Redevelopment (TOOR) and enlisted support from outsiders, such as community workers, volunteers, and most importantly, aggressive public interest lawyers. Although the primary aim of TOOR ideally would have been to stop the project altogether, it thought that planning had gone too far, that there was too much concentrated power behind Yerba Buena, and that, therefore, its best hope was to secure comparable subsidized housing in or adjacent to the project area. This, of course, conflicted with the strongly held views of the redevelopment agency.

After more negotiations failed, including renewed efforts to get HUD to force the redevelopment agency to come up with an adequate housing relocation plan, TOOR filed suit, in 1969, against the redevelopment agency and HUD. After several hearings, the court finally ordered a stop to all demolition and relocation until a relocation plan could be agreed upon. For the next three and a half years, there were numerous court hearings and appeals, a vicious press and media campaign against TOOR, its lawyers and the federal judge, but the court held firm. In the meantime, with the advent of the Nixon administration, HUD began to reconsider massive urban renewal programs. But the real leverage in the case was the court injunction. The land was held hostage, and eventually it dawned on the redevelopment agency

[33] Quoted in Hartman (1974, p. 90).

and city hall that they would have to bargain seriously with the resident organization and the lawyers.

It was finally agreed that the redevelopment agency would provide a substantial number of subsidized housing units adjacent to the project. The housing would be financed in part by the federal government, but mostly out of the city's hotel tax. The agreement also had some unique features. TOOR was reconstituted as a nonprofit community organization, receiving $50,000 annually from the tax, which would enable the organization to develop and maintain a staff. Under the agreement, TOOR was to select the architect for the housing (from a panel of five selected by the city), and participate in the design and development of the housing. The settlement agreement was carefully constructed so that it would proceed step-by-step and would be self-enforcing. In the meantime, there were to be no evictions until basic steps were taken to guarantee the housing.

By the time the Yerba Buena settlement was reached, the economic picture of the area had changed and the project has not yet gotten under way. Therefore, the residents do not have their subsidized housing. On the other hand, except for those who fled or were pressured to leave before the court injunction, the residents are still in their community. Great damage was done to the community before the lawyers were able to stop the juggernaut, but it was stopped.

In addition to Yerba Buena there have been other court victories in the housing area. State courts invalidated large lot restrictions, minimum floor areas, minimum building sizes, and various restrictions on apartments, age and number of inhabitants. Several state courts no longer automatically bow to local discretion in zoning matters. Some courts have even gone beyond traditional judicial remedies; instead of simply outlawing an existing zoning provision and waiting for development to proceed (or further litigation), these courts have ordered specific changes to allow for subsidized housing or have ordered towns to produce specific plans. One court retained planning consultants and then ordered zoning changes on the basis of the consultants' reports. Without doubt, the most far-reaching zoning case was decided in New Jersey in 1975 when the court held that a town could not zone out the poor. Moreover, it ruled that local zoning laws must promote the general welfare by providing "for adequate housing of all categories of people." The towns had to take into account not only local housing needs, but regional needs as well (Danielson, 1976, pp. 175–189).

Open Suburbs Movement leaders and lawyers hail these new developments, but there are great difficulties in implementation. In the past, and we can expect similar conduct, towns have been exceedingly resourceful in resisting court victories. As each zoning restriction is invalidated, the local communities can reach for other devices—changing lot sizes, or set-back requirements, or house size, or yard coverage. Delays, footdragging, and legal maneuvering not only sap the strength of the plaintiffs but also can alter the financial considerations in the proposed development. The costs of delay are even more severe when subsidized housing is involved. Federal money usually requires evidence of local support and by the time this support is ultimately commanded by the court, the federal program may no longer be available. This is what happened in the Black Jack case. The litigation took 5 years and at final judgment, the federal subsidy program was no longer in existence and no other federal funds were available for the project (Danielson, 1976, pp. 165–167).

One can also have doubts as to how far judicial activism will go. Most courts will not become de facto planning boards for local communities, especially in view of the fierce opposition in the suburbs and almost uniform political hostility. Again, the demands on the Judiciary, as an institution, are too great and this is especially true with regard to subsidized housing, the only housing that can be made accessible to lower-income families. The reason for this is that too many other factors in addition to outlawing exclusionary zoning have to be put together before such housing can be built. As one noted New Jersey official, who labored long to provide low-income housing, put it: "The plain fact is that you could zone all of New Jersey for low-income housing and unless you had the money, manpower, technology, and a vast variety of other legal powers, you could not build one unit of low-cost housing."[34] There are some things that courts can do, but as one public-interest lawyer said, "Ultimately the courts cannot build houses." The great difficulty then for the social-reform groups is that while their goals of opening up the suburbs for the poor and minorities are most persuasive with the courts, these victories are the hardest to implement because they require subsidized housing. As stated before, when the suburbs have been opened up, it has not been for housing the poor.

The frustrations encountered by the law reformers in the housing area have taken their toll. The tangible results have been slight and the reform groups have suffered. The Suburban Action Institute, the most aggressive, litigation-oriented, ambitious, and active of the organizations, has had no tangible success except in generating the publicity that accompanies lawsuits. In every major case, local opposition

[34] Paul Ylvisaker, quoted in Danielson (1976, p. 307).

always prevailed. The groups were unable to obtain support from anybody, and that includes suburbanites, local churches, builders, and the federal government. They had to rely on social-action foundations. Eventually this source dried up and by 1975, the Suburban Action Institute became moribund (Danielson, 1976, pp. 120–122).[35]

Employment Discrimination

Discrimination in employment shares the same characteristics of the other civil rights issues discussed in this chapter. Despite gains in recent years, employment discrimination remains widespread and pervasive.[36] As a result of employment discrimination, white males are overrepresented in the higher paying or prestigious occupations, they earn more than others doing the same work, and they are more successful than others at both finding jobs and keeping them.[37] Furthermore, even when women or nonwhites obtain the better jobs, they are paid less than the white males who have the same jobs. For example, in the "professional" occupational category (the highest category for women), women earned only two-thirds as much as males. In addition, females and nonwhites experienced considerably higher rates of unemployment than white males. Through the years, there have been some changes. For example, there has been an improvement in the relative position of nonwhite males, although with females, there not only has been no improvement, but their relative position has worsened. But whatever the trends, there are enormous disparities between employees of different races and sexes, and there is some evidence that about 60–70% of the earnings difference between whites and nonwhites, and perhaps the entire difference between males and females is attributable to employment discrimination (Blinder, 1973).

We have seen that the role of government in the previous civil rights examples varied. In school integration, the federal government

[35] The Ford Foundation in 1976 announced a grant of $50,000 to The Suburban Action Institute to help it develop political strategies. See Trubek (1976, p. 131).

[36] Much of the factual data and analysis is condensed from Handler, Edgar, and Settle (1978). In addition to the usual documentary sources, that chapter relied on extensive interviews with civil rights, public interest, and government lawyers.

Employment discrimination is defined as work-related behavior toward others that is not motivated by objective market considerations, such as differences in training, experience, or natural ability. Such behavior may be (a) an unwillingness to hire or work with certain types of people; (b) paying unequal compensation for equal work; and (c) denying access to jobs in certain professions or above certain levels.

[37] For example, as of 1972, 64% of whites worked in the three highest paying occupations as compared with 38% of nonwhites. With regard to the top two occupations (in terms of median earnings), 21% were women as compared with 48% men.

was passive during the Eisenhower years, and then actively supported the efforts of social-reform groups. In voting rights, the efforts of the federal government under Kennedy and Johnson were even more vigorous. In housing, the situation was the reverse; the federal government, especially through its various subsidy programs, reinforced segregation. In employment discrimination, although the record is mixed, for the most part, the federal government and other public agencies are either discriminators themselves or they fail to enforce the law either through ineptitude, backlogs, or what the social-reform groups claim are restricted interpretations of the law.

There is a lot of antiemployment discrimination law on the books, extending back to the nineteenth century. Starting in 1941, the federal government began to approach problems of employment discrimination outside the government through an Executive Order prohibiting racial discrimination in federal and defense industry, but there was minimal enforcement. This pattern was repeated with other public agencies charged with enforcing antiemployment discrimination laws. Either existing agencies, such as the National Labor Relations Board, were given antiemployment discrimination authority, or new agencies were created (for example, state Fair Employment Practices Commissions), but most commentators agreed that before the 1960s the influence of the various federal and state efforts to combat employment discrimination was negligible (Sovern, 1966).

Starting in the 1960s, a more vigorous approach began in the federal government. The Executive Order was strengthened to prohibit discrimination on the part of contractors doing business with the federal government and required contractors to come up with affirmative action plans to implement nondiscriminatory employment practices. All federal contracting agencies were charged with enforcement, under the supervision and coordination of the Office of Federal Contract Compliance. The most significant legislation was Title VII of the Civil Rights Act of 1964 that prohibits employment discrimination (hiring, discharge, compensation, terms, conditions, or privileges of employment) because of race, sex, color, national origin, or religion. The statute covers all employers with more than 15 employees, employment agencies, labor unions (with more than 15 members), governmental agencies, training programs, and educational institutions. The Equal Employment Opportunities Commission (EEOC) hears individual complaints, but can also initiate "pattern and practice" suits against discriminators. Most states also have agencies similar to the EEOC.

Thus, in addition to the state laws and agencies, there are federal laws, and numerous federal agencies charged with eliminating employment discrimination including the EEOC, the Office of Federal Contract Compliance (OFCC), the Justice Department, the NLRB, the Wage and Hour Division (authorized by the Equal Pay Act), and the Civil Service Commission. Nevertheless, enforcement efforts on the part of government have been weak. For the most part, the government agencies are reactive in that they rely on individual complaints on a "first-come, first-served" basis. Either the agencies have too few complaints or they are jammed with backlogs. For example, during fiscal 1976, the EEOC received 97,674 complaints, resolved 82,537, and had a backlog of 122,000 cases. In addition, practically all of these agencies suffer from inefficient procedures, poorly trained and inexperienced staff, and lack of adequate financing.

In an effort to stem its mounting backlog problems, the EEOC started a program of "pattern-centered" complaints, that is, proceedings involving discriminators against whom there were large numbers of complaints. But this, too, has raised troublesome issues. The most prominent actions were consent settlements obtained from American Telephone and Telegraph Corporation and the steel industry. The AT&T settlement provided for $15 million in back pay, another $23 million annually to equalize the pay between women, minorities, and white males, and an affirmative action plan. In return, the EEOC agreed to drop all existing complaints against the corporation and to declare that it conformed with existing federal laws. The consent agreement with the steel industry also provided for back pay and a reform of the seniority system. Both actions, although hailed as great victories by the EEOC, were bitterly attacked by social-reform groups as "sell-outs" or "sweetheart" agreements.[38] They claim that the back pay awards were low and that the affirmative action plans were weak; in short, the discriminators settled cheap. Moreover, social-reform groups, such as the NAACP, had been completely excluded from the negotiations and were unable to obtain judicial relief. From the industry and government point of view, it would be far more difficult to reach a settlement agreement if more parties (especially social-reform groups) participated in the negotiations, and there would be no point in reaching a settlement agreement if it did not give the companies protection. From the point of view of the social-reform groups, the AT&T and steel settlements exemplify precisely the pattern that they fear from the government: The EEOC is under great pressure to reach a settlement because it saves scarce resources by avoiding long, drawn-out litigation, receives publicity, and is supported by the industry itself.

---

[38] Interviews with Carol Polowy, Womens Equity Action League, June 21, 1974; Herbert Hill, Executive Director, Labor Committee, NAACP, December, 1974; Maslow (1974, p. 28).

In addition to public enforcement, Title VII of the Civil Rights Act also seeks to encourage private enforcement of antiemployment discrimination laws by providing that counsel fees can be recovered for prevailing plaintiffs. Antidiscrimination litigation can also be brought under the civil rights statutes, which also provide counsel fees. The theory of these alternative remedies is that individuals should not be forced to rely on government agencies alone for relief but that victims of employment discrimination should be able to get financing for needed litigation. Under Title VII, private attorneys can take the cases on speculation. So far, these financing provisions have not had the intended effect, at least as far as the individual complainant is concerned. The economics of employment discrimination cases are such that private attorneys, representing individual clients, can only gamble on the "best" cases, the sure winners. Even so, unless there is a large back-pay award, the courts have not been generous in the rate of compensation. There are other problems with awards to attorneys of fees, such as long delays before the money is actually received, which puts a strain on the resources of small firms. For the individual victim of employment discrimination, the attorney fee provision is not much help, but attorneys' fees are of considerable importance to the efforts of social-reform groups that are involved in large class action cases and are financed by outside contributions.

The early, formative law-reform work on employment discrimination was done by the NAACP, which, since its inception, has concentrated on achieving group goals through appellate court litigation. The NAACP's first major victory was a Supreme Court decision holding that unions, designated as exclusive bargaining agents under the National Labor Relations Law, had a "duty of fair representation" of minority workers.[39] The NAACP continued to litigate this issue, but expanded its activities with the passage of Title VII in 1964 to include a wide range of class actions and complaints before the EEOC. After the passage of Title VII, the NAACP Legal Defense Fund also became quite active in employment discrimination. LDF concentrated on seniority and testing issues as well as litigating several of the procedural issues involved in the laws. Probably its most famous case was *Griggs* v. *Duke Power Co.*[40] where the Supreme Court held that intent to discriminate can be demonstrated by a seemingly neutral, nonaccidental practice that, in fact, results in an unfavorable impact on minorities. Currently, the LDF has more than 200 class action suits against various public and private entities.

[39] *Steel* v. *Louisville & Nashville Railroad Co.*, 323 U.S. 192 (1945).
[40] 401 U.S. 424 (1971). On the significance of this case, see Jones (1976).

Some of the new public-interest law firms have also been active in challenging employment discrimination. Their cases are invariably on behalf of large, mass or paper membership organizations. In fact, in many of the cases, the same organizations appear as plaintiffs.

As with other civil rights examples, the *characteristics of the social-reform groups* do not favor successful activity. The groups are either mass membership (for example, the NAACP) or paper organizations, or really have a nonexistent membership. The law-reform organizations are not able to finance their litigation activity out of membership dues. The goals of the activity are purely collective goods; no minority applicant or employee has to be a member of the organization or make any contribution whatsoever to the activity of social-reform groups to participate in the fruits of victory. Selective incentives, for members, are minimal.

The *distribution of benefits and costs* also does not favor successful activity by social-reform groups. Benefits are widely distributed. Costs appear to be concentrated on the discriminators, although on a theoretical level, there is disagreement as to why employment discrimination occurs. One explanation is that it is costly for employers to obtain accurate information on the productivity of minorities and, therefore, they will rely on sketchy, stereotypical information. Although this may lead to the hiring of less productive white male workers than more qualified minority or female workers, it still may be more efficient than obtaining more accurate information (Arrow, 1972). Another explanation is a "taste for discrimination," that is, discriminators simply dislike working with minorities or women and are willing to pay for it in the form of less productivity (Becker, 1971). A third explanation views the white labor force as a "collective monopolist" that uses its monopoly power to maintain its position relative to minorities and women (Thurow, 1969, pp. 130–143). Whatever the reason, discriminators act as if, in fact, the cost of ceasing to discriminate is concentrated. Employers resist efforts to change employment practices, and, of course, unions dominated by white males are even more bitterly opposed to the actions of social-reform groups.

The *bureaucratic contingency* also poses serious problems for social-reform groups. As noted, employment discrimination is found throughout society in both public and private employment, and among large and small employers. Moreover, the basic remedy involves challenging individual, discretionary decisions involving particular applicants or employees. Under normal legal theory, an aggrieved member of a minority group or a female, would prosecute a claim against the alleged discriminator and claim that the defendant violated the antiemployment discrimination laws in either failing to hire, or failing to provide equal pay, promotion, or other important conditions of work. The defendant would claim that there was a work-related reason for the decision; for example, that the plaintiff did not score high enough on a particular test, which may be objective or subjective, or was not as productive on the job, or lacked the requisite personal qualities to be promoted. The plaintiff would have the burden of proof on all the elements of the case, including proving that the defendant intended to discriminate.

It is obvious that under these circumstances the bureaucratic contingency would present an insuperable obstacle in battling employment discrimination. It would be impossible for the victims of discrimination to challenge a significant number of employment decisions. For this reason, social-reform groups and law reformers have been pressing for a routinized test of employment discrimination which would be analogous to the routinized tests pressed for in school integration and finally accomplished in voting rights. In employment discrimination, the principal solutions sought are the following: If it is determined that minorities and/or females are not proportionately represented in various job categories, then the antidiscrimination laws will be held to have been violated. If employment tests have a disproportionate impact on minorities and/or females, then the employer has the burden of proving that they are job-related. The most desired remedy is a combination of goals and timetables under which discriminators are ordered to come up with affirmative action plans that provide that, within specific time periods, certain percentages of jobs in various categories will be filled by minorities or females. In addition, the employers have the burden of justifying any failure to meet the goals and timetables. The aim, of course, is to attempt to substitute a statistical test for discretionary employment decisions.

Needless to say, all parts of the remedy are extremely controversial.[41] Although such a remedy is being sought by social-reform groups and some government agencies, and has been ordered by some courts, the law and the policy are far from settled. But as far as social-reform groups are concerned, the issue is directly analogous to other civil rights issues. With statistical tests of discrimination, and the burden of proof shifted to the employer, social-reform groups will have some chance of accomplishing their goals. If the issue of employment discrimination has to be resolved through the examination of in-

---

[41] Compare Glazer (1975, chap. 2) with Bell (1976a) and Edwards and Zaretsky (1975). See also Nickel (1975), Jones (1970, 1976b), and Dworkin (1977).

dividual discretionary decisions, then the efforts of the social-reform groups are doomed.

The efficacy of the *judicial remedy* follows the analysis of the bureaucratic contingency. If the courts are willing to take a hard line on employment testing, and impose goals and timetables, then the remedy has the potential for becoming effective. If the courts are not, then as far as the social-reform groups are concerned, the effort will be lost. This point is well illustrated by a case brought by Public Advocates, a public-interest law firm in California, against the University of California, Berkeley, alleging sex discrimination. The suit was filed in 1972. The university has been very successful in thwarting the efforts of HEW and the plaintiffs in seeking access to employment records. After a long period of time, HEW finally issued a report that found sex discrimination but contained no information about individual cases. In the meantime, the court would not take any action against the university. The plaintiffs found themselves hamstrung. The court refused to grant access to records or issue any preliminary injunctions and the suit had to be abandoned. If the court had been willing to use a statistical approach, the university would at least have had to come forward and justify its employment situation. Under the current state of law, at least as far as HEW requirements are concerned, affirmative action means that a university or college only has to show a good-faith effort to recruit minorities or women in its search for the "best qualified" person for a particular position.[42] The employment decision remains discretionary since each case has to be litigated individually. And, the burden of proof is on the plaintiff. The practical effect of this result is to make the bureaucratic contingency an insuperable obstacle.

Although the statistical approach may be a necessary condition for successful activity by social-reform groups, it is not a sufficient condition. This is because of the *characteristics of the law reformers*. The law reformers have independent financing and so can engage in large-scale employment discrimination suits. They also are independent of their clients, so they can pick and choose their cases and their strategy. The law firms deal mostly with the leaders of the social-reform groups, which either have no membership to speak of or do not exert significant control over the leaders. The leaders invest little or no resources in the litigation but reap the publicity that comes from any victory. This

[42] HEW's, Memorandum to College and University Presidents, December 1974, quoted in Edwards and Zaretsky (1975, p. 34). There is litigation pending against HEW concerning discrimination in higher education.

freedom of action has allowed some of the law firms to achieve impressive results, at least on paper. For example, settlement agreements providing for goals and timetables have been reached with the banking and savings and loan industry in California, with Pacific Telegraph & Telephone, as well as other large utilities. Public interest law firms have been particularly adroit in using publicity as leverage against these entities.

On the other hand, the law reformers have structural weaknesses that limit their effectiveness in the employment discrimination field. It has been noted that while law reformers have the resources to overcome the free-rider problem for certain kinds of litigation, they lack the resources for the long haul—the bitterly fought, factually complex case. This same weakness appears in employment discrimination cases, especially against public employers, such as police and fire departments or other bureaucracies. With rare exceptions, most of the active public interest law firms encounter most of their difficulties when a public employer is recalcitrant. Under the best of circumstances, large public bureaucracies are sluggish and bound by various civil service and other rules and regulations. Courts are usually reluctant to intervene with other branches of government. Also, dominant white male employees in these agencies usually are politically potent. For these and other reasons, the law reformers usually find that suits against public employers are fraught with political problems and are expensive.

Another weakness has to do with relations with public enforcement agencies, particularly the EEOC and the state agencies. Given the weaknesses in the social-reform groups, the small number of law-reform organizations, as well as both groups' slender resources, the lawyers have long recognized that they alone cannot make a significant dent in employment discrimination. Consequently, a major effort has been made to try to enlist the support of public enforcement agencies. The most successful employment discrimination cases have been those where public agencies have joined forces, in a vigorous manner, with the law reformers and where there has been an activist court. In these situations, the public agencies can use their power to gather the necessary information and lend their support to the social-reform groups. The public agencies can thus help the social-reform groups overcome difficult resource problems. When the opposite happens, social-reform groups and law reformers have a much more difficult time. This was one of the main problems in the Berkeley litigation. HEW had the initial responsibility for investigating sex discrimination at the university and issuing a report. The judge would not move until HEW did, and that agency stalled and eventually issued an inadequate report.

The role of the public enforcement agencies is vital, yet the prospects for the future are not promising. Relations between the principal social-reform groups and law reformers and the EEOC cooled considerably as a result of the AT&T and steel settlements, and the law reformers are worried that what they regard as sweetheart agreements may be the wave of the future. In addition, there are growing doubts about the effectiveness of the EEOC in carrying out its normal duties. The backlog continues to grow, the state FEPCs continue to fail to assume their responsibilities, and there is a feeling of crisis concerning the future effectiveness of public antiemployment discrimination efforts (Greenberger and Gutmann, 1977).

A final weakness of the law reformers has to do with monitoring compliance. The point was made that statistical tests, especially goals and timetables, were a necessary but not sufficient condition for successful activity by social-reform groups. The task of supervising enforcement of the goals and timetables remains. For most important employment discrimination cases, enforcement is a long-term proposition and already law reformers are reporting difficulties in holding discriminators to goals and timetables that are part of a court order or settlement agreement. The primary monitoring mechanisms are quarterly reports, which vary in terms of specificity and other kinds of information. These reports are filed with the court and the plaintiff's attorney. Most attorneys admit that these reports are not a satisfactory monitoring mechanism but that neither they nor the clients have the resources (and, in the case of the attorneys, the interest) to pursue the matter further. As one lawyer admitted, the lawyers assume that the employer is in compliance unless the client complains.

There have been some exceptions to this pattern. In some instances, more information is required in the employer reports and this makes monitoring somewhat easier. In other cases, employee groups have been able to monitor performance. In still others, the lawyers have asked, as part of the relief, that funds be paid to client groups to give them a monitoring capacity. But generally speaking, these are exceptions, and monitoring remains a critical weakness. In the meantime, it is reported that several of the large, industrywide agreements are being violated, that companies are coming in and offering excuses for failure to comply, and that social-reform groups and law reformers are struggling to enforce their remedies. Finally, the prospect of goals and timetables as a remedy appears to be rapidly diminishing, and may even be undercut altogether by the Supreme Court; if this happens, enforcement of antiemployment discrimination laws will become even more difficult.[43]

Summary and Conclusions

Table 4.1 summarizes the results of the case studies. At the risk of oversimplification, I have divided the school integration cases into three categories: straight litigation efforts prior to the 1964 Civil Rights Act; post-1964 Civil Rights Act cases; and those cases where courts have ordered extensive busing plans. After the 1964 Civil Rights Act, the federal Executive through the Justice Department and especially the funding powers of HEW at least had the potential for significantly altering the outcome of the struggle. Although the record of school desegregation is very mixed, and subject to conflicting interpretations, I think that most observers will agree that when the federal government did intervene actively, results were changed, and this intervention has an important bearing on our theory. It is quite evident that the social-reform groups could not accomplish their goals through the legal system alone. As the first column indicates, there were some outside resources for the groups, and the law reformers were affiliated with the organizations, but every other variable was unfavorable to successful action. The intervention of the federal government reduced the costs of litigation, but, more significantly, it took the campaign out of the courts and used administrative remedies (such as cutting off HEW funds). The goals of the social-reform groups and the law reformers, during this phase, included publicity, consciousness-raising, and focusing political pressure. While important, these goals did not include the seeking of group goals through litigation.

The busing cases also serve to illustrate a different kind of situation. Here, the court is willing to assert extraordinary remedies. Whether courts should, in effect, become administrative agencies is of course a controversial question, but the point is that without the active intervention of the federal government, the courts had to assume extraordinary remedies to achieve at least the potential for success. When social-reform groups and law reformers are able to persuade courts to assume such a role, there is at least the chance of winning; if the courts are unwilling, the bureaucratic contingency of field-level discretion becomes an insuperable obstacle. This is not to say that school integra-

[43]*Regents of U. of Cal. v. Bakke,* 98 S Ct 2733 (1978).

Table 4.1 *Civil Rights, Summary of Theory Variables*

Variables	School Integration				Voting	Housing	Yerba Buena	Employment discrimination	Goals and timetables
	Pre–1964	Post–1964	Busing	Montgomery					
Groups									
Small size							+		
Outside funding	+	+		+	+		+		
Selective benefits							+		
Large size	−	−	−	−	−	−		−	−
No outside resources			−			−		−	−
Collective goods only	−	−	−	−	−	−	−	−	−
Distribution									
Benefits concentrated; costs distributed									
Benefits distributed; costs distributed									
Benefits concentrated; costs concentrated					+		+		
Benefits distributed; costs concentrated	−	−	−	−	−	−		−	
Bureaucratic									
One time					+				
Top solution					+				+
Technically simple		+		+	+				+

Discretion reduced	+				+	+		+	
Long-term	−	−	−	−		−		−	−
Field-level implementation		−	−	−					−
Technically complex									
Discretion required	−	−	−	−					−
Judicial									
Preventive injunction			+		+	+	+	+	
Court solution	+		+		+	+		+	+
Order can be monitored	+		+		+	+		+	+
Regular injunction	−	−		−		−		−	−
Remand to agency	−	−		−		−			−
Order complex	−	−		−					−
Law Reformers									
Affiliated	+	+			+	+		+	+
Technical resources		+			+		−		
Political resources		+			+	+	−		
Independent	−	−	−	−		−	−		−
No technical resources	−	−	−	−		−	−		−
No political resources	−	−	−	−		−	−		−

151

tion will automatically be accomplished through court-imposed busing plans; there still has to be long-term implementation that will require staying power on the part of the groups. It is only to point out that in this area (as well as in other civil rights areas), *normal* judicial remedies will be inadequate.

A similar analysis applies to the employment discrimination area, which is separated into two categories: a standard employment discrimination case where the court orders an employer to stop discriminating and use good faith efforts to employ more minority persons and females, and the situation where the court imposes goals and timetables. In the former situation, the bureaucratic contingency becomes insuperable; in the latter situation, the social-reform group may still eventually lose, but potentially unfavorable characteristics may have been changed to favorable ones.

Only a word need be said about the housing cases. The courts have been unwilling to take an unconventional role and there has been minimal federal government help; every variable is unfavorable to successful activity by social-reform groups.

Aside from the Montgomery bus boycott case, where the litigation was used for the limited purposes of face-saving, legitimacy, and publicity, there are only two situations in the civil rights area that could be counted as victories for the social-reform groups. The one clear case is in voting rights, but this is not really an apt case, since the solution came about through legislative change and federal executive enforcement rather than law-reform litigation. But that, of course, underscores the point. Initially, there was classic-style law-reform litigation (for example, Supreme Court cases outlawing discrimination in voting), which did not accomplish group goals. There was also activity by social-reform groups without law reformers—such as the SNCC campaigns—which also failed to accomplish goals. These activities were important for consciousness-raising and legitimacy. However, it was only when these activities were combined with the Kennedy administration's decision to push the campaign that tangible results were forthcoming. But even this effort would not have been successful without a legislative and administrative solution that was truly draconian by American standards. In an area that was historically and constitutionally committed to local discretion, discretion was not only eliminated by the substitution of a rigid, routinized standard, but administration was replaced, if necessary, by federal officials. And even this solution was only successful where social-reform groups were active in urging citizens to register.

The voting rights area may represent a clear victory for minorities in a substantively important area (there has been a redistribution of political power in many areas of the South) but its uniqueness casts doubt on efforts by social-reform groups in other civil rights situations. So many combinations had to fall into place, including lack of threat to northern and western liberal Democratic support, that one doubts whether social-reform groups would be able to achieve similar successes elsewhere.

The other successful situation was that of Yerba Buena. As compared with voting rights, this was a small case, but it was significant for the residents involved, and it was a large political controversy in the San Francisco Bay area. Some of the variables in Yerba Buena were favorable to successful activity. For example, the group was small, and although collective goods were involved, there also were present powerful selective incentives: The residents knew that their housing and precarious way of life were in jeopardy. The real difference, however, in this case, had to do with the federal district court judge. The injunction was preventive and thus capable of being monitored, but what made the case unique, was that the court kept the injunction in force, and this gave the social-reform groups and the law reformers the leverage that they needed. Without that injunction, the groups would have failed, which is what usually happens in most relocation cases. The court orders more complete compliance with the law, but the problem is referred back to the agency, which then exercises discretionary authority. In this case, the judge was persuaded not to trust the agency, and this made the difference. The Yerba Buena decision was not extraordinary in terms of legal doctrine or the appropriateness of the judicial role; by itself, there is nothing unusual about a preventive injunction. What was extraordinary was the courage and tenacity of the particular judge assigned to the case. That changed the outcome.

5

Social Welfare

This chapter presents cases in three areas: welfare reform, health and mental health, and occupational health and safety. The principal hurdle that the social-reform groups and the law reformers face is the bureaucratic contingency. In these areas, especially, implementing rule changes often requires changes in large numbers of field-level discretionary decisions. However, although the problem is the same as the one encountered in civil rights, the chapter is not redundant. Law-reform activity by social-reform groups in social welfare has been and continues to be an important area. Activity here grew out of the civil rights struggle of the 1950s; it antedates the environmental and consumer movements, and there are many lessons to be learned from these efforts. Although this book does not purport to be a comprehensive account of all law-reform activity by social-reform groups during the past two decades, it would be seriously deficient if it did not include activity in social welfare.

The social welfare case studies have an importance beyond their historical significance. They have been selected to illustrate particular attempts to overcome the bureaucratic contingency. Some of the techniques have been discussed before (for example, the substitution of a routinized solution), but each substantive area presents its own particular difficulties. As we shall see, one of the most important problems in the social welfare area involves human services, and so far defies solution.

Welfare Reform

The special benefit campaigns of the National Welfare Rights Organization (NWRO), particularly in New York City, and litigation to raise welfare benefits in California, provide us with two examples of welfare law-reform activity.

The idea of the NWRO grew out of the experience of a storefront service agency in New York City, Mobilization for Youth (MFY).[1] As poor people began to come into MFY for help, it was discovered that many people were eligible for welfare but not enrolled, or were on welfare but did not receive what they were entitled to. The MFY staff rapidly became skilled in aggressive advocacy on behalf of their clients. At this time, under welfare, recipients were legally entitled to a variety of benefits in addition to their basic allowance. For example, it was New York City policy to allow an extra benefit of about $150 per family of four for winter clothing. In fact, however, these extra benefits were rarely granted. Most recipients did not know about them; if they did and requested the benefits, welfare case workers either refused the requests or gave less than the prescribed amounts. The administration of special benefits was handled on a case-by-case, item-by-item basis.[2]

MFY handled a number of special grant request cases, then decided to bargain with the welfare department on behalf of groups of welfare recipients. At this time, there was a great deal of unrest in the urban ghettos. The organization backed up its demand with mass demonstrations, and demands for administrative hearings as required by federal law. In the first confrontation, the New York City welfare department gave in. Shortly thereafter, hundreds of families received checks for winter clothing. Naturally, word spread rapidly. Within six months, thousands of welfare families joined the campaign for extra benefits, and, thus, signaled the birth of welfare rights organizations.

[1] For a political and social history of the National Welfare Rights Organization, see Piven and Cloward (1971, chap. 10); Kotz and Kotz (1977).

[2] The general lack of use of the special needs program was not, of course, confined to New York City. For an analysis in Wisconsin, see Handler and Hollingsworth (1971, pp. 96–100).

At the height of the campaigns, NWRO workers would station themselves outside welfare centers with checklists of various benefits that recipients were entitled to. When recipients came into the outer office, they were asked to check the items they had not received. Then, they went in to see the welfare case workers and demanded the items. If they were refused, the NWRO worker went back in with them to help present their case. If the demand was still refused, requests for hearings were filed and lawyers were available for this purpose. These campaigns were backed up by marches, demonstrations, sit-ins, conventions, platforms, and lobbying. In New York City, at least, the campaigns were very effective. In June 1967, special grants in New York City were close to $3 million; one year later, they had reached $13 million (Gellhorn, 1967).

Although NWRO was interested in immediately increasing benefits for its members, and attracting new members, this was not its major goal. Its effort was part of a larger strategy to reform the welfare system. The strategy, developed by Professor Richard A. Cloward, a founder of MFY, and Frances Fox Piven, and adopted by NWRO, envisioned a massive drive to recruit all the eligible poor to demand the maximum benefits to which they were legally entitled. This, it was hoped, would disrupt state and local welfare agencies, create a fiscal crisis, and force the federal government to take over and reform welfare (Cloward and Piven, 1966; Cloward and Elwan, 1966).[3]

Eventually, welfare agencies struck back in two ways. First, they eliminated special grants. At a stroke of the pen, NWRO was robbed of its principal organizing tool and its power to create a fiscal crisis. Welfare departments also resisted at administrative hearings by employing delaying tactics or simply by continuing to deny requests after hearings. Welfare organizations lacked the resources to pursue judicial remedies on a massive scale.

In California, as is true in every state, under the program of Aid to Families with Dependent Children (AFDC), the State Department of Social Welfare determined each recipient's minimum need by computing budgets containing allowances for housing, food, clothing, personal needs, recreation, and other needs. County welfare departments calculated the amount of income the family had available.[4] If the family's need exceeded its available income, then AFDC paid the difference between the family's income and its need standard, unless the

---

[3] On the adoption of the Cloward–Piven strategy by the NWRO, see Kotz and Kotz (1977, chap. 21) and Piven and Cloward (1977, chap. 5).

[4] The California example is based on Sitkin (1973).

difference would exceed a fixed maximum amount for a family of that size.

Congress then enacted legislation under which, by July 1, 1969, the states had the duty to increase their need standards and their maximum grants to reflect changes in the cost of living. There was a long controversy over the precise meaning of this law, and particularly whether a state could avoid complying through various techniques, but from the beginning, high officials in the California welfare department understood that these techniques did not apply to California.[5] They knew exactly what the new law meant and that they were required to raise the maximum grants in the state. Nevertheless, when the statute was passed by Congress, and despite the fact that the states were given 18 months to meet the requirements, California did nothing to implement the statute. The July deadline passed, California did not comply, and HEW did nothing to enforce the law. On August 6, 1969, a class action on behalf of all California AFDC recipients was commenced in federal district court to require California to comply with the statute, but the state strenuously resisted the lawsuit and tried to delay the judicial decision. In the fall and spring of 1969 and 1970, HEW wrote letters of inquiry to California about its noncompliance, but took no concrete action. The National Welfare Rights Organization then filed suit against HEW to force it to take steps to make the states comply. Apparently in response to this lawsuit, HEW began proceedings against several states, including California. On August 25, 1970, 13 months after Congress had required compliance, HEW held a hearing on California's noncompliance. California then tried to convince the federal court to defer any action in the lawsuit until HEW had had an opportunity to act, but the court refused.

In September 1970, the court ordered an immediate increase in the maximum grants to conform to federal law. The HEW hearing examiner also issued a proposed decision finding California in violation of federal law and noting widespread malnutrition and suffering on the part of welfare children. Nevertheless, California continued to refuse to increase the grants. Instead on November 24, California submitted to the court a proposal that would permit the state to avoid a real rise in grants. And, at the same time, California appealed the federal court order to the state appeals court. Later, on January 8, 1971, HEW issued its final report, holding California in violation of federal law and ordering a termination of federal funds to California, effective April 1, 1971, unless the state complied. Immediately, Ronald Reagan, then governor

---

[5] See Rabin (1970); *Rosado v. Wyman*, 397 U.S. 397 (1970).

of California, conferred with Vice President Agnew and HEW Secretary Eliot Richardson. The following day, HEW withdrew its decision to terminate federal funds.

In March 1971, the California Supreme Court, in a unanimous decision arising out of a state lawsuit, held that the state had authority to increase the maximum grants to conform to federal law. The court also recognized a clear and continued violation of federal law by the state. Plaintiffs continued to press HEW to reissue its nonconformity decision and they brought suit to force HEW to act. One week after the California Supreme Court removed any doubt about California's ability to comply with federal law, HEW issued its decision and once more ordered a termination of federal funds. Finally, faced with imminent termination of federal funds, California's welfare department raised its grants, effective July 1, 1971, 23 months after Congress had ordered the increase, and almost a year after HEW had notified California that a conformity hearing would be held.

The *characteristics of the social-reform groups* were unfavorable to successful action. When NWRO was at the height of its power, there were selective incentives for the leadership, although never to the degree that was present in civil rights organizations. Beyond this, incentives were weak. The recipient groups had large, inert memberships; they were weak and unstable. As long as the leaders could offer specific, immediate, tangible goods (i.e., special need items), recipients flocked to the welfare offices. But dues-paying membership or other kinds of contributions to the organization were not made a condition for special needs services. The leaders hoped that recipients who had been helped would remain loyal to the organization, but when the special grants were sharply reduced, welfare rights organizations withered. NWRO exactly fit Wilson's view that organizations with lower-class memberships usually have to rely on material incentives rather than purposive incentives; moreover, the supply of material incentives has to be maintained or interest will fade (Wilson, 1973, pp. 65–66).[6]

In the California welfare litigation, there was little pretense at organizational membership. This was class action litigation on behalf of all welfare recipients in the state. The goals were pure collective goods; the increase in welfare benefits applied to all who were on welfare regardless of whether they joined the organization, and even if they were opposed to the organization.

[6] For the decline of NWRO, see Kotz and Kotz (1977, chap. 32), and especially p. 291 on the importance of material incentives as well as the difficulty in providing purpose incentives.

The *distribution of benefits and costs* did not favor successful action. The benefits were widely distributed. In the long run, costs are also distributed, but in the short run they are concentrated since welfare officials resist the demands made on their budget. This was clearly the case in California under the Reagan administration, which bitterly fought the litigation. This was also true in New York City. At first, the city capitulated to the demands, but then the state came to its aid by eliminating special grants. The state was not willing to distribute this additional cost of welfare.

The California welfare litigation represents a favorable *bureaucratic contingency*. Once the state gave up, the rule change could be implemented at the top; no field-level discretionary decision making was involved, only a recomputation of welfare grants by computer. Compliance was easily monitored. The NWRO case was a different story. Under normal circumstances, the administration of special grants is not a favorable bureaucratic contingency. The benefits are not granted automatically. Recipients have to request and justify them; lower-level officials have to be persuaded that the special benefits are due. These decisions are discretionary and of low visibility. Furthermore, although each particular benefit is discrete, the issue, even as applied to a single welfare family, is long term. Special needs arise all the time, so even if an official complies with the rules in a particular instance, there is no guarantee that compliance will be forthcoming the next time around. Under normal circumstances, recipients are at a disadvantage, and the empirical findings confirm that the special grants systems had been working poorly. The bureaucracy held too many of the cards (Handler and Hollingsworth, 1971, chap. 4).

The NWRO sought to overcome the bureaucratic contingency by attempting to routinize the process. The leaders and workers prepared check lists of what each recipient was entitled to under the applicable rules, and then would demand all of the items that were checked. Massive demands, backed by militancy, did in fact routinize the process for a time. Officials, more or less, paid on demand. But after awhile the welfare department was able to reinstate the discretionary system; applications for special needs were decided on a case-by-case basis and disappointed recipients were required to go through the hearing procedures. The bureaucratic contingency became unfavorable again, and the welfare rights organizations began to have trouble handling the massive numbers of individual decisions.

The *judicial remedy* worked in the California case. Finally, the various courts ordered the state to increase the benefits according to an easily ascertainable statutory formula. By this time, HEW had no alternative but to announce a cut-off for failure to comply, but since HEW had not enforced a cut-off in 30 years, the real lever in the case was the courts. Monitoring compliance would not be difficult.

In the NWRO case, courts would not order special grants except in unusual circumstances; even then, the decision would only apply to the particular parties before the court for the specific request at issue—for example, that these plaintiffs were entitled to a winter clothing allowance. In the normal case of judicial review, and especially with class actions, the court would remand to the agency, and ask the agency to exercise its discretion under different criteria. Thus, in most situations, the parties would be forced to confront field-level officials.

The *characteristics of the law reformers* were favorable in the California example. This is one of the clearest cases where the subsidized law reformers (in this case, Legal Services) can overcome the free-rider problem. The social-reform group could not have supported this lengthy appellate court litigation, and it was exactly the type of law-reform work most suited to law reformers.

The NWRO case presented a different situation. In a customary dispute over special grants, a lawyer would be competent, if not overly qualified, and many Legal Services lawyers did take such cases. The NWRO campaigns, however, were much different; this was mobilization by social-reform groups that used special grants as an organizing technique. The usual type of law reformer was not likely to have the skills that the group needed; litigation skills were needed less than advocacy and negotiation skills at the community level. For a time, Legal Services lawyers did, in fact, work successfully in the NWRO campaigns, but these were a special breed of young, militant lawyers, far more interested in community organization than appellate court litigation (Wexler, 1970).

In more recent years, two trends are noted for social-reform groups and law reformers in the welfare area. The groups themselves, especially on the national level, have probably died. In isolated parts of the country, welfare rights organizations exist, and, although systematic data is hard to come by, one suspects that they are small, led by a few activists, and most likely interested in community-based, individual problems of daily living and survival, rather than larger issues of social change.[7] At the same time, law-reform litigation continues apace. This is primarily undertaken by Legal Services lawyers, and although welfare rights organizations often appear on the pleadings, it

---

[7] For example, there is a local welfare rights group in Madison, Wisconsin that is small, stresses personal help to new and old recipients and members, and works closely with some trusted Legal Services lawyers, but generally eschews grandiose law-reform efforts.

is doubtful whether the local social-reform groups play an active, serious role in the litigation efforts.

The law reform efforts cover a wide range of welfare issues. The states and the federal government are constantly changing welfare laws and rules, and especially AFDC, which, in turn, stimulates legal challenge. In recent years, issues include relitigating the residency rules, the treatment of payments to older children, methods of obtaining information from clients, procedures for chasing absent fathers, calculating the resources of unrelated adults, the collection of overpayments, alternative methods of calculating budgets and work-related expenses, and state–county funding arrangements, to name only a few. The Supreme Court, in recent years, has become unsympathetic to the arguments of the law reformers, and, as a result, more litigation has taken place in state courts.[8]

On the basis of the analysis so far, one can predict the likely consequences of much of the litigation. Enforcement is more likely for cases falling closer to the California example, that is, where uniform, statewide cutback rules are enjoined. One example would be attempts to restrict residency. There are other rules that prevent reductions or cutbacks, but these rules are complex, of low visibility, and are historically ignored, violated, or prone to error. The prime examples here are the various budget, taxing, and work-related expense rules. I doubt whether court cases have much of an impact here since communication, monitoring, and enforcement problems are so difficult.[9] It is even difficult to predict whether statewide budgetary rules will be enforced. For example, it took 5 years and several more court cases before New York State would acknowledge the applicability of a Supreme Court decision dealing with substitute parent budgetary rules. Law reform work in welfare has become exceedingly difficult. Hard-fought legal victories are often nullified by statutory or administrative changes; on other occasions they are ignored, and in still other situations, no one knows what the subsequent effects are (Capowski, 1976).

Health and Mental Health

All of the problems of law-reform activity by social-reform groups in welfare become exacerbated in the health and mental health areas.

---

[8] For a current listing on welfare and poverty litigation, see *Poverty Law Reporter* and the *Clearinghouse Review*; for a recent history of law reform litigation in California, see Doolittle and Wiseman (1976).

[9] On the other hand, cases involving intergovernmental relations would be enforced, but these examples are not within the scope of this study.

Client groups are weaker, costs are more concentrated, implementation is more difficult, basic decision making has to remain at the field level, and the law reformers are even less equipped to deal with the issues involved. My examples are the litigation that seeks to raise the quality of medical care in the D.C. General Hospital, the right-to-treatment litigation in Alabama (*Wyatt* v. *Stickney*), and efforts to protect patients in federal sterilization programs.

In 1970, a public interest law firm, representing a senior citizen group, several individual plaintiffs, and some health professional organizations, brought suit against the D.C. General Hospital for its alleged failure to provide quality care for its patients.[10] The plaintiffs won. The district court held that the hospital is "required by law to provide comprehensive medical care for indigent residents of the District of Columbia . . . including inpatient services, outpatient services and emergency room treatment." The quality of care "is measured by the degree of care, skill, and diligence customarily exercised by hospitals generally in the community."[11] The plaintiffs in the case produced voluminous records, government reports, and expert testimony establishing the care provided in neighboring hospitals in the district as compared with that provided by D.C. General. The defendants did not seriously contest the facts, but argued that the failure to provide such care was due to budgetary and political constraints, an argument that the court specifically rejected.

To capture the full complexity and difficulties involved in trying to realize this victory, it is necessary to discuss in some detail what was wrong with the D.C. General and what remedies were called for. There was a critical shortage of personnel in the medical records department that resulted in large numbers of misplaced records and backlogs, making appropriate and timely diagnoses difficult. The situation became so serious that one department had to set up, informally, its own record system. In the outpatient department, patients sometimes had to make two trips to the hospital in order for the physician to be sure what medication the patient was receiving and should take.

The radiology department was understaffed in clerical, technical, and nursing assistant positions, resulting in low-quality work performed by overworked technicians, delays in moving patients to and from other areas of the hospital for X-rays, inability of doctors to obtain X-ray reports and films in time, and needless repetition of pro-

---

[10] The case study is based on court papers of *Greater Washington, D.C. Area Council of Senior Citizens et al.* v. *District of Columbia Government et al.*, Civil Action No. 275–71 in the United States District Court for the District of Columbia and interviews with the plaintiffs' lawyers, The Center for Law and Social Policy, Washington, D.C.

[11] Opinion filed Sept. 11, 1975.

cedures. Over the years, demand for X-ray diagnostic and therapeutic services increased significantly, and at the same time, the number of essential staff declined. There was also a serious maintenance problem with the equipment. Machines often broke down and remained out of repair for considerable periods of time. There was no preventive maintenance program, and bureaucratic redtape hampered repair.[12] Weekend, evening, and night coverage were inadequate, and film retakes were necessary about 25% of the time.

The emergency room lacked sufficient physician and support staff, including the necessary observation of potential suicides, or persons subject to seizure, or otherwise dangerous to themselves or others. The lack of supervision contributed to several deaths. There was also lack of radiology personnel for the emergency room, especially in the evenings and during weekends and holidays. The court found that D.C. General has the only major hospital emergency room in the country without the services of a radiologist. The result of this deficiency was that physicians, with no special training, had to read the X-rays. They sometimes could not recognize poor quality films or recognize medical problems in films, which resulted in incorrect diagnosis and lack of adequate treatment.

There was a large and persistent shortage of registered nurses. The nursing staff had to spend most of its time preparing and distributing medication and had little or no time for patient education and observation. The staff could not perform ordinary patient care or prevent complications from arising. The nursing shortage was particularly serious when patients were transferred from intensive care to the regular wards but still needed nursing care. There was an incomplete charting of physiological and other vital signs, which made diagnosis and treatment by physicians more problematic. The shortage of nurses in the renal-dialysis unit necessitated that physicians perform dialysis.

There were also chronic shortages of drugs and personnel in the pharmacy department, which exacerbated the nursing shortage since the nurses had to shop around in other departments for the medication or locate a physician for a substitution of medication.

There was no effective preventive-maintenance program and an insufficient number of maintenance personnel to repair breakdowns in equipment and buildings. Malfunctioning of electrical equipment for the diagnosis and treatment of heart patients posed a serious health

---

[12] For example, administrative regulations required that the in-house staff be called in first before the manufacturer's repair team could be summoned, even though the in-house staff rarely fixed the complicated machines.

hazard. Fallen ceilings and leaky roofs went unrepaired for considerable periods of time.

The hospital lacked an adequate infection-control program or sufficient laboratory staff. Physicians felt that they could not rely on single test results, and because of staff shortages, doctors and interns often had to perform messenger services to ensure prompt testing.

In addition to all of the above problems, which only have been sketched, the D.C. General Hospital is a public institution, which means that it is subject to the normal governmental bureaucracy, red tape, and, in recent years, budgetary squeeze. In fact, one of the major difficulties was a citywide hiring freeze.

Needless to say, despite its initial court victory, the law firm has been back to court repeatedly seeking to force changes in the hospital. There have been administrative changes at the top level and some improvement in the staffing, but the problems are complex, and obtaining reliable information and verifying results nearly impossible. Without trying to belabor the point, I will review briefly one of the stipulations entered into between the parties to illustrate what is involved. This stipulation only covers problems of supplying information to the plaintiffs. It requires the hospital to file monthly reports on the following matters: (a) hospital staffing—lists, by job title, of employees in nursing, medical records, radiology, pharmacy, maintenance, laboratory, emergency room, and administrative staff showing number of positions filled, number of vacancies, number of new employees hired, number of terminations, number of requests to fill positions, number of requests to fill positions granted and pending; (b) nursing—lists of all requests to fill positions initiated, pending, and granted during each month by job title and unit assignment, and a list by job title of all staff positions that have been transferred each month from D.C. General to other agencies in the district; (c) volume—monthly reports on average daily inpatient census, total number of outpatient visits, and total number of emergency room visits; (d) recruiting efforts—monthly number, place, date, and job title of recruiters and applicants interviewed for each job category; name of each newspaper, journal, or other periodical where job openings are advertised, and the amount of money spent on recruitment activities.

There were many more items covered in this one stipulation including information requests on staff coverage per unit, administrative reorganization, and other matters. The reasons for the stipulation are self-evident; despite what plaintiffs concede to be efforts on the part of the hospital, there remained serious staffing deficiencies in most essential services, and lack of information as to what was going on.

The lawyers, after a considerable effort, have been able to make some structural changes in the administration. Slowly, the hospital has gained more control over its personnel policies, and this has led to some improvements. For example, the new administrator has been able to make improvements in the staffing of the radiology department. But even with control located more in the hospital, the task of reform remains monumental.

The D.C. General Hospital is a 700-bed facility with an annual budget of about $35 million. Hospitals are complex organizations, with large amounts of discretion and weak lines of communication and chains of command. Even under the best of circumstances, it would be difficult for top management in such an organization to institute bureaucratic reforms, and, as noted, a large municipal hospital does not present ideal administrative conditions. Reform at the hospital is a continuous problem; there is constant movement of staff, equipment failures, breakdown, and the like. The court will not supervise its order. If there is to be reform, it will only come about through the constant pressure of the law firm, since, for all practical purposes, the client group does not exist, and other plaintiff groups will only lend professional and technical help on a voluntary, sporadic basis. At the present time, sole responsibility for ensuring compliance rests on the shoulders of one relatively young attorney, who does not devote full time to the case, but who is helped from time to time by other attorneys in the office.

There is a final point to be emphasized about the D.C. General Hospital case. The complaint is about the quality of care, but the litigation only deals with this issue indirectly. The law reformers are only concentrating on staffing ratios; they are assuming that this is the first step toward adequate health care, and while this is a plausible assumption, it does not necessarily meet some of the major objections that the poor have concerning the way they are treated in hospitals. The poor complain of inadequate education and information, lack of sensitivity, lack of consideration as human beings, and other kinds of anxiety-producing experiences. The D.C. General litigation does not reach any of the issues that involve the relationship between health professionals and patients. The litigation is aimed at getting a certain number of nurses in a ward; it says nothing about the care that the nurses should give the poor.

The distinction between numbers of staff and dollars spent and the quality of service that is actually performed must be emphasized. In the human-services area, the numbers are necessary but not sufficient to accomplish the result sought by the social-reform groups, namely, decent professional treatment. Yet, most law-reform activity is directed at the former and not the latter. For example, there has been an extensive amount of litigation seeking to force hospitals to provide a certain percentage of their resources to the poor under the terms of the Hill-Burton Act. Without this obligation, the poor would be without service in particular localities, but even with the obligation imposed, nothing is said about the quality of service actually delivered.

The task of obtaining a quantifiable health-service resource for the poor is a first step, and as the D.C. General case illustrates, it has proven to be truly formidable. Even with outcomes that can be quantified (for example, the number of nursing vacancies per month), compliance still involves monitoring long-term, field-level discretionary decisions. Administrators always come back with excuses for failure to comply, and checking the validity of the excuses requires detailed factual investigations. Without such investigations documenting that the excuses are invalid, the court will not impose coercive sanctions on the administrators. Without such sanctions, compliance will inevitably slip, especially since the administrators are under other pressures to hold costs down. Imagine the task, then, if the litigation also involved the quality of care more directly. That one lawyer would have to reinvestigate and challenge the actual professional interactions that transpired between the patients and the staff in this large municipal hospital. Yet, this is what is involved in our other two examples in the health and mental health areas.

Major activity in the mental health area involves right-to-treatment litigation. Starting in the 1950s, a series of cases were brought seeking to establish the proposition that persons who were involuntarily committed to a mental institution, but who had not committed any crime, had a right to treatment in a therapeutic institution rather than a prison. Gradually, the courts became receptive to the idea. One of the most important cases was *Wyatt* v. *Stickney,* which held that as a matter of constitutional law, the right to treatment applied in three Alabama mental health institutions.[13]

The litigation initially stemmed from a labor dispute between professional employees protesting their discharges on the ground that as a result of the reduction in staff, the mental institutions would no longer be able to adequately treat the patients. Public interest lawyers joined the litigation representing patients and professional mental-health organizations. The court found that the treatment methods at the in-

[13] *Wyatt* v. *Stickney,* 344 F. Supp. 373, 344 F. Supp. 387 (M.D. Ala. 1972) enforcing 325 F. Supp. 781, 334 F. Supp. 1341, aff'd. in part. 503 F.2d 1305 (5th Cir. 1974).

stitutions were "inadequate" and "shocking." There was a lack of individualized treatment, a lack of privacy, unsafe and unsanitary conditions, malnutrition, inadequate staff, and inappropriate staff attitudes. The court held that there was a right to treatment guaranteed by the due process clause of the Constitution and that to fulfill this right, there had to be (*a*) a humane psychological and physical environment, (*b*) a qualified staff in sufficient numbers, and (*c*) individualized treatment plans. After a further series of hearings, the court adopted over 80 standards that had to be applied; these ranged from specific minimum staff–patient ratios, to more general requirements such as the "right to privacy and dignity," the right to receive prompt and adequate medical treatment, and the requirement that for each patient there had to be an individualized treatment plan.

The most interesting part of the court order was the creation of a seven-member Human Rights Committee (HRC) for each of the three defendant institutions to monitor compliance with the comprehensive standards. Each HRC was given power to review all programs to "ensure that the dignity of the human rights of the patients are preserved." They could advise and assist patients who felt their legal rights had been violated or that there had been failure to comply with the court-ordered guidelines, and could consult with independent specialists who were to be compensated by the defendants. The HRCs had no direct implementation powers, which remained with the institutions, but rather were to serve as the "eyes and ears" of the court. The HRCs were composed of laymen active in the mental health field, but did not include any mental health professionals. One included a minister, a newspaper editor, three parents of mentally impaired children, and a former patient.

In addition to ordering the creation of the HRCs, the court ordered the hiring of a professionally qualified and experienced administrator.

In 1975, a study was completed on the first 2 years of the operation of the Human Rights Committee at one of the three mental institutions.[14] There was an initial correction of hazardous and unsanitary conditions, the hiring of 300 additional staff members, and an acceleration in the reduction of the patient population. From the very start, the HRC assumed an "aggressive stance" concerning investigation and reporting, and held biweekly meetings to discuss findings and confer with staff and administrators. There quickly developed considerable hostility and conflict between the committee and the hospital

[14] The study was based on extensive interviews with persons on all sides of the litigation, as well as documentary sources (*Yale Law Journal*, 1975).

staff and the head of the state mental health department. There was frequent resort to the press to air differences and grievances. There also had to be further court orders to prevent the state superintendent from interfering with the HRC activities. After a time, the court authorized the HRC to employ a psychiatric specialist at state expense to help in evaluation and to enlarge the committee's jurisdiction.

The study reached the following conclusions: There was a great improvement in the personal cleanliness of the patients and the sanitary conditions of the facilities and "most life-endangering conditions were removed." On the other hand, the odor of urine and excrement still permeated some of the wards. Patient–staff ratios had been improved, but there still remained old-time staff that regretted the fact that they could no longer use electric prods on the patients. Most patients had planned rehabilitation programs, but they were limited. Most of the waking hours were spent in rocking chairs. "The major change that the decree brought these patients was that they previously sat on benches." It was difficult for the court and the HRC to determine the extent of compliance because of the difficulty in obtaining reliable information. Nevertheless, the study concluded that the court and the HRC did accomplish considerable improvement in the conditions of the Alabama mental institutions, although the extent of the improvement could not be ascertained.

There were other factors in the *Wyatt* litigation that resulted in changes in the state's mental-health program. Prior to the litigation, there had been a decline in the patient population, and although this may have continued, the rate clearly accelerated as a result of the litigation. The HRCs accused the hospitals of dumping the patients out of the community, but this charge has not been substantiated. In fact, preliminary research indicates the opposite (Leaf, 1978). As compared with other states, for example, New York and California, Alabama did make some effort at increasing community resources to receive patients, and although the quality of care was uneven in the communities, on the whole, community integration seemed to be better than elsewhere. There was also a significant increase in public expenditures for mental health, and this was directly attributable to the litigation. Prior to the litigation, the state mental health department had been singularly unsuccessful with the legislature, and Alabama ranked among the lowest in patient expenditures. After the litigation commenced, public appropriations rose considerably. Alabama's per-patient expenditures soon exceeded those of neighboring states and even approached national averages. On the other hand, the state achieved far less success in recruiting the kind of professionals that the court ordered, and it may be that this part of the order is impossible to meet.

In important respects, the *Wyatt* litigation is unique. The district court judge was Frank Johnson sitting in Montgomery, an activist judge of great courage and determination who fought Governor George Wallace in the bitter school desegregation battle and other civil rights controversies. Judge Johnson threatened to appoint a master to take over the state's mental health institutions if his orders were not obeyed, and the Alabama government knew that these threats were not idle. While Governor Wallace loudly attacked the federal court for interfering in state matters, he also vigorously supported the mental health department's request for increased appropriations.

The other unique feature of the case was the appointment of the Human Rights Committees to oversee implementation. Other courts, faced with implementation problems in large, complex bureaucracies dealing with human services, have also fashioned new remedies, such as "hybrid masters" (combining the fact-finding role of the traditional master with the supervisory role of a receiver), monitors, and ombudsmen.[15] On the whole, though, these are extraordinary remedies and most courts will not assume these burdens. As a result, implementing decrees and monitoring performance in human services institutions remain formidable tasks,[16] so much so that the principal public interest law firm in the mental health field recently decided to halt systemwide litigation while it reassessed compliance capabilities.

In the *Wyatt* and D.C. General cases, the law reformers were seeking changes in professional–client interactions in specific institutions. The problems they faced become even more difficult when decision making is decentralized, as is true in many health and mental health areas. Federal family-planning, and especially sterilization programs, are illustrative of these problems.[17] Federally financed family planning is administered by the Public Health Service to state health agencies and private agencies and through the Medicaid and Aid to Families with Dependent Children program. Thus, in both instances, actual family-planning programs are administered by state, local, and private agencies with federal funds pursuant to federal rules and guidelines.

[15] *Pennsylvania Association for Retarded Children* v. *Pennsylvania*, 343 F. Supp. 279 (E.D. Pa. 1972); *Gates* v. *Collier*, 501 F.2d 1291 (5th Cir. 1974); *Morales* v. *Turman*, 364 F. Supp. 166 (E.D. Tex. 1973).

[16] For the difficulties in finding out what goes on in mental institutions, see Sullivan (1977).

[17] This case study is based on the litigation of *Relf* v. *Weinberger*, 372 F. Supp. 1196 (D.D.C. 1974); 403 F. Supp. 1235 (D.D.C. 1975), and court papers filed in subsequent proceedings, *Relf* v. *Mathews*, Civil Action No. 74–243, supplemented by interviews with the lawyers in the Women's Rights Project, Center for Law and Social Policy, Washington, D.C.

Through the family-planning funding, sterilization is provided. It is an extensive program. For example, between 100,000 and 150,000 low-income people have been sterilized under federally funded programs. Most are adults. Between 2000 and 3000 are under 21, and only a few hundred under 18. No statistics are available for the mentally incompetent.[18]

Although the statute authorizing federally sponsored family planning insists that participation be purely voluntary, there is ample evidence that minors and mental incompetents have been sterilized with federal funds and that poor people have been coerced into sterilization operations under threat of assistance cut-offs. The most frequent targets are mothers receiving Medicaid assistance at childbirth; assistance is refused unless the mother agrees to a sterilization procedure after the birth.

Social-reform groups that are concerned with the poor and the mentally incompetent, of course, had been aware of these practices, but matters came to a head after a particularly notorious incident involving two young black girls in Alabama. HEW declared a moratorium on the federally sponsored program for nonemergency sterilizations for persons under 21 or legally incapable of consent, and then issued guidelines. The first approach taken by HEW was to establish different procedures depending on whether the patient is, under state law, a legally competent adult, a legally competent person under 18 years of age, a legally incompetent minor, or a mental incompetent.[19] Legally competent adults must give their "informed consent," as shown by a written and signed document that must include the fact that if the patient withdraws from the operation, there will be no loss of federal benefits. With legally competent persons under 18 there must also be written consent, but in addition, consent has to be passed upon by a review committee of independent persons who must also make the determination that the sterilization is in the best interests of the patient. With legally incompetent minors, the same review committee procedure applies, but in addition, a state court must determine that the proposed sterilization is in the best interests of the patient. With mental incompetents, the review committee and state court rules apply, but personal consent is not required, only that the patient's "representative" requests sterilization. The regulations applied to non-therapeutic sterilization but did not define the difference between a therapeutic and a nontherapeutic sterilization.

The regulations were challenged by the National Welfare Rights

[18] *Relf* v. *Weinberger*, p. 1199.
[19] The description of the HEW regulations is in *Relf* v. *Weinberger*, pp. 1199–1200.

Organization and individual plaintiffs. The district court held that the regulations were invalid because there was no statutory authority to fund the sterilization of persons who could not consent because they were minors or mentally deficient. In addition, the court ruled that the regulations failed to adequately protect patients from coercion. At the minimum, with adults, the court would require oral as well as written notification that federal benefits would not be withdrawn if the patient decided against sterilization.

HEW went back to the drawing board and eventually came up with new regulations. Concerning mentally incompetent persons, the regulations authorized nontherapeutic sterilization where an interviewer certified that the patient appeared to understand what was going to happen, voluntarily requested sterilization, and gave informed consent; a physician certified that the patient voluntarily accepted the service; and a committee certified all of the above. There were other procedural requirements, including state court approval if the patient had been adjudicated incompetent and was in an institution. Again, the court found the procedures defective. Among other things, there was no definition of a nontherapeutic sterilization, no provision for counsel, and lack of uniformity or consistency with state law.[20] HEW has appealed.

What impressed the district court and what was really at issue in the sterilization case was the lack of ability of HEW to monitor the regulations. For some 18 months, interim regulations had been in effect and it was quite clear from the record that the responsible officials at HEW had little or no idea what was happening with the sterilization regulations, that there was little funding and even less interest in supervision, and that, in fact, gross violations of the regulations had been occurring with considerable frequency. Minors and incompetents continued to be sterilized. Informed consent forms had not been prepared or distributed in many states, court-ordered cautionary language had not been included in the forms, and coercive tactics had been used. The initial problem started with HEW; it delayed in addressing the problem and issuing regulations. Its laxness in requiring states to prepare and file compliance plans is notorious; and for years its enforcement of federal rules for grant-in-aid programs has been minimal.[21]

---

[20] *Relf* v. *Mathews*, 403 F. Supp. 1235 (D.D.C. 1975).

[21] For example, The Health Research Group of Public Citizen found in a survey of United States hospitals that 76% were in violation of the HEW regulations. Thirty-one percent had never seen the interim regulations and the same percentage was unaware of the cautionary language. According to the government's figures, 37% of the sterilizations failed to reveal voluntary consent forms, 44% failed to meet a 72-hour mandatory waiting period, and 160 sterilizations were performed on persons specifically included in the moratorium. Brief for NWRO in *Relf* v. *Mathews*, U.S. Court of Appeals, D.C., Nos. 74–1797; 76–1053 (1976), p. 12, N. 8, p. 5.

At the state and local levels, there are strong reasons to oppose restrictions on sterilization. With mental incompetents, sterilization removes the necessity of other more costly methods of preventing pregnancy by birth control, abortion, or by providing separate institutional facilities for each sex. Sterilization allows for greater use of furloughs or release to the community. With the welfare poor, racist and antiwelfare attitudes run strong. In addition, the people in charge of sterilization are used to having their own way. They are professionals who generally think they know best and do not like to be questioned or bothered by bureaucrats, patients, and, especially, lawyers. Paternalistic, if not authoritarian attitudes, are manifest.

What the social-reform groups and the law reformers are trying to do in the sterilization controversy, then, is to establish procedures that will somehow guarantee that judgmental discretionary decisions involving the patient's best interest, understanding, and voluntary agreement are made carefully and accurately. Moreover, these decisions are made throughout the country in hospitals, clinics, and mental institutions. Who will sit on these review committees? Who will certify that the patient understands the written form or the oral instructions and voluntarily consents? Even if lawyers are allowed to participate, who will ask for the lawyers and what lawyers will be available? These are not hypothetical questions. In other areas, especially in the mental health field, there are elaborate procedural safeguards, but they are paper rights only. The clients have neither the knowledge nor the resources to take advantage of procedural due process and violations are widespread (Handler, forthcoming; Kirp, Boss, and Kuriloff 1974). The same will apply to the sterilization regulations.

The social-reform groups, of course, are aware of these problems but face a dilemma. Some of the organizations argue for the exploration of other alternatives; others see no way out and argue for a flat prohibition—no sterilization whatsoever for minors and mental incompetents. Of course, there is no guarantee that such prohibition will be enforced; indeed, HEW's moratorium was violated. But it also may be an unwise rule. There probably are cases where minors and mental incompetents would be better off sterilized and should be sterilized. In any event, it is doubtful whether such a rule will be enacted. There are strong pressures for sterilization and ultimately these organizations would have to rely on the hopes of a Supreme Court constitutional decision. In the meantime, the other groups continue to press for better procedures.

In terms of the variables of the theory, the health and mental-health examples are probably the most unfavorable for successful law-reform activity by social-reform groups. In the health and sterilization examples, the groups are virtually nonexistent. The common identifiable bond between similarly situated people is episodic—isolated visits to hospitals, doctors, and clinics—and without massive community education efforts does not form a basis for common activity. Because of its crisis-oriented, unplanned-for nature, it is difficult to organize groups on the basis of material incentives. Lower-income people are unlikely to join an organization to help solve a future health episode, and community organizers report that it has even been difficult to enlist the support of people who have had encounters; either they want to forget about the events, or a halo effect sets in. In the mental health area, there are active groups among relatives of mental health patients, but these are usually middle-class groups seeking publicly supplied benefits (for example, the right to a public education for the mentally retarded). For situations such as *Wyatt v. Stickney,* there are no social-reform groups of beneficiaries although there are purposive professional groups. The law-reform activity is on behalf of an institutionally defined class. Again, although the incentives are material, there is no capacity for the mobilization of beneficiaries.

The *distribution of the benefits and costs* does not favor activity by social-reform groups. The goods are collective; whatever reforms are accomplished can be enjoyed by all regardless of contribution to the cost of obtaining the goods. Even though most of the institutions are public, the costs are still concentrated in the short run. Bureaucrats and professionals are forced to change their ways and seek increased funding.

The most important point in these examples has to do with the unfavorable *bureaucratic contingency*—the delivery of human services. Routinized solutions can work at the edges of the problem (for example, increasing funding and improving staffing ratios), but ultimately, what is involved is the quality of the professional–client interaction, a process that is most often hidden from view, or when exposed, shrouded in vague standards and professional jargon. It is difficult to find out what is going on, and even more difficult to develop meaningful standards of performance that can be communicated and enforced. In the sterilization case, some social-reform groups, out of frustration, have pressed for a routinized solution, an absolute ban for certain clients, but this is obviously an unsatisfactory solution.

Because of the nature of the bureaucratic contingency, *judicial remedies* are also largely unsatisfactory. The courts can order certain things, such as increased resources, and, under limited conditions, can even persuade the funding sources that the courts, if disobeyed, will take coercive action. But this is not usual. It is a rare court that will enforce a contempt order against a hospital administrator, let alone a legislative body or public executive. In most situations, the defendants will keep coming back to court with evidence of half-hearted attempts and more excuses. In the sterilization situation, the courts only can order more and better procedures. Follow-up will have to depend on the parties involved in each individual case.

The major exception, and it really proves the general point, is the *Wyatt* v. *Stickney* litigation, where the court took extraordinary measures. The evidence indicates that there has been considerable change in the administration of the mental institutions and that the situation of the patients has improved. But to accomplish these results, the court had to operate in a nontraditional manner; it proved that change could come about through a judicial remedy but only if the court no longer acted like a court.

The *characteristics of the law reformers* did not favor successful activity. As distinguished from civil rights lawyers, there were no groups to which the lawyers could belong. They were independent, free-floating firms that had the legal expertise to handle the law-reform activity in court, but no special expertise or resources in the enforcement stage.

Occupational Health and Safety—Coal Miners

The last two examples deal with health and safety issues in the coal mines. The first example, compensation for black lung victims, is analogous to the voting rights example in the previous chapter. It involves inadequate procedural remedies at the field level and law reform through legislative solutions. As with voting rights, the example is not entirely apt since solutions are coming from Congress rather than primarily through the courts and administrative agencies as a result of law-reform activity. The example is used to show attempts at routinized solutions for common and persistent problems in administering social welfare benefits.

In 1968, an explosion in a Pennsylvania coal mine focused national attention on the unregulated dangers facing coal miners and the lack of compensation to disabled miners or their families. Congress responded with the 1969 Federal Coal Mine Health and Safety Act.[22] In

[22] See McAteer (1975). For a description of the statutory and administrative history of the black lung program, see *Talley* v. *Mathews*, 550 F.2d 911 (4th Cir. 1977). The case study is based primarily on United States Congress (1973).

addition to providing for protection of miners against physical dangers, it also sought to protect miners from lung diseases caused by years of exposure to coal dust (black lung or pneumoconiosis). The act ordered the Secretary of the Interior to establish maximum respiratory dust levels for all coal mines and a dual-compensation scheme for miners who were or would be disabled for having inhaled coal dust in the past. First, the federal government would allow disabled miners or their heirs to file claims with the Social Security Administration for disability benefits until December 31, 1972. These benefits would be paid out of general tax revenues, and eligibility would be based largely on rules promulgated by the secretary of HEW. Second, claims of miners filing after December 31, 1972, would be processed under state workers' compensation plans. The Department of Labor (DOL) would determine if a state plan met minimum federal standards. If it did not, the secretary was authorized to seek payment from any liable mine operator.[23]

Although HEW was given discretion to fashion rules and standards for benefits, Congress legislated a series of presumptions to aid the miners; it would be presumed that pneumoconiosis of miners who had worked for 10 years or more in an underground coal mine had been caused by their employment, or that miners who worked 10 years or more in an underground mine and who died of a respiratory disease died of pneumoconiosis, or that any miner who suffered a chronic dust disease of the lung diagnosed by lung opacities on X-rays, by massive lesions of the lung discovered by autopsy or biopsy, or by any method that would duplicate the X-ray or autopsy-biopsy diagnoses, was totally disabled by pneumoconiosis.[24]

Despite congressional efforts to provide a liberal compensation scheme for miners suffering from black lung, the program did not work. In 1973, a congressional committee heard testimony from miners who had worked between 20 and 50 years in the mines. All complained of shortness of breath and coughing fits, so severe that phlegm was often coughed up and was often black. Their breathing capacity was so impaired that they were unable to walk up stairs, hills, or slight inclines. They found it difficult to breathe in a prone position. Most had to have their heads elevated when they slept, and some even had to sleep in reclining chairs rather than in beds. All said they needed fresh air or oxygen regularly, and mentioned they were unable to tolerate anyone in their presence smoking because the smoke caused them great difficulty in breathing. All had been taking medication for their breathing problem for several years.

[23] 30 U.S.C. §863 (1970).
[24] 30 U.S.C. §921(c)(1)(2)(3) (1970).

The miners had worked many years under conditions where dust was extremely thick and said their shortness of breath had been noticeable after 10 to 15 years of working in the mines. Many had been diagnosed as having pneumoconiosis or other chronic and disabling dust diseases of the lung by local doctors. Nevertheless, they had to continue working to support their families. Those testifying had been refused benefits by the Social Security Administration (SSA) because medical studies have been unable to prove a direct connection between the exposure to coal dust while working and chronic lung disease. X-rays, blood-gas tests, or breathing tests cannot adequately establish whether a miner is disabled. It is this lack of an objective standard that caused and continues to cause many of the difficulties of the black lung program for these miners.

There were other problems with the black lung program. Immediate bottlenecks developed because Congress had neglected to give HEW additional personnel to handle claims for black lung benefits. Much of SSA's administration of benefits was done in Baltimore, and not only claims but simple requests for information had to be done by mail. The understaffing problem caused massive delays throughout the system, with even simple inquiries going unanswered for months.

Although HEW received considerable criticism for delays in processing claims and appeals, more fundamental criticisms were made of its eligibility standards and procedures. HEW was hostile to the program and was concerned primarily with denying benefits unless claimants were totally disabled. "Total disability" was narrowly construed. Panels of HEW doctors, pressed for time, gave only superficial review (usually just the rereading of an X-ray) and any doubt about the claim was resolved against the claimant. Claims initially denied but later granted on appeal by an administrative law judge (ALJ) were subject to discretionary, unilateral review by the Appeals Council, which could reverse the ALJ's finding. The Department of Labor administration was also criticized. Since few states amended their workers' compensation laws to allow for black lung benefits, DOL was obligated to investigate most claims filed after December 31, 1973. It approved about 20% but could find a liable coal mine operator only in about half the cases, and the operators invariably appealed, making compensation even more problematic for disabled miners.

Congress responded by mandating increasingly less discretionary standards. In 1972, after extensive hearings in both Senate and House committees, amendments were passed to include all miners, not just those working in underground mines.[25] A new presumption was added,

[25] 30 U.S.C. §921(c)(1)(2) (1972).

further reducing discretion: If a miner were employed in an underground mine for 15 years or more, and medical evidence indicated a
"totally disabling respiratory or pulmonary impairment" despite the
negative evidence of an X-ray, there would be a rebuttable presumption of pneumoconiosis and the miner would be entitled to benefits. In
addition, the authority of HEW was amended to forbid the denial of
benefits solely on the basis of a negative X-ray.[26]

Nevertheless, HEW continued to deny benefits to any miner who
could not demonstrate conclusively either that he was totally disabled
by pneumoconiosis or that he had been totally disabled solely by inhal-
ing coal dust. Reacting to HEW's continuing reluctance to follow congressional directives, the Ninety-fourth Congress considered bills to
reduce agency discretion even further. The House passed a bill that
provided that miners who had worked for 30 years or more in an
underground coal mine or that had worked for 25 years or more in an
anthracite mine be eligible for black lung benefits. The definition of
"totally disabled" was broadened, and HEW was forbidden to review
the findings of its ALJs unless the claimant requested review. Both DOL
and HEW were ordered to abolish their review boards. HEW was
ordered to develop a plan to contact all potential victims of black lung
to inform them of their possible eligibility for federal benefits. Senate
bills contained similar provisions, but included additional sections as
well. The Senate called for transferral of all HEW rule-making authority to DOL, the establishment of DOL offices for processing benefits in
the coal fields, and a plan to introduce a severance tax on each ton of
coal mined to finance a federal coal miners' compensation plan for
black lung (most states had been unwilling to extend their workers'
compensation to black lung benefits).[27]

The new proposed legislation died in the Senate committee, but is
pending. The analogy with voting rights is quite clear. The black lung
program provided miners with certain rights to benefits, but those
rights were contingent on information and resources to prosecute a
claim that required discretionary decisions by a hostile administration.
Given the poverty and other social conditions of the disabled miners, it
was predictable that the program would fail. A great many would be
unaware of their rights, and others would have difficulty in proving
their cases, especially since appeals were necessary. The solution that
Congress seems to be moving toward also resembles the voting rights

[26] 30 U.S.C. §921(c)(4), §923(b). The new provisions were made retroactively effective [P.L.
92–303(4)(g)]. HEW opposed all attempts to liberalize the 1969 Act. See, United States Senate (1972).
HEW has also opposed every subsequent attempt to liberalize the act.

[27] H.R. 10760.

case: The discretion of HEW is being curtailed or removed and a routinized test (a certain period of working time in particular mines) is being substituted for a discretionary decision.

The last example deals with the law-reform efforts of social-reform groups in enforcing safety provisions of the Federal Coal Mine Health and Safety Act of 1969 in the unorganized coal fields in eastern Kentucky. The example illustrates an imaginative, broad-gauged attack on a severe bureaucratic contingency. The examples of this book have stressed the ultimate importance of the social-reform group at the implementation stage. Groups varied in their capacity to meet this challenge. Some organizations, such as the Sierra Club and the NAACP, are maintained to some considerable degree through purposive incentives and can carry out some implementation. In the consumer area, there were also some cohesive groups. In another example, dealing with cash discount sales involving credit cards, before the law-reform activity was started, the law reformers and the organization worked out an implementation plan. In welfare and health, the groups become far more tenuous, and even nonexistent.

With occupational health and safety, the strength of the group varies. In many situations, there are well-established unions which, if they decided to pursue occupational health and safety issues, would have no difficulty in mobilizing support. The example chosen is at the opposite end of the spectrum. The nonunion coal miners probably represent, along with migrant workers, some of the most oppressed labor in America. For the most part they work for small operators or absentee owners; it is a society where labor disputes are settled peremptorily through firings and violence. There is a persistent labor surplus in the area subjecting miners to constant job insecurity. There is also the widespread tradition of blacklisting troublemakers, which further chills the exercise of rights.

The Federal Coal Mine Health and Safety Act provides that safety standards can be enforced either through the federal government or by private groups. If a federal inspector finds an "imminent danger," he can close the mine or the section affected. An imminent danger is defined as "[t]he existence of any condition or practice in a coal mine which could reasonably be expected to cause death or serious physical harm before such condition or practice can be abated."[28] Lesser regulatory actions include notification of violations of safety or health rules and closure orders for failure to obey. Then, for recalcitrant operators, there are "unwarrantable failure closure orders" for re-

[28] 30 U.S.C. §802(j) (1970).

peated and unwarranted violations. The Mine Enforcement Safety Administration (MESA) is in charge of enforcement. When orders are issued, there are administrative proceedings with appeals to the Board of Mine Operations Appeals and judicial review.

There are a number of problems with federal enforcement efforts.[29] At least until the Carter administration, the Department of Interior had the reputation of being captured by the coal operators. The Board of Mine Operations Appeals has been strict in its interpretations of federal power, and the department has been singularly unaggressive in appealing cases. The federal inspection system is especially weak. There are insufficient numbers of inspectors, and for the most part, they operate in an extremely hostile environment. In 1976, 88 federal inspectors petitioned the head of MESA for protection against operators. Inspectors were subjected to verbal abuse, threats of bodily harm, gunfire, and tire-slashing. In some instances, inspectors were simply run off the property. Despite legal protections for federal inspectors, the laws are seldom used and the harassment of federal inspectors has continued to be a major problem in mine safety enforcement.

There are about 750 federal inspectors and over 5000 coal mines. It is obvious, and well-recognized by Congress, that the federal inspectors can only inspect a fraction of the number of mines. For this reason, there are also provisions for the private enforcement of health and safety regulations. Private safety rights under the 1969 act are granted to representatives of miners and the individual miner. A representative is any person or organization who represents two or more miners at a particular mine. Under the act, a representative is for safety purposes only, although the representative may also be the collective bargaining representative. The representative has the right to demand an immediate inspection whenever he suspects a violation or imminent danger. He also has "walkaround" rights with federal inspectors, the right to administrative hearings on withdrawal orders and notices and to contest the termination of those orders and notices, and the right to seek modification of safety standards. In addition, informal practices have developed where safety representatives participate in meetings between management and MESA on safety matters.

Of the more than 5000 operating coal mines, over 4000 are nonunion, and, at the present time, there are only 11 safety representatives in these unorganized mines. In other words, there are virtually no safety representatives for nonunion miners. Even in the unionized coal mines, this is a little used provision. Several unions have never filed as a safety representative; only three company unions have filed during

[29] The material on enforcement is based on Galloway and McAteer (1977).

the 6 years of the act. One company union filed only after two explosions. A major reason for the lack of use of this provision is undoubtedly lack of information. MESA has taken inadequate steps to inform miners and unions about the provisions of the law. For example, an entitlement brochure, which seems to be MESA's major effort in informing miners of their rights, merely reproduces sections of the statute without any explanations or comments.

Individual miners are also granted safety rights. The most important one is the right to refuse to work in unsafe conditions, which is backed up by the right of compensation if the company retaliates against a miner for exercising safety rights. The United Mine Workers have had the right to refuse to work in an unsafe condition written into their contracts; beyond this, it is doubtful whether any other miners know of this right. It is not expressly stated in the 1969 act or any of MESA's educational material. It is a matter of case law, and except in the course of legal pleadings, MESA has never explicitly acknowledged that the right exists. The few cases that have arisen show that the knowledge gained was, for the most part, purely fortuitous. No one knows how many miners are fired for refusal to work in an unsafe condition and merely walk away. Similarly, there are very few applications for compensation when a mine is closed for safety reasons. In the unionized mines, the right is acknowledged and payment is made without the need for applications. In the nonunionized mines, the best evidence is that the miners are ignorant of this right.

There is also a "hot line" between the individual miner and MESA, which is a toll-free number that any miner may use anonymously to call the Washington office to report a safety violation. In theory, at least, upon receipt of the call, the district office is to investigate the complaint within 24 hours. In the first 6 years of the act, the hot line has been used only on an average of about 80 times per year. One district has not had a single call; only 1 of 10 districts has had more than 100 calls in more than 6 years. The only information that MESA requires to be disseminated about the hot line is a poster on the company bulletin board.

In the meantime, coal mining continues to be an unsafe, dangerous occupation. It is estimated that federal inspectors are at the coal mines only about 3% of the time that the mines are in operation; yet, during that small fraction of time, over 20,000 safety orders have been issued, and 400,000 notices of violations. During that same 6½-year period, 1000 miners have died, and over 100,000 have been injured.

The law-reform activity seeking to strengthen coal mine safety and health administration represents a sophisticated approach that is especially sensitive to the problems of implementation. The law reformers themselves grew up and were educated in the coal fields of Kentucky and West Virginia. One of them previously served as a United Mine Workers organizer and lawyer and the other worked as a lawyer for the coal companies before becoming a public interest lawyer. The law reformers are concentrating in the unorganized mines for several reasons. One is that because of the weakness and internal divisions of the United Mine Workers, it is a tricky, delicate matter to engage in community organization work without becoming embroiled in the internal politics of the union. The other reason is that the law reformers feel that the unorganized miners are in the greatest need of law-reform activity and pose the greatest challenge. If the law reformers can succeed in these areas, the techniques they use can more easily be applied where there is less violence, oppression, ignorance, and fear.

From the very beginning, the lawyers have established and nurtured contact with whatever community organizations exist. To a considerable extent, they established and maintained their credibility through service work; for example, they provided immediate help to the families of the Scotia Mine disaster victims, helping to explain legal rights and administrative processes, providing limited representation to the families, and obtaining counsel for them. The law reformers have kept in close touch with the local community organization, have maintained pressure on the Department of Interior and provided expert assistance at the administrative hearings.

The law reformers have also undertaken a series of law-reform cases designed to clear out some of the underbrush, particularly in seeking judicial liberalization of the crabbed, legal interpretations of the administrative agency. One case seeks to establish the authority of the Department of Interior to set up administrative safety procedures in the unorganized fields similar to the ones that exist in union mines. Another case seeks to lower the imminent-danger standard that the law reformers feel has been set too high by the Board of Mine Operations Appeals. And several cases deal with strengthening protection from retaliation.

The law reformers are also putting forth extensive proposals for the dissemination of information and the education of miners as to safety rights during safety training sessions that are now required by law. They have prepared course materials and pamphlets to be distributed to every miner. There are also plans to train instructors and safety representatives, and to establish monitoring systems. The law reformers are also pressing for changes in regulations to require more input by the miners in the various administrative proceedings dealing with safety issues and compensation for representatives of both individuals and groups. In two of the most violent counties, miners have been secretly contacted and safety representatives have been designated. The safety organization efforts have been made public and the law reformers are in a bitter struggle to establish the viability of the safety representative program.

There is also a program under way under which the law schools in the affected areas are establishing student clinical programs to train law students and lay advocates to handle safety cases. The Department of Interior has granted permission for law students to handle administrative appeals before the appeals board.

The outcome of these efforts, is, of course, still very much in doubt. The law reformers consist of two full-time lawyers, a paralegal, some law student interns, and some foundation financial resources. At the same time, they enjoy good relations and credibility with what local community groups exist and the top echelon at the Department of Interior and Bureau of Mines. The Carter administration appointees have expressed sympathy and support for the safety efforts. On the other hand, the task itself is formidable. The decision-making process is discretionary as each case involves findings of fact and the application of rules and standards. What are the environmental conditions? Are they sufficiently serious to justify an "imminent danger?" Was the notification proper? Was there retaliation for the exercise of safety rights? And so forth. Under the best of circumstances, the answers to these questions are often not clear-cut, and the weak social and economic conditions of the unorganized coal miners militate strongly against the fair, objective determination of the issues. In the end, it may turn out that the coal mine operators in these areas will prove to be too strong, and that the national political leadership will back off or turn to other interests. This example shows what is involved in seeking to overcome this kind of bureaucratic contingency. There not only has to be law reform but also an effective dissemination of information and a method for creating and strengthening local client groups to exercise their rights.

In terms of the variables of the theory, the coal mine cases perhaps represent a different picture than the other examples in this chapter. The *characteristics of the social-reform group*, although weak, are potentially more favorable to mobilization. Olson (1965) argues that, in general, workers cannot be organized into unions unless there is coercion (for example, pickets, a union shop); otherwise the free-rider problem discourages workers from contributing to the cost of the improved working conditions that are collective goods. These tendencies could apply to the unorganized miners, but there are countervailing incentives. Mine health and safety does have a saliency that is more personal and enduring than the issues of patient care at hospitals or the safety of factory workers. The miners and their families are long-term community residents, so there are communal bonds and perhaps purposive incentives as well as the material incentives of health and safety.[30] Moreover, the incentives are continuing, which is considered to be important in mobilizing lower-income groups. In one sense, the costs of contributing to the group are small. In the safety case, there is little that the law reformers and the leaders are asking the miners to do. They simply want them to receive, understand, and act on safety information, elect a safety representative, and provide communal support. Elaborate union structures, participation, and dues are not called for. If this were all that is involved, one would think that mobilization would be relatively easy. In fact, however, the costs are high because of the vulnerability of the miners to the hostility of the coal mine operators. The miners take great risks in addition to losing their jobs for collective goods.

In the black lung case, the characteristics of the groups are probably more varied. No doubt, where communities are long standing and integrated, there is a dissemination of information and mutual help in pressing claims; moreover, as distinguished from the D.C. Hospital case, the health issue is chronic, not episodic, and participation in the benefit program is generally long term. These factors would help overcome the free-rider problem; solidarity and purposive incentives would provide some cohesion for local groups. On the other hand, many victims of black lung are also dispersed and lack information and resources; once on the program, they would have little or no incentive to work for the benefit of others. Miners in this situation would resemble other clients and patients of welfare and health programs.

The *distribution of the benefits and costs* does not favor successful action. Safety rights and safe working conditions are widely distributed. Welfare benefits are selective to the individual applicant, but widely distributed to the class as a whole. The costs are concentrated. The large operators would no doubt pass on safety and health costs, but many operators are small and marginal. In any event, the operators act as if costs were concentrated, especially in the safety example, and strenuously object to the sharing of any management control with miners or government inspectors. The role of the government varies. In

---

[30] Miners in these communities would most likely have the solidarity necessary for mobilization that Fireman and Gamson (1978) emphasize.

the black lung case, SSA acted as if the costs were concentrated. It opposed the program, and it has treated applications for benefits restrictively. In the safety case, the government is acting differently. The Department of the Interior, under the Carter administration, has been responsive to the program of the social-reform groups and the law reformers, which helps ease the problem of the distribution of the costs and benefits. For some reason, the Carter administration and its appointees in Interior think there are political benefits to them that are selective benefits.

As noted, the *bureaucratic contingency* is severe. Most cases require factual determinations and the interpretation and application of standards are often vague. These are discretionary decisions that are made at the field level and throughout the various administrative stages. In the black lung case, the groups hope to avoid the discretion by routinizing eligibility by establishing that a certain period of work time in a particular location qualifies for benefits, period. In the safety case, the social-reform groups and the law reformers hope to overcome this hurdle by redressing the balance of power in the bargaining situation through the organization of miners around safety representatives, increased knowledge of rights among the miners, increased advocacy resources, and a more effective and responsive federal bureaucracy. If, for example, the revitalization of the Department of Interior continues and it assumes a position something like the Justice Department's civil rights enforcement under Robert Kennedy, the miners would be in a much stronger position at the field level and throughout the administrative process. This proposed solution to the bureaucratic contingency does not seek a restructuring of the rules to reduce or eliminate discretion. Rather, it accepts the basic structure of decision making but seeks to overcome its negative impact by changing the relative position of the participants. For a short time, the National Welfare Rights Organization was able to accomplish this in its special benefits campaign. Whether the miners will be able to achieve sufficient power and sustain that power is still uncertain.

When cases have come before the courts, the courts have been sympathetic and liberal in their interpretations of the act, but, generally speaking, *judicial remedies* are not very helpful for the day-to-day field-level decisions. These are for the administrative agency.

The *characteristics of the law reformers* are unfavorable in the black lung case. Although lawyers are competent to handle disability cases, law reformers are simply not available to handle the massive numbers of cases involved. The situation is similar to other large welfare programs that require adversarial administrative hearings to

Table 5.1 *Social Welfare Cases, Summary of Variables*

Variables	NWRO	California Welfare	D.C. General	Wyatt v. Stickney	Sterilization	Black Lung	Coal Mine Safety
Groups							
Small size							+
Outside funding							
Selective benefits							
Large size	–	–	–	–	–	–	
No outside resources	–	–	–	–	–	–	–
Collective goods only	–	–	–	–	–	–	–
Distribution							
Benefits concentrated; costs distributed							
Benefits distributed; costs distributed							
Benefits concentrated; costs concentrated	–	–	–	–	–	–	+
Benefits distributed; costs concentrated							–
Bureaucratic							
One time		+				+	
Top solution		+				+	
Technically simple		+				+	
Discretion reduced		+				+	

Long-term	–	–	–	–	–	–
Field-level implementation	–	–	–	–	–	–
Technically complex				–		
Discretion required	–	–	–	–	–	–
Judicial						
Preventive injunction			+		+	
Court solution			+			
Order can be monitored			+			
Regulatory injunction		–		–		–
Remand to agency				–		
Order complex				–		
Law Reformers						
Affiliated	+					
Technical resources	+					
Political resources	+					+
Independent		–	–	–	–	–
No technical resources		–	–	–	–	–
No political resources		–	–	–	–	–

vindicate client rights. On the other hand, in the safety case, the characteristics of the law reformers are favorable even though they are independent of any organization and supported by foundations. The reason for the favorable characteristics are the unique skills of the lawyers themselves, especially their social and cultural ties to the region and its people and professional expertise in union organizing and the specialty of coal mine health and safety law.

Summary and Conclusions

The seven examples discussed in this chapter are summarized in Table 5.1. The California welfare litigation represents a clear-cut victory for the social-reform groups. If the black lung program is amended to provide a routinized solution, then that also will become a victory. Two others look like there might be some chance of success, *Wyatt* v. *Stickney* and coal mine safety. Each of these four examples has a change in a variable that makes the difference. In the California welfare and black lung cases, the crucial variable is a favorable bureaucratic contingency. The problem can be solved by the top, on a one-time basis, with no discretion or technical complexity involved. In *Wyatt* v. *Stickney,* the unusual behavior of the federal district court accounts for the difference. In the coal mine safety case, a combination of factors may make the difference. Those factors include the small size of some of the groups, the existence of immediate, tangible incentives, assistance from the federal government in easing the distribution of costs and benefits, and the favorable characteristics of the law reformers. In effect, the lawyers are affiliated with the social-reform groups, and they have technical and at least some political resources because of the receptivity of the Carter administration.

In the other examples, success does not seem likely. Virtually all the characteristics of the variables are unfavorable, but the one that has been emphasized is the critical importance of the bureaucratic contingency of human service administration.

In evaluating reform activity, I continue to focus on the achievement of specific, tangible goals such as increased welfare benefits, improved health or mental health care, accurate and informed decisions concerning sterilization, and coal mine health and safety. There are, however, less tangible methods of evaluating law-reform activity by social-reform groups, particularly consciousness-raising. The welfare rights campaigns played an important role in dramatizing the inequities and inconsistencies of the welfare system, and in placing welfare reform on the national agenda. Health and mental health law-reform litigation and cases involving mine safety and health have also served similar functions. Cases have created publicity and focused attention, and there has been some movement. It may be unrealistic to evaluate any one piece of litigation in terms of specific, tangible benefits; rather, evaluation of social change efforts should be looked at in terms of many cases, over a long period of time, eventually changing the climate of public opinion. This idea was raised in Chapter 1 on the discussion of the meaning of success and will be discussed more fully in Chapter 6.

6

Social Change
and Law Reform

The theoretical perspective set forth in Chapter 1 was intended to provide a framework for evaluating law-reform activity on behalf of social-reform groups. In subsequent chapters, 38 case studies were discussed in terms of that framework. While the studies have not been selected quantitatively, they are drawn from real-life situations and represent important examples of law-reform activity by social-reform groups in four principal areas—environment, consumer rights, civil rights, and social welfare. In this chapter, the implications of the case studies will be analyzed and law-reform activity by social-reform groups will be evaluated from three perspectives. The three perspectives are not discrete categories, but they emphasize different evaluative criteria.

The first perspective looks at direct gains and losses. To what extent have social-reform groups accomplished tangible benefits as a direct result of law-reform activity? In the short run, have the groups gained or lost something specific as a result of changes in the rules? This perspective evaluates social-reform groups' use of the courts in traditional terms: They sued because they wanted something. Did they get it?

Social-reform groups also use the legal system for nontraditional purposes, such as publicity, fund raising, leverage, and conscious-raising. Although courts have always been used for such purposes, they are considered nontraditional in the sense that they are "extralegal" because courts are not supposed to be used this way. The nontraditional or extralegal use of the legal system is more indirect than the first set of criteria for evaluation because the social-reform groups are using the legal system to help them in their nonlegal strategies and tactics rather than relying on court or agency rule changes to accomplish their goals. Under what circumstances are social-reform groups successful in achieving their goals with this nontraditional, indirect use of law reform?

The third perspective addresses the broader issues of power in the decision-making processes of American society. Chapter 1 noted that the fundamental premise of the law reformers was that by obtaining access to the decision-making processes on behalf of underrepresented groups, the pluralist system of government would be revitalized. Law-reform action by social-reform groups represents a challenge to the alliance between public agencies and vested interests. What do the theoretical framework and the case studies tell us about the likelihood of this endeavor?

Direct Results from Traditional Law-Reform Activity

In reviewing all of the case studies, it is clear that the most crucial variable is the bureaucratic contingency. Practically all of the social-reform groups have unfavorable characteristics. They are large, dispersed, and, whether they have purposive or material incentives, the goods they seek are collective and they face the free-rider problem. In practically all situations, benefits are dispersed and costs are concentrated on the adversaries. Access to the law reformers and availability of some other outside resources help the groups overcome the free-rider problem for the law-reform activity. But, if the judicial remedy will not solve the problem and the matter ultimately rests on administration, the group will not achieve direct, tangible results, especially if the administration needed is long-term, discretionary, at the field level, or complex.

In looking at cases where social-reform groups have failed or are likely to fail, the unfavorable bureaucratic contingency has several variations. In situations like the Trans-Alaskan Pipeline[1] and the D.C. General Hospital cases[2] social-reform groups are required to monitor

---

[1] See Chapter 2 for full elaboration on the Trans-Alaskan Pipeline case.

[2] See Chapter 5 for full elaboration on the D.C. Hospital case.

low-visibility decisions that are made on a day-to-day basis. Factual determinations of officials have to be uncovered and then challenged. How is this stream-crossing consistent with the environmental stipulations? Why hasn't the hospital fulfilled this month's quota for hiring registered nurses? And so on. Not only must the factual determinations be uncovered, examined, and challenged, but if the officials or developers refuse to negotiate, the social-reform group has to file an administrative proceeding or return to court. It is easy to see what a costly, time-consuming process this becomes. The defendants can easily wear down the social-reform groups and the law reformers.

Other situations not only involve long-term, field-level discretion but also the active participation of clients, and, typically, the clients are usually those least likely to know about their rights or how to assert them. Major examples of this were the sterilization[3] and Equal Credit Opportunity cases. Neither the social-reform groups, which are generally paper organizations, nor the law reformers have the capacity to monitor these decisions at the field level. All they can hope for is the establishment of proper procedures, which, as we know from other administrative systems dealing with dependent populations, is almost meaningless.[4] The problem of making the client population aware of its rights and acting on them applies to several other examples, including employment discrimination where the employer only has to use "good faith" efforts,[5] the availability of refunds in consumer cases,[6] most welfare rights,[7] and antidiscrimination laws in housing and public accommodations.[8]

A third type of agency discretion does not involve field-level discretion but is complex and long term, and this saps the law-reform strengths of social-reform groups. Most rate regulation poses this kind of problem.[9] Other examples are the FTC's ad-substantiation rules,[10] the FDA's drug laws,[11] the Federal Reserve Board's disclosure rules on bank loan rates,[12] and court rulings on power plant sites.[13] Cases on power plant sites and rate regulation are usually very costly and difficult in terms of mustering the expertise to challenge the industry.

[3] See Chapter 5 for a full description of this case.

[4] There is extensive literature on this point. See Handler (forthcoming) and Rubenstein (1976).

[5] See Chapter 4 on employment discrimination issues.

[6] See Chapter 3 for further information on consumer protection.

[7] See Chapter 5 for further information on welfare litigation.

[8] See Chapter 4 on housing discrimination.

[9] See Chapter 2 on rate regulation.

[10] See Chapter 3 on the FTC rules.

[11] See Chapter 3 on the FDA drug laws.

[12] See Chapter 3 on the Federal Reserve Board rulings.

[13] See Chapter 2 for rulings on power plant sites.

With the FTC, the FDA, and the Federal Reserve Board, effective implementation requires that the social-reform groups stay with the agencies
constantly to monitor decision making. The groups and the law
reformers that were involved in these cases simply lacked the capacity
or the will to engage in this long-term activity.

In the above cases, it is doubtful whether social-reform groups and
law reformers will achieve much in the way of tangible results for their
members. It may be, however, that other kinds of benefits are derived
from these cases, a matter which will be discussed in the next section.
But now the question is, under what circumstances can social-reform
groups achieve tangible benefits through law-reform activity?
Specifically, in what ways can they avoid the various types of unfavorable bureaucratic contingencies discussed above? There were a
number of case examples where success was attained.

The most favorable situation is where the bureaucratic contingency is not involved at all, that is, the rule change by itself will trigger
the redistribution of tangible benefits, or virtually no significant discretionary implementation is required. The most significant example
presented was the. California welfare litigation where, after a bitter
struggle, the law reformers were able to prevent a cutback in benefits.[14]
There were a number of important points about this example that
make it such a special case. The group was, in fact, made up of welfare
recipients in the state of California, the benefits were purely collective
and the state administration, under orders from Governor Reagan,
treated the costs as concentrated. The defendants not only fought the
case vigorously in court, but also used all of their considerable influence with the Nixon administration to sustain their position. For the
social-reform group side, this was pure law reform, the *only* effective
weapon was court litigation. They won. This victory occurred because
the judicial remedy, a prohibitory injunction, was completely effective
in this type of situation. The state finally conceded that it lacked the
authority to cut benefits. So, because they were not cut, the welfare
recipients received tangible benefits.

Other cases were discussed that presented a similar situation. The
Wisconsin court decision outlawing high interest charges by retailers as
a violation of the state usury law would have this effect; interest rates
would have to be automatically lowered; otherwise there would be stiff
criminal and civil penalties.[15] The court decision outlawing the
Virginia ban on prescription drug advertising would have this effect if
we assume competitive market conditions and before long, the large

[14] See Chapter 5 for more detail on the California case.

[15] See Chapter 3 on this aspect of consumer protection.

Washington, D.C., discount drug companies will cross the Potomac.[16] In the California milk price-fixing case, market forces did lower prices after the rule change.[17] Although the ban for host selling on children's television programs was not strictly a law-reform case, it does illustrate, as do the cases just mentioned, that the rule prohibiting the activity provides the tangible benefits that the group seeks.[18] In these cases there may be some monitoring, but violations are relatively easy to detect because, for the most part, they occur at the top or otherwise are readily visible and clear-cut.

In the environmental area, similar results can be achieved if the bulldozer is stopped, or if a major modification is agreed to, as in the case of *Calvert Cliffs* (a pipeline for a pier, and the dedication of some shore for a park)[19] and *Scenic Hudson* (substitution of cooling towers for open-cycle cooling).[20] In the housing area, the Yerba Buena case involving urban renewal in San Francisco eventually worked out this way, although that was not the original intent of the social-reform groups.[21] The injunction was designed initially to secure adequate relocation housing for the residents, a result that would have involved an unfavorable bureaucratic contingency. But, eventually, the whole project stalled and the injunction served to preserve what neighborhood was left. Other housing cases did not result in such tangible benefits because even though injunctions were granted, extensive administration was required, and this was not forthcoming.[22] The Yerba Buena residents won because, in their situation, stopping the bulldozer was enough for the tangible benefits that they wanted. Most other people who need low-cost housing are not so fortunate.

There are a number of examples, then, where the bureaucratic contingency can be avoided because a rule change practically accomplishes the result. This usually means a prohibitory injunction, which stops action that will be harmful for the social-reform group. In most of these cases, the law reformers are a sufficient resource to overcome the free-rider problem and see through the rule change. These are usually cases that fit the characteristics of the law reformers, that is, they involve court motions and appeals.

However, as effective as prohibitory injunctions are, they are also

[16] See Chapter 3 on the discount drug companies.

[17] See Chapter 3 on the California milk-pricing issue.

[18] See Chapter 3 for further detail on this case.

[19] See Chapter 2 for description of *Calvert Cliffs.*

[20] See Chapter 2 on the *Scenic Hudson* case.

[21] See Chapter 4 on the *Yerba Buena* case.

[22] See, *The Kennedy Park Homes* case, Chapter 4.

as rare. Ordinarily, government is not so outrageous or the law so clearly violated that a court will order a permanent (or even a temporary) injunction. An unusual combination of events occurred for the Trans-Alaskan Pipeline injunction to be issued. It was issued during the initial phases of NEPA and the environmental impact statement was clearly inadequate. For a considerable period of time the Department of Interior as well as the oil companies refused to take NEPA seriously, and the case was finally decided on a violation of the Mineral Leasing Act. Disregarding the technical violation of the Mineral Leasing Act, there is little doubt that if the initial impact statement bore any resemblance to the final impact statement, an injunction would never have been granted, and the pipeline would have been built years earlier. In subsequent NEPA cases, agencies got past the appellate courts by submitting bulky documents purporting to touch all of the bases because the courts did not want to get into the merits of the arguments and facts.[23] Injunctions to halt projects or other large-scale government programs are hard to get, and, with the retreat of the activist judicial period, will probably become even harder to get in the future. Social-reform groups and law reformers have to seek other ways of getting results.

One method of overcoming unfavorable group characteristics and the unfavorable distribution of benefits and costs is to form alliances. In the *Scenic Hudson* case, the Oak Ridge Laboratory staff of the Atomic Energy Commission entered the contest quite early, and throughout the entire controversy supplied the costly technical data necessary to support the environmentalists' position. Without this government assistance, it is difficult to see how the social-reform groups could have mobilized the resources to pursue this long, technically complex litigation. The alliance with the government overcame the free-rider problem. Government has also been involved on the side of social-reform groups when large numbers of field-level discretionary decisions are involved, such as in voting rights, school desegregation after the enactment of the 1964 Civil Rights Act, and employment discrimination.[24] In these three cases, the federal government assumed part of the litigation burden, but mainly supplied administrative remedies to help overcome the bureaucratic contingency. In voting rights, it was registrars and lawyers to protect blacks; in school desegregation, it was lawyers, but also HEW's power to promulgate guidelines and cut off funding; in employment discrimination, the EEOC assumed the burden of factual investigations and litigation.

[23] See Trubek (1977).

[24] See Chapter 4 on these three issues.

These cases also show the dangers of alliances. In most action by social-reform groups discussed, the government is the enemy, along with developers, manufacturers, and employers. With alliances, the government can switch back to this role and subtly undercut the social-reform groups' position. In school desegregation, the pace of desegregation was influenced by the attitudes of the Justice Department, which changed considerably with the Nixon administration. In voting rights, the Kennedy administration was uneven about the counties in which it would enforce the law, and where the Justice Department held back, the results were far less favorable to the social-reform groups. In employment discrimination, the EEOC, for a variety of reasons, would vacillate, and one of the major criticisms subsequently made against it is that it entered into sweetheart agreements with large discriminators. It has been argued that not only do these agreements let discriminators off lightly, but, more importantly, the social-reform groups and the law reformers are frozen out of negotiations.

As noted, the injunction, even if only a preliminary one, is often vital to law-reform activity, but the willingness of the court to grant such an extraordinary remedy depends on how serious the situation is. One of the best arguments that the social-reform groups have is to show that the responsible government agency is defaulting in its lawful obligations. If, however, the government is purporting to enforce the law and can make any showing that it is trying, then the court is not likely to grant an extraordinary remedy against a coequal branch of government. This is illustrated by the difference between the antidiscrimination lawsuit against the University of California, Berkeley and the *Adams v. Richardson* case.[25] In the Berkeley litigation, it will be recalled, HEW purported to be on the side of the plaintiffs and attempted to investigate allegations of sex discrimination at the university. HEW's performance was incompetent. There were long delays, essential information was not obtained, and the final report was tepid. Yet, the court refused to move actively in the case as long as HEW was going through the motions. Eventually, the delay and inability to obtain information sapped the strength of the law reformers and the suit died. In *Adams v. Richardson*, HEW took the unprecedented step of announcing that it was refusing to enforce sex discrimination laws in secondary and higher education. Here the government was clearly the enemy and defaulting in its lawful responsibilities. The court granted an injunction. In short, the role of the government can be crucial in the tactics and strategies of law-reform litigation. If the government does form an alliance with the social-reform group and vigorously fulfills that role, then the position of the social-reform group may be vastly im-

[25] See Chapter 4 for more detail on *Adams v. Richardson*.

proved. For one thing, the difficult problems of mobilizing resources for staying power can be lessened considerably. On the other hand, if the government vacillates in its support, or, in effect, covertly supports the other side, then the social-reform groups and the law reformers are at a great disadvantage, and they may be even more weakened than in cases where the government is clearly the enemy.

The danger of alliances with the government has increased under the Carter administration because noted leaders of social-reform groups and law reformers have moved into important government agencies, particularly in the consumer area. Heads of these agencies are realizing that they no longer have the freedom to be completely partisan. If they are members of independent regulatory commissions, such as the FTC, they have to strike bargains to form majority decisions, and maintain relations with key congressional committees, the White House staff, and certain segments of the industry. If they are heads of executive agencies, they may be under more pressure to be responsive to the political needs of the administration. Whatever the cause, it is safe to assume that these government officials are seeing the issues in a somewhat different light, and this different perspective will inevitably lead to collisions with their old friends in the social-reform groups. These conflicts arose quickly and sharply between Governor Jerry Brown's administration in California and the social-reform groups and law reformers. Brown professed to be an advocate of consumers and citizens and appointed some of the most prominent leaders of social-reform groups and law reformers to key government posts. Yet, it was not long before roles conflicted with values and, eventually, friendships. However, despite what social-reform leaders and law reformers might think of their former friends, Carter appointees present an image of being more consumer-oriented and environmentally aware than their predecessors, which makes their arguments and demonstrations of reasonable efforts to enforce the law more plausible. And this makes law-reform efforts more difficult in the courts and agencies.[26]

Alliances can also be formed with private groups. The case examples were the Center for Auto Safety,[27] the litigation involving the lock and dam construction on the Mississippi River,[28] and the Open Suburbs Movement.[29] The presence of private interests on the side of

[26] Apparently many of the 20 or so consumer, environmental, and public-interest advocates who joined the Carter administration are already experiencing role conflicts and frustrations, and some have already drawn the fire of Nader (*The New York Times*, 1977, p. 1).

[27] See Chapter 3.

[28] See Chapter 2.

[29] See Chapter 4.

the social-reform groups changes the characteristics of the groups to small groups with selective, material incentives instead of only collective goods. In addition, benefits are concentrated as well as costs. On the other hand, such alliances can also cause problems for social-reform groups and law reformers. Social-reform groups that rely on purposive incentives might find themselves compromised if they form alliances with certain groups. In the Mississippi Locks and Dam 26 case, some of the environmental organizations dropped out when the railroads joined.

The presence of vested interest groups can also damage the credibility of social-reform groups in court. At least, some of the social-reform groups in the OSM felt that they were less persuasive in court when they were joined by developers. Vested interest groups, if they are paying substantial amounts of the cost, will inevitably have a say in the conduct of the litigation, which may conflict with the needs of the social-reform groups and the special needs of law reformers. In the OSM, developers joined the lawsuit for the purpose of outlawing exclusionary zoning, but once that was accomplished, lost interest in pushing for the development of subsidized housing because they were more interested in building middle-class housing. As noted in Chapter 1, law reformers view litigation differently than private practitioners. Litigation has to serve their purposive, publicity, and fund-raising needs, which may conflict with the litigation needs of private developers. There also may be conflicts in goals. In addition to the OSM example, we have Ralph Nader and the Center for Auto Safety being criticized for remaining silent on the no-fault auto insurance controversy.[30] Although a separate organization, the Center for Auto Safety is, in fact, identified with Nader whose credibility is sufficient to withstand any suggestion of compromise. But other social-reform groups may not enjoy this luxury, and alliances with private interests will likely remain troublesome.

Another method of overcoming the bureaucratic contingency is to substitute a quantifiable measure for field-level discretion. The outstanding example was voting rights;[31] although the quantification came about through legislation rather than litigation, the case does serve to illustrate the point. Eligibility for registration was made dependent on attaining a certain level of formal schooling rather than passing various kinds of tests. Similar results will be accomplished if pending legislation for black lung benefits is enacted.[32] Courts have also im-

[30] See Chapter 3 on the no-fault insurance issue.
[31] See Chapter 4 on voting rights.
[32] See Chapter 5 on black lung legislation.

posed quantified measures, although not in the same draconian fashion as the voting rights legislation. In school desegregation, school board plans were assessed according to statistical results rather than good faith efforts or proof of evil intentions. Somewhat similar results may be achieved if courts impose goals and timetables to end employment discrimination. Here, the picture is still unclear, since failure to meet goals and timetables often only serves to switch the burden of proof, with the litigation still turning on factual determinations of the employer's good faith efforts. Although quantification may not solve the bureaucratic contingency, it may lessen its impact, especially in the bargaining between social-reform groups and their adversaries. Certainly, egregiously poor statistical results for employment tests or hiring practices put employers in a bad light and make their good faith arguments less credible.

As a general proposition, the problem of enforcing rights and monitoring discretion becomes easier to the extent to which substantive relationships can be simplified and measured in quantifiable terms. Thus, although there are many pros and cons about a simplified welfare system (i.e., a negative income tax), one of its virtues would be fairly simple measures of client rights, which would ease the task of social-reform groups and law reformers. On the other hand, quantifiable measures can distort relationships. Law reformers may be driven to insist on such measures because of an inability to cope with field-level discretion; however, the measure may be unwise, or at best, a very poor fall back position. It was noted that some of the social-reform groups in the sterilization controversy were driven to this position.[33] Because they felt that there was no way to establish a fair procedure for informed consent and monitor such a procedure, they pressed for a flat prohibition on the sterilization of minors and mental incompetents. It is also predictable that the D.C. General Hospital case, will develop into a battle over statistics. Staffing ratios, number and type of personnel in various units, and organizational charts will serve as proxies for the quality of medical care. This is not to say that adequate staffing is not important or that if more nurses, aids, doctors, and technicians are employed, the law reformers will not have accomplished anything. These figures only address part of the problem of what kind of medical care the poor are receiving at that hospital.

The school busing[34] and Alabama mental health litigation[35] represent still another method of coping with the bureaucratic contingency. Here again, we find an extraordinary situation where courts act in a

[33] See Chapter 5 on the Alabama sterilization case.

[34] See Chapter 4.

[35] See Chapter 5.

most unusual fashion—in effect, becoming administrative agencies and closely supervising implementation. Results are being accomplished for social-reform groups in these situations, but it is not a technique that law reformers can count on. The law reformers in the D.C. General Hospital case asked for a court-appointed master to supervise implementation, but the hospital director threatened to resign and the court backed off. In the Alabama litigation and some of the busing cases, the courts were easily persuaded that the responsible governmental authorities could not be trusted to implement court orders, but the facts in those cases were compelling. Defendants can probably avoid masters or other kinds of court-appointed officials if they make a colorable showing of compliance and say the right things about good intentions. Courts are normally very reluctant to assume extensive administrative roles.

The final method discussed for coping with the bureaucratic contingency involves participation of social-reform groups. In the credit card case, where the law reformers succeeded in having removed the ban on cash discounts, the law reformers wisely declined to get involved in the case until they were assured that Consumers Union had a viable plan for disseminating information about the rule change.[36] The coal mine health and safety case illustrates a more concerted effort at grass-roots involvement.[37] Here, the law reformers have no illusions about the problems of obtaining tangible benefits for the members. The unorganized miners need to be made aware of their rights and then be afforded effective protection for the exercise of those rights. Establishing safety rights and procedures in courts and administrative agencies is only the first step. The bureaucratic contingency can only be overcome if the individual miners have sufficient strength in the day-to-day, field-level discretionary decisions. Whether the law reformers and the groups will be able to succeed in this case is, of course, unknown. What is important is that they recognize the full dimensions of problems of field-level implementation and decide their strategy accordingly.

There are ways in which social-reform groups can overcome unfavorable conditions and succeed through law-reform activity. The subsidized lawyers can overcome the free-rider problem at least for purposes of litigation or similar kinds of advocacy. Alliances help mitigate the unfavorable effects of the usual distribution of benefits and costs of action by social-reform groups, and, on occasion provide staying power to monitor results. There are also instances where the most serious obstacle, the bureaucratic contingency, can be avoided by

[36] See Chapter 3 on the credit card issue.
[37] See Chapter 5 on this case.

injunctions or rule changes. But how important are these particular techniques for overcoming unfavorable conditions? Because the case selection was not random, quantifiable conclusions cannot be made, but the case studies show that there are large areas of concern where the bureaucratic contingency is formidable and judicial remedies are inadequate. Many of the most significant examples in all four substantive areas were of this nature; social change required long-term changes in field-level discretionary or technically complex decisions. For these kinds of problems, the social-reform groups, even with the subsidized law reformers, simply lacked the staying power.

The vulnerability of law-reform action by social-reform groups to the bureaucratic contingency raises doubts about one of the most talked about benefits of law-reform activity—gaining access for the underrepresented in American society. In discussing the characteristics of the law reformers, one of the principal justifications advanced for public interest law was the improvement of decision-making processes. The rationale behind public interest law, was to give the underrepresented in American society an opportunity to be heard in procedures where decisions are made affecting their interests. Public interest law would further the goals and ideals of due process. It would revitalize pluralism; the rigidities of institutionalized pluralism would be softened by the introduction of new groups seeking social change. Through public interest law, underrepresented groups would not only obtain access but they would be listened to (Rabin, 1976). For some of the proponents of public interest law, participation in itself is a tangible benefit to the social-reform group. It is a conferring of legitimacy and a fair opportunity to be heard, while not necessarily meaning that the social-reform group would ultimately prevail on the merits.[38] Although this is the official or establishment justification of public interest law, it is not the most important motivation. Law reformers and their clients are interested in procedural justice, but not as an abstract proposition; they believe that if they have access and are listened to, different decisions will be reached, that the "public interest" will be taken into account.

During the past decade, there has been a remarkable increase in formal access for social-reform groups. One of the earliest examples was the participation of the poor in the War On Poverty's Community Action Agencies.[39] This trend has continued for other kinds of under-

---

[38] Gamson (1975) uses official invitations to speak as a measure of success for efforts by social-reform groups.

[39] A great deal has been written on the participation of the poor in the CAP program. See Moynihan (1969) and Peterson and Greenstone (1977).

represented groups. Doctrines of standing have been expanded and groups have been allowed full participation rights in judicial and administrative proceedings. In recent years, there has been some cutback on standing, but, on the whole, the rules remain much more liberal than previously. There have also been changes in various environmental and consumer protection laws that enjoin the decision makers to take account of social-reform interests. The first, and probably still the foremost example, is the National Environmental Policy Act (NEPA), which requires government agencies to file environmental impact statements. Statutes such as NEPA allow social-reform groups to challenge alleged failures to follow statutory duties. Also, social-reform groups have gained membership status on decision-making bodies. Sometimes, statutes provide for membership representation; but even without statutory membership, environmentalists, consumers and other representatives are often invited to participate in policymaking or supervisory groups. In *Wyatt* v. *Stickney* (the Alabama mental health litigation), members of interested groups, including parents and a former patient, were included in the Human Rights Committees. Environmentalists have participated fully in the Law of the Sea Conferences. And these examples are not unique. Although one cannot be sure of how widespread the practice is, decision-making bodies have become far more sensitive to the participation rights of affected interests.

How important are formal participation rights? As noted, one can take the view that the right to participate is a tangible benefit in itself, and that if law-reform activity has succeeded in obtaining access for the social-reform groups, there has been a redistribution of benefits. But rights of access are hardly sufficient for the kinds of controversies and struggles that social-reform groups are engaged in; they are concerned with a cleaner and safer environment, product safety, civil rights, and social welfare benefits. The test of procedural justice is not to be found in its formal properties alone; ultimately it must prove fair to the participants in substantive results. Those who argue for the benefits of access sense this. They argue that social-reform groups not only must have access but they also must be listened to, their claims and arguments must be taken seriously. But that is the rub.

Prior to the recent advent of law-reform activity, the problem of the sham hearing was familiar. In zoning matters, for example, statutes require public hearings. But all of the important decisions were actually made by local officials and the developers involved before the hearings. The public hearings were, at best, a public relations exercise (Plager and Handler, 1966). The same complaints are made today even with full participation rights in administrative proceedings. In contests over power plant sitings, or most other important NEPA cases, the planning process has been under way for many years before social-reform groups become involved. By the time social-reform groups have the chance to exercise their right to participate, the key decisions have been made, the bureaucracy is in a fixed position, and the social-reform groups are placed in the difficult position of trying to get the agency to change its mind. The groups submit their position, which is formally received and formally listened to, but how does one make sure that the agency is seriously considering the arguments?

A few appellate courts have recognized that standing and access can be a sham, and they have tried to establish procedural rules guaranteeing meaningful participation. For example, the agency will have to show, in the record, that all serious arguments made by participants have been considered by the agency, and that the participants have had full access to important information and arguments that the agency is considering prior to its decision (Pedersen, 1975). But how useful are such requirements? Already, reviewing courts have shrunk back from close examinations of environmental impact statements. Clever and sophisticated agencies, such as the Corps of Engineers, quickly learn how to touch all of the procedural bases. It is far cheaper for an agency to prepare a bulky, statistics-laden, impact statement than to engage in extensive litigation. It is even in the interests of the agency to confess ignorance about certain issues but assure the court that it is doing the best it can. The early NEPA victories were based on administrative recalcitrance, stupidity, and ignorance. Agencies refused to file impact statements or filed only incredibly sloppy ones. But that day is over. Now the Corps of Engineers files hundreds of impact statements. Agencies have all types of environmental specialists—staffs of biologists, geologists, and populations experts.

There are several reasons why the most likely prediction is that the agencies will be able to undermine the access rights won by the law reformers. One is the role of the reviewing court. By law and tradition, the merits of these controversies are committed to administrative discretion. The courts know this and believe it, and for a long period of time, court–agency relationships were such that if the courts were satisfied that the agencies were exercising their discretion in a fair and reasonable manner, the reviewing court would not interfere in the merits. This relationship broke down during the activist period because courts lost confidence in the fairness of the administrative agencies. However, this was an aberrational period for the Judiciary (Stewart, 1975, 1977). Judges do not want to interfere in administrative processes and have already shown a willingness to listen to agency assurances, if they are of the right kind.

The second reason has to do with the weakness of the social-reform groups. The social-reform group participates in an administrative proceeding. The agency then reaches its decision, and files its impact statement, which follows the procedural steps outlined by the reviewing courts. The social-reform group then has to demonstrate before the appellate court that although the agency said it took the group's position seriously, in fact it did not. This is a very difficult burden to sustain unless the matter is clear-cut. The group, in an appellate brief and oral argument, has to persuade the court that no reasonable person could have reached the decision that the agency reached. If there is room for argument, if the issue is a question of judgment, then the court will not reverse because unless the court is persuaded that the agency acted unfairly, in a procedural sense, substantive judgments are for the agency. Finally, even if the social-reform group is able to persuade the reviewing court that the agency did not pay enough attention to the group's arguments, the reviewing court still will not decide on the merits. Rather, it will send the case back to the administrative agency and tell it to take another look, and the process starts all over again.

There have been situations where the court has been so outraged at administrative decisions that substantive results have been changed. There also have been cases where the courts have repeatedly returned the matter to the agency and after awhile, the agency has given up. But it must be emphasized that these are rare cases. Most important cases, especially those involving the environment, rate-making, or economic regulation, are highly complex, and there is a great deal of uncertainty about future impact. In these situations, the agencies continue to hold the cards. The social-reform groups simply lack the resources to engage in these kinds of protracted struggles, especially if the cases continue to be returned to the agencies.[40]

Social-reform groups and law reformers are well aware of the problem of making sure that their arguments are listened to seriously. One indication of awareness has to do with their attitude toward reform of administrative procedures. In administrative decision making, efforts are being made to relax the necessity of having trial-type hearings. Instead, more informal notice-and-comment, rule-making procedures are being used. A trial-type hearing, as the name implies, resembles a formal trial. Affected parties have full participation rights, which include

---

[40] Graphic illustrations of the enormous disparity in resources between developers and social-reform groups may be found in Committee on Governmental Affairs, United States Senate (1977).

the right to present oral testimony and, most importantly, the right to cross-examine opposing witnesses. There are other rights in trial-type hearings, but these two—oral testimony and cross-examination—are the most troublesome.[41] In traditional legal procedure, they are considered to be the most important rights constituting the basic right of the opportunity to be heard, but, and this is the problem, they produce great delay. It is difficult for courts and administrative hearing examiners to cut off repetitious oral testimony and cross-examination, which gives parties interested in delay considerable advantage. The problem becomes monumental in large, complex cases that are highly technical and involve multiple parties. Administrative cases have truly reached Bleakhouse proportions resulting in great delays, and ineffective planning and administration.

The misuse of trial-type proceedings has become one of the most serious problems in the breakdown of the administrative process, and an important reform is the substitution of notice-and-comment rule-making for trial-type hearings. Under notice-and-comment rule-making, interested parties are only entitled to submit written comments in agency proceedings. There can be some oral testimony and some cross-examination, but these rights are limited and only available for special cases; they are not granted as a right for the entire case. The reviewing courts, as noted, will then see if the agency has taken the written comments seriously in its decision.

Social-reform groups and law reformers scorn notice-and-comment rule-making procedures, and it is easy to see why (Stewart, 1975). They view the right to submit written comments as almost worthless and are fully aware of the futility of reviewing court supervision. They know that the trial-type procedures give them much more protection. Why is this so? If social-reform groups lack the resources for staying power, how can they muster the resources to fully participate in extensive trial-type proceedings? The answer is that, for the most part, they cannot. In the *Scenic Hudson* case, it will be recalled, the environmentalists had to rely on the Atomic Energy Commission for the factual issues in the case. In rate-making procedures, the groups cannot sustain the fights in the administrative agencies (United States Senate, 1977). The reason why the social-reform groups want to retain trial-type rights is that it gives them leverage. They can threaten to block, or at least seriously delay, development by use of delaying tactics in the administrative process. Notice-and-comment is a streamlined, efficient, quick administrative proceeding, which is precisely the kind of proceeding that one does not want if one expects to lose to the agency. Of

---

[41] See, for example, Boyer (1972), Hamilton (1972), and Robinson (1970) on trial-type hearings.

course, the use of delay as a tactic is a time-honored technique in American law. The drug companies, for example, have been very successful in thwarting FDA regulation through the use of trial-type hearings on drug safety and efficacy, and the social-reform groups and law reformers are only borrowing tactics from the other side. In the next section, the use of the legal process as leverage will be discussed more fully. It is used here to illustrate that social-reform groups and law reformers are not naive about the problems of access in administrative agencies. Notice-and-comment gives them access, but they know that those kinds of rights are no guarantee that their position will be listened to and respected.

This is not to argue that agencies will always ignore the positions of social-reform groups. It may be that some agencies have become more responsive to environmental, consumer, or poverty interests, and have adjusted their programs accordingly. This issue will also be discussed shortly. The point is that if the agencies are doing this, there are probably other reasons behind such actions than the formal participation rights of the social-reform groups. When one considers the major problems of group characteristics, mobilization of resources, and especially the bureaucratic contingency of countering administrative discretion, formal participation rights in administrative proceedings seem very tangential to the task of obtaining tangible benefits.

A similar analysis applies to other kinds of participation rights. As noted, the poor were given membership status on Community Action Agency boards during the War On Poverty. Aside from many problems of selection, a major problem was that community representatives lacked the capacity to make their participation relevant. They lacked the technical resources and knowledge to cope with the professionals, administrators, politicians, and other experts who were fellow members. Consequently, they became co-opted and passive, figureheads rather than important spokesmen for their communities. Although OEO may have encouraged black leadership and political participation generally, practically all studies agree that participation in CAP agencies failed to accomplish substantive changes for the poor (Peterson and Greenstone, 1977). Other kinds of social-reform representatives may not, of course, suffer from the same kinds of disabilities as the CAP community representatives, but the disparity is relative. An intelligent, middle-class, concerned housewife still lacks the technical resources to question environmental, consumer, or mental health experts. To prevail in a committee, advisory group, or board, one has to be either politically or socially powerful or *persuasive*; and in order to be persuasive, one has to back up one's position with reasoned arguments and facts, which are not easy to come by for social-reform groups.

There are remedies to the participation problem. In the Yerba Buena settlement, one of the important points was that the community organization (TOOR) was to have full participation rights in the selection and design of the relocation housing. This is an important issue for the elderly, since the designers and developers are usually not sufficiently sensitive to the social and living requirements of the elderly. The law reformers and group leaders not only built in rights to select the architect, but also provided for the continued funding of the organization so that it could hire its own staff and acquire its own technical resources. Similarly, the Human Rights Committees in the Alabama mental health litigation were given authority and funding to hire their own professional staff. And, in some of the large employment discrimination cases, lawyers are attempting to negotiate funds, independently administered, to finance social-reform groups for outreach, training, and monitoring.

The importance of building in permanent technical and professional resources to make participation effective is so obvious, yet it seems so often neglected by law reformers and social-reform groups. For example, there has been litigation establishing the rights of community residents to membership in health planning boards.[42] These are important boards that have extensive powers over the allocation of public funds for the construction of health facilities, yet provisions for providing *independent* resources for the community members have not really been addressed.[43] And without resources that are under their control, it is difficult to imagine how these people will have much of an impact on the boards.

Most important administrative decisions are on-going. For participation to be meaningful, formal rights of access are needed but, most crucially, the mobilization of technical and professional resources, and staying power are required. At any given time, a knowledgeable law reformer can present an effective argument in a Law of the Sea Conference, or in a rate proceeding, or in a health plan-

---

[42] *Texas Acorn* v. *Texas Area 5 Health Systems Agency, Inc.*, U.S. District Court, E. D. Texas, Civil Action No. 5–76–102–CA, March 1, 1977 (5th Cir., 1977).

[43] A Consumer Coalition for Health has been formed recently to take advantage of the new rights of participation. There seems to be considerable interest in a national organization, but how much support it will be able to provide to consumer members in actual decisions is decidedly unclear at this time. Without a great deal of resources, such an organization would probably be restricted to lobbying and publicity at the national level and the dissemination of educational and informational materials to local organizations. While this will be helpful, it will clearly not redress the inbalance of resources in specific fights over the allocation of health resources that will occur throughout the country.

ning board meeting. But how long will this influence last? After a time, these controversies lose their newsworthiness, and law reformers and reform leaders need publicity and find new dragons to slay to maintain purposive incentives. There is the never ending problem of mobilizing personnel and resources to maintain credibility. And in the meantime, the bureaucrats and developers remain. The costs and benefits are concentrated for them.

In sum, social-reform groups find it difficult to obtain tangible results directly from law-reform activity. It can be accomplished, and numerous cases have been discussed where such results have been obtained, but, on the whole, special circumstances are needed. The optimal situation is where the problem can be solved (i.e., the benefits distributed) on the basis of a rule change. This avoids the all-important bureaucratic contingency. While this can happen, most important controversies in the four areas considered (the environment, consumer protection, civil rights, and social welfare) are not amenable to this kind of solution. Instead, they require hard-fought, long-term battles. This result should not be surprising. The judicial process is best suited to resolve discrete disputes between two parties. The system comes under increasing strain in direct proportion to the complication of the dispute. Most of the cases brought by social-reform groups are complicated, involve administrative discretion, and are not readily susceptible to judicial resolution. Social-reform groups seek out the courts because they are weak and have lost in the political process, and there is only so much that courts can do by way of direct, tangible benefits.

But, of course, there is a great deal more to the story than seeking tangible benefits directly from law-reform activity. Social-reform groups and law reformers use the legal system for many other purposes, and the success or failure of a movement cannot be judged on the basis of single battles. We turn now to the more indirect uses of law-reform activity and look more in terms of campaigns rather than discrete court battles.

Indirect Results from Law-Reform Activity

Most law-reform activity serves multiple purposes. Even if the social-reform groups and the law reformers are counting on direct tangible benefits from litigation, the litigation usually will help publicize the organization and the law reformers, legitimize values and goals, stimulate purposive incentives, and hopefully result in obtaining outside resources from elites, foundations, other organizations (for example, labor unions), and public agencies. In this section, though, for purposes of evaluation and analysis, lines will be drawn between direct and indirect effects, and then between the various kinds of indirect effects. These divisions are artificial, but they will aid in the analysis. Indirect effects arise out of situations where social-reform groups and law reformers are using litigation as part of a broader campaign, which may or may not include additional litigation, but, more significantly, the campaign uses nonlitigation techniques such as lobbying, direct action, community organization, and public relations. A prime example is the use of litigation by the Center for Auto Safety which, as we have seen, has a variety of other strategies, and, clearly, its administrative and legislative lobbying and educational campaigns are considered far more important than its litigation. Nevertheless, the center has engaged in litigation for certain limited purposes. For example, from time to time it is necessary to demonstrate to the government and the automobile manufacturers that the center, if pressed, is ready, willing, and able to sue. It also uses litigation for publicity.

Three types of indirect effects will be distinguished: (a) Where litigation is used to clear the underbrush (subsidiary to nonlitigation strategies); (b) for leverage to enable the group to mobilize resources and increase the potency of its other tactics; and (c) for publicity, fund raising, mobilizing outside resources, consciousness-raising, and legitimacy. Each of these uses will be specified and evaluated in terms of the case studies and the theoretical framework. It will be recognized, however, that as we move farther away from focusing on direct, tangible results, the use of the theoretical framework and evaluations will become increasingly imprecise. While lack of precision is regrettable, the indirect effects have to be discussed. They are an important part of law reform by social-reform groups; indeed, they may be the most important part of all.

Clearing the Underbrush

There are some situations where social-reform groups rely on nonlitigation techniques but along the way have to change legal rules that impede mobilization. A common example is removing or lessening the threat of criminal prosecutions. When civil rights moved from the courts to direct action with the start of the sit-ins at the lunch counters, the black students were allegedly violating the criminal trespass laws, and law reformers were used, initially, to obtain their release.[44]

The most elaborate use of law reform to clear the underbrush was in the voting rights example.[45] Law reform, here, covered the full range

---

[44] See Chapter 4 for more detail on the sit-ins.

[45] See Chapter 4 on voting rights.

of legal services. Supreme Court and other appellate court litigation was needed to rule on major issues, such as invalidating the white primary and the poll tax provisions, and to clarify the important powers given to the Justice Department under the Voting Rights Act of 1965. Lower court services were also needed to protect black registrants from criminal and economic sanctions, and other kinds of harassment.

In desegregation and voting rights, the bureaucratic contingencies were severe and, in both situations, the social-reform groups were not relying on law-reform activity to overcome these hurdles. In this particular phase of the desegregation campaign, direct action was considered far more important.[46] In voting, principal reliance was placed on an aggressive Justice Department administration and local community organization. How, then, does one evaluate the result of law-reform activity in these situations? For the most part, the cases were successful at the law-reform level: Rules were changed. Also, where applied, they were successful in obtaining the release of blacks who were arrested; after this point, direct, tangible effects became more difficult to evaluate. In areas where legal and other kinds of support were available, direct and indirect benefits were realized; the threat of criminal sanctions was removed. However, where such resources were not available, no direct or indirect benefits from this law-reform activity resulted. An illustration is the lack of civil rights enforcement or progress in the town of Shaw.[47]

Evaluation of law-reform activity that clears the underbrush depends, then, on how important the reduction of the threat of criminal sanctions is to the mobilization efforts of the social-reform group and, if it is important, whether local legal resources are available to help members of social-reform groups if local officials continue to enforce a clearly illegal law or try other forms of legal harassment. In most mobilization efforts, reducing the threat of criminal sanction probably is important and necessary.[48] On the other hand, there are many situations where social-reform activists prefer jail to demonstrate the injustice of the system that they are fighting, or where passions are so inflamed and purposive incentives so strong that the formal legality of the activity is irrelevant.

In sum, the effectiveness of clearing the underbrush depends on how much of the bureaucratic contingency still has to be overcome by additional law-reform activity. Social-reform groups and law reformers

---

[46] In fact, after a short time, the arrested students refused legal services and chose to remain in jail to make more visible and dramatic their campaign.

[47] See Chapter 4 on the *Shaw* case.

[48] Wilson (1977) thinks that the threat of criminal sanctions is an important inhibiter on mobilization.

use other strategies to overcome field-level discretionary decisions, but additional law-reform activity may still be needed if local law enforcement officials continue to disobey the law or use other means of harassment. In that situation, more direct benefits from law-reform activity are needed. It ceases to play a subsidiary role and its effectiveness in accomplishing group goals becomes more doubtful.

Leverage

There are a number of case examples where law-reform litigation was used as leverage. The most dramatic situations are where the social-reform group is able to stop action, and by doing so enormously increases its bargaining power. This occurred in the Yerba Buena urban renewal case.[49] Although the social-reform group's ultimate hope was to be left in peace with no development at all, the lawsuit was not filed for this purpose, which would have been seeking direct tangible results from the litigation. Rather, it was filed to force the urban renewal authority to take seriously the housing relocation laws and provide decent, safe, comparable housing for the displaced residents. The social-reform group was not asking the court to draw up a relocation plan and implement its order; it wanted the agency to do this, with court approval. But without the injunction, the social-reform group would have been powerless to overcome the bureaucratic contingency. The distinguishing feature of the leverage situation is that the social-reform group is not necessarily interested in obtaining its benefits directly from the court order; rather, it uses the court order to increase its bargaining power in its nonlitigation strategies.

The other example of this use of leverage was in the Wisconsin usury litigation.[50] The social-reform group was willing to bargain away any possible tangible benefits from the lawsuit, which probably would not have been realized, in return for a strong consumer protection statute. The consumer groups had powerful allies, the state attorney general (an elected official courting consumers) and the governor, among others, and therefore it is difficult to outline direct causal relationships that produce a particular result. Most often consumer groups cannot accomplish significant results without help, and this is true in the Wisconsin usury case. But most observers agree on the leverage aspect of the Wisconsin lawsuit. And, without the leverage of that court decision the consumer bill would not have been enacted, regardless of the support of the governor, the attorney general, and other officials.

In large, complex matters where direct results are not at issue, it is

[49] See Chapter 4 on the *Yerba Buena* case.
[50] See Chapter 3 on Wisconsin usury litigation.

easy to note the law-reform activity, have some feeling that it is important in the politics of the case, but yet be unable to be precise as to the
exact role it has. In the Kaiparowits power plant controversy where,
after many years of planning, the huge project was abandoned, one of
the reasons given was pending litigation, and the threat of future litigation.[51] But it is doubtful whether litigation could have stopped a project
of this size (no other power plant has ever been stopped). The litigation
was one of a number of reasons, including opposition from the state of
California, rising costs, a changing financial situation, and a decline in
the rate of demand for electricity. At this point, it cannot be said which
reason or reasons were decisive. The environmental groups and law
reformers waged a long and bitter struggle against the project. No one
can claim that their roles were crucial, but they were probably not in-
significant either.

It is not always necessary to obtain an injunction to gain leverage
because the effects of injunctions can be obtained in other ways. For
example, in Wilmington, Delaware an urban hospital announced plans
to relocate in the suburbs. The plans were challenged by social-reform
groups on the ground that the hospital would no longer be able to serve
the poor, which, they alleged, was in violation of the federal funding
laws.[52] It is quite clear that an ordinary lawsuit seeking either to block
the removal of the hospital or to provide adequate services in the poor
neighborhoods would fail. In this case, the effect of filing the lawsuit
was to completely stop the program financing the construction through
the sale of bonds. There was no court order, no injunction, but as long
as the bonds could not be marketed the social-reform group and the
law reformers happily found themselves in exactly the same position as
the plaintiffs in the Yerba Buena litigation. The project was halted and
the bargaining position of the groups had been increased a thousand-
fold. Now they are negotiating with the hospital, HEW, and others as to
what kind of facilities and arrangements will be made to provide service for the poor. Other law-reform attempts to block the relocation of
hospitals to wealthier neighborhoods have failed. This one looks promising for the social-reform groups because they were able to gain what
was effectively an injunction.

In the Allegheny Airlines bumping case, a different kind of
leverage was gained even though the case was ulimately lost.[53] In that
case, Ralph Nader was bumped, but instead of merely claiming the
tariff remedy he sued and won punitive damages in the trial court. The

[51] See Chapter 2 for more detail on the case.

[52] *NAACP et al.* v. *Wilmington Medical Center et al.,* Civil Action No. 76–298 (D. Del.). Interviews
with plaintiffs' lawyers, the Center for Law and Social Policy, Washington, D.C., 1977.

[53] See Chapter 3 on Nader and Allegheny Airlines.

damage award was later reversed on appeal. Nader was not interested in the damages or in having the court promulgate new bumping rules, which he knew a court would not do. Instead, he was using the litigation as a way of forcing the Civil Aeronautics Board to take action where previously it had rebuffed Nader's demands. And, shortly thereafter, the CAB announced that it was reconsidering the bumping rules.

In cases such as Wisconsin usury, the Wilmington Hospital and Allegheny Airlines, the social-reform groups still have to face the bureaucratic contingency if they hope to obtain tangible rewards for the members. The distinction made is that they are not using the law-reform activity, specifically, the litigation, to overcome the bureaucratic contingency. They intend to use nonlitigation strategies, and the law-reform activity is used only to increase their power so that they are in a better position to apply nonlitigation strategies.

Publicity, Legitimacy, Consciousness-Raising

Most law-reform activity by social-reform groups is newsworthy and, in most cases, the groups and lawyers are seeking publicity. In some cases, publicity is used to obtain direct benefits from the litigation. One public interest law firm, which is particularly adroit in using publicity, brought an antiemployment discrimination suit against Pacific Telephone and Telegraph Company seeking 10,000 additional jobs for Spanish-Americans. However, instead of filing a conventional complaint with the state Fair Employment Commission (FEPC) or the EEOC, the law reformers challenged license renewals before the FCC and filed for a rate reduction before the state public utilities commission.[54] These were unusual actions, which were newsworthy and, simultaneously, the firm conducted a massive public campaign against the company, which quickly entered into an affirmative action agreement specifying goals and timetables. This firm has been successful with similar publicity techniques against other discriminators that feel themselves particularly vulnerable to effective public relations campaigns, such as banks and savings and loan associations (Handler, Edgar, and Settle, 1978). The tactic that distinguishes these cases is that the law reformers do not expect to achieve results through a court or administrative order; such proceedings will take too long or become too costly for the firm. Rather, they use legal proceedings to generate harmful publicity that will force the discriminator into a settlement. If successful, this technique has a number of advantages. The parties themselves are in control of the settlement, which is important if the

[54] This case is discussed in Handler, Edgar, and Settle (1978).

law reformers think they have more power than a weak and vacillating government agency. The other principal advantage is that this kind of publicity is relatively cheap for social-reform groups and law reformers, and costs are always an important consideration.

The use of courts for publicity is, of course, a time-honored technique. Probably the oldest and most dramatic example is the political trial where defendants will forego technical defenses or choose to remain in jail for propaganda reasons. There are many forms of political trials; here, we mean cases where the defendant deliberately eschews technical, legal defenses, using the trial as a forum for publicizing his cause. Lenin is quoted as saying, "The supreme rule of a political defense is propagation of the doctrine rather than the fate of the individual defendants."[55] An example in the recent past involves the Black Panther Party, for a time a militant and activist social-reform group. During the early days of the party, when its leader, Huey Newton, was trying to establish the rights of blacks to carry arms for self defense against the police, he was arrested and tried for the murder of a police officer. This was Newton's first trial as the party leader, and he specifically told his lawyer, Charles Garry, "If there is a conflict between a move that will further the cause politically and one that will serve Huey Newton personally, pursue the political motive. Let no tinge of racism pass unchallenged for fear the challenge will offend a juror; let nothing discriminatory about the system go unexposed even should the exposure make defense more difficult."[56] The Panthers immediately launched a Free Huey campaign, which attracted support from white radicals. Newton used the trial to explain his background, the reasons for forming the party, and what the party stood for.

Other civil rights leaders have chosen to remain in jail for various periods of time to dramatize their causes. It was noted earlier that when the direct action, sit-in campaigns first started, the students sought legal services and were released from jail but quickly changed strategy, adopting the "jail without bail" tactic to dramatize the repression, stimulate northern white liberal support and, at the same time, lessen the problems of soaring legal and bail costs. Under certain conditions, indirect benefits can be obtained even though the litigation is technically unsuccessful. The publicity of the prosecution, a forum in which to defend the cause, and the martyrdom of political prisoners and young, black, civil rights students and famous activists served the publicity needs of the groups.

Most environmentalists, consumer advocates, and other social-

[55] Quoted in Kirchheimer (1961, p. 245).
[56] Quoted in Marine (1969, p. 43).

reform leaders are not willing to go to jail to dramatize their cause, but law-reform activity is still used for similar, albeit less dramatic, public relations purposes. It was noted that the law reformers are quite explicit about not only the value but the necessity of publicity. They, along with social-reform groups, are interested in building a program, obtaining visibility, and justifying their existence to their financial backers. As one of the law reformers wryly put the matter, "A case without publicity is our *pro bono* contribution," meaning, of course, that such a case has no tangible benefit to law-reform lawyers.

Law-reform publicity performs a number of crucial functions for the social-reform groups. Although these functions merge and reinforce each other, for analytic purposes they will be described separately. Public relations used for fund-raising purposes is addressed to existing or potential contributors.[57] One of the most successful examples was the Environmental Defense Fund (EDF) litigation to stop the use of DDT. EDF was interested in stopping DDT and it eventually succeeded after an extremely long, costly, and hard-fought struggle, thus achieving direct tangible benefits for the members (and society). But the DDT litigation was always conceived in broader terms. From the very start, EDF used the litigation to dramatize the dangers of environmental degradation and to launch a massive, and successful, fund-raising drive. The use of law-reform activity has become a major device for the funded social movement organizations that McCarthy and Zald described. Through the drama and newsworthiness of the litigation, the groups and the law reformers publicize their cause and demonstrate their worth, and thereby hope to stimulate conscience beneficiaries (foundations, unions, and liberals) to support their cause. Other groups, of course, use different techniques. Martin Luther King, Jr. used nonviolent direct action. Caesar Chavez and the United Farm Workers were able to use the boycott and other kinds of public relations techniques. And Ralph Nader has been able to use a variety of nonlitigation techniques with considerable publicity. But these were especially charismatic leaders. The heads of most environmental, consumer, welfare, and health groups and the law reformers, are only known in small circles. The lawsuits, especially if they are large ones seeking huge changes, with dramatic allegations in the complaint, serve similar purposes. On the whole, with the exception of Ralph Nader, a 20-page complaint and a temporary injunction are worth more than a 300-page report in the media.[58]

Law-reform activity is used to communicate to elites and other

[57] On the importance of addressing elites, see Dolbeare (1969, pp. 244–245).

[58] See Sive (1977).

sources of outside resources, but what exactly is communicated? What are the specific symbols communicated by law-reform activity? Students of American politics have agreed that legal pronouncements, and especially those emanating from the highest courts, have important symbolic content in American political ideology (Scheingold, 1974, pp. xi, 13-19; Edelman, 1964, pp. 37-38; Turk, 1976). It is an American characteristic to cast political conflicts in legal terms, and especially the basic constitutional values of fundamental fairness (due process) and equality (equal protection of the laws), and to identify constitutional values with social justice. Americans have a penchant to impute rules to social relationships; they always feel it necessary to invoke a rule; "moral conduct is equated with rule-following, and moral relationships consist of duties and rights determined by rules." There seems to be a difference between making a demand and claiming a right founded on a rule. A claim of right is dignified; it is based on a principle that transcends the interests of the claimant and applies to all similarly situated citizens; it fixes responsibilities on others to respond to the claim, but at the same time it commits the claimant to work within the system. Claims of legal rights envision a process of peaceful, orderly adjustment that can be confidently left in the hands of professionals. They appeal to the use of reason, of change within a framework of continuity. For all of these reasons (and probably others as well), "law furnishes American politics with its most important symbols of legitimacy (Scheingold, 1974, p. 48)."

The claims of social-reform groups and law reformers fit within this long tradition in American political life. These claims fall into three categories, all of which have their roots in fundamental constitutional values. One is the opportunity to be heard. Social-reform groups, as underrepresented interests, are seeking procedural due process. A second is equality before the law—to be given a fair chance at the good life that is supposed to be due to every American regardless of race, creed, or national origin. A third is enforcement of the law, a right that every citizen should be able to demand of a government founded on the rule of law. When appellate courts, legislatures, or administrative agencies, but especially the Supreme Court, agree that the demands of a social-reform group are within one of these basic, fundamental con-

---

[E]nvironmental decision-making is frequently *political* in nature . . . litigation . . . holds great drama for the public; points made in speeches about important controversies may attract little media notice, but achieve page-one status if set down in the language of a court-filed complaint. Controversy attracts journalists, and media attention attracts lawyers and litigants [pp. 640–641].

stitutional principles, then the goals and values of the group have received the important symbols of legitimacy.

The legitimation of values is supposed to affect attitudes toward the claims of the social-reform groups. When the claim is validated, elites will become more sympathetic to the claims of the group and contribute money and other kinds of political and social resources.[59] But does this happen? Theories of legitimacy tell us little about the circumstances under which attitudes are changed, how much they are changed, and with what consequences.[60] We know, for example, that attitudes toward law and legal institutions are not uniform throughout society but vary in terms of socioeconomic characteristics. We also know that throughout history, responsible leaders as well as large segments of society have not changed their views as a result of Supreme Court decisions. The *Dred Scott* decision, for example, probably did not change many attitudes.[61] Legitimacy is said to be a powerful force, but it may be that, in fact, people are selective in the kinds of laws that they will approve, and that legitimacy merely bolsters existing attitudes about right and wrong (Friedman, 1975).

The view that legitimacy is selective, in that it reinforces rather than changes attitudes, and may, on the whole, be diffuse and weak, fits the McCarthy–Zald and Wilson views of the nature of the commitments of elites to social-reform groups. Incentives are purposive (even when legitimated); grievances are felt only vicariously. These scholars view such support as unstable, fickle, and easily lured away by other social causes. The fact that the demands are validated in terms of legal entitlements would reassure the elites of the moral worth of the group and their support; it would probably encourage their support, which scholars think is essential if the claims of social-reform groups are to succeed. The effect of legitimacy on elites is probably true, and certainly law reformers think so, but it is questionable how much additional, concrete, long-term support legitimacy produces. There is nothing in the empirical literature to suggest that legitimacy is very powerful.

Legitimacy also speaks to the membership or society at large. It performs a consciousness-raising function. The principal example used is school desegregation. Prior to 1954, segregation was the explicit policy in the South and the implicit policy in the North but in the two decades since, the articulated goals of our public policy with regard to

---

[59] See Rodgers (1973, p. 644) citing Dolbeare and Hammond (1971).

[60] In addition to Scheingold (1974), see discussion of legitimacy in Friedman (1975, pp. 113–125).

[61] See Bickel (1962, pp. 29–33, 65–72) for a discussion of the legitimacy role of the Supreme Court and Lincoln's treatment of the *Dred Scott* decision.

segregation have completely changed, in both the North and the South. These goals may not have been reached, but certainly the entire climate of public opinion and public policy is markedly different, and it was law-reform litigation that led the way to this change.[62]

There are a number of strands to the consciousness-raising argument. The legitimation of demands can overcome the acquiescence of oppressed groups. As Murray Edelman (1971) observes, "Perception of deprivation . . . like all perceptions, is a function of social cues regarding what is to be expected and what exists; it does not correlate directly or simply with objective conditions or with any particular measure of them [p. 107]." And court orders are "powerful shapers of perceptions [p. 111]." The judicial decision not only recognizes the demands but converts them into legal entitlements, it raises them in status, they are expected to be granted, they are a claim of right, in short, they are legitimated. Social-reform groups no longer have to accept the status quo; they now have entitlements authoritatively validated. They have a right to environmental protection, or safe products, or better medical care.

Law reform may raise consciousness, but what does it mean? Does consciousness-raising speak at all to the problems that social-reform groups have in overcoming unfavorable characteristics, altering an unfavorable distribution of benefits and costs, or overcoming the bureaucratic contingency? These are the stubborn conditions of successful action by social-reform groups. Legitimating grievances can make members feel better (or more aggrieved), and can perhaps strengthen purposive incentives somewhat, but it is doubtful that legal symbols are that powerful for the long term. After all, in the great civil rights struggles, the Supreme Court early, clearly, and repeatedly legitimated the demands of blacks for equal protection of the laws. The Court spoke to elites and no doubt helped mobilize their support, which was essential. While the Court no doubt raised the hopes and desires of the ordinary southern black, there was still extraordinary difficulty in mobilizing social-reform groups at the grass roots. Legal symbols may serve to raise grievances, diminish acquiescence, and build hopes, but they are not sufficiently strong enough to overcome the barriers to mobilization. For the most part, legal symbols of substantive and procedural fairness speak to the most powerless in American society, the victims of racial, social, and economic discrimination; yet, they are the most difficult to mobilize. Legal symbols are most effective

---

[62] Many commentators make this point. See, for example, Scheingold (1974, pp. 100–102), and Rodgers and Bullock (1972, chap. 4). On the other hand, how much blacks have actually gained will always be a controversial question. For an empirical study, see Farley (1977).

as purposive incentives; yet, purposive incentives are least effective among the poor, weak, and disenfranchised.

Consciousness-raising, however, may not only be looked at in the short run; it also has to be considered over a longer period of time. James Q. Wilson, as well as others, argue that social change only really comes about by dramatic events, political entrepreneurs, or the gradual change of public opinion. It is to the latter cause of social change that consciousness-raising speaks. Elites, the media, and other opinion formers are affected by the pronouncements of basic constitutional rights and, gradually, these new attitudes and perceptions about social relationships filter through the society and opinions change. This seems to have been the case with school desegregation, although clearly other sources of opinion and legitimacy (i.e., legislation) played influential roles. It was also noted in Chapter 2 that although social-reform groups and law reformers through law-reform activity have not been able to stop a single nuclear power plant, recently an influential blue ribbon-report adopted such a position, and, more recently still, President Carter halted the construction of a fast breeder reactor on environmental safety grounds. It was argued that in some way the publicity generated by the litigation, as well as other activities of the social-reform groups, gradually began to make itself felt at least among certain important segments of society. This is difficult to prove, but most knowledgeable insiders doubt whether that report on nuclear power would have reached the same conclusion 3 years ago.

The legitimacy claim for law-reform activity by social-reform groups for the long term has a plausible ring, but there are a number of serious theoretical and methodological problems with this theory of social change. The theory is too broad and does not discriminate among cases. In most of the examples discussed in this monograph, claims were vindicated in court, or in administrative rules, or by statute, and thus legitimacy was attached. Yet, in a great many cases, the law-reform activity was unsuccessful, certainly in the short run, and probably in the long run (although there is less confidence about the latter). But there is no way to tell when legitimacy was important. Legitimacy stimulates purposive incentives on the part of elites and other sources of outside resources, but we know that this support is unstable and variable; when does the legitimation of values make a difference? Conceptual and methodological problems become even more difficult the farther away in time one moves; symbols become more abstract and diffuse and chains of causality more complex. We somehow feel that the Supreme Court played an important role in changing the articulated values concerning racial discrimination, but there is no theory explaining what that role was and how it affected attitudes and expressions of public policy. President Carter has ordered increased safety requirements for oil tankers, thus adopting most of the position that social-reform groups had been unsuccessfully urging on the Coast Guard.[63] Was the President's change in position due to the steady publicity of the social-reform groups, the recent tanker spills (especially the one off Nantucket Island), or both, or other causes as well?

The more general and diffuse the symbols become and the more reliance there seems to be placed on general consciousness-raising, the more it would seem that social-reform groups would be prey to symbolic reassurance rather than the actual redistribution of benefits. Edelman has pointed out that when matters are complex and technical, and social-reform groups lack the organizational capacity to pursue their interests in the details of administration, they tend to seek out and cling to the symbols of reassurance that all is well, that the complex technical matter is safely left in the hands of experts, professionals and government. Situations where consciousness-raising is brought about through legal symbols are particularly apt examples of Edelman's thesis. He uses major regulatory programs of prior decades—antitrust, the Federal Trade Commission, as examples. Today, there has been a general consciousness-raising concerning environmental quality, and the Corps of Engineers, after a shaky start, is piously assuring the public of its new found faith and issuing scores of impact statements. Commercials from lumber and energy companies lay great stress on conservation and public service. Regulatory agencies are opening their doors to give interested persons and groups an opportunity to be heard. We are also being told that we have substantially achieved the goals of equality and that the normal workings of the American legal system can be counted on to iron out the last remaining trouble spots (Glazer, 1975). These are all symbols of reassurance. The claims and entitlements of the social-reform groups have been validated by the courts; their morality has been accepted by the influential opinion makers and others who control the sources of information. The articulated goals of public policy have changed, but how much behavior has changed in fact?

The theoretical and methodological paradoxes of law-reform activity by social reform groups become apparent. In some respects, the indirect effects of such activity are the most interesting. Law-reform litigation is used for leverage, for strategic moves in larger campaigns,

[63] The maritime pollution case is discussed in Chapter 2.

for publicity, fund raising, and other kinds of mobilization, for legitimacy, and for consciousness-raising. The indirect uses are imaginative, for the most part nontraditional, if not heretical from the perspective of the legal profession, and seem to speak more directly to the mainsprings of social change. At the same time, it is more difficult to pin down, either theoretically or empirically, what precisely the indirect effects are. Insiders claim they are happening—for example, that developers (public and private) are less likely now to propose projects that are truly damaging to the environment. This may be true, or it may be wishful thinking. There seems to be a consensus, at least among leaders of social-reform groups, law reformers, and their supporters, that times have changed. Maybe they have, or maybe we are entering into another period of symbolic reassurance.

Pluralism or Corporatism?

Throughout the monograph, one of the most important claims for law reform activity by social-reform groups has been discussed—that of gaining access for underrepresented groups to important decision-making procedures. There are three strands to this claim. At one level, the law reformers address the organized legal profession and foundations, and the claim is cast in conventional, fairly narrow, legalistic due process terms: Interested people and groups should have an opportunity to be heard. This level of the claim represents an addition to accepted legal doctrine; as a technical matter, it amounts to expanding the doctrine of standing. At the second level, it was noted that the law reformers were not primarily interested in reforming the law of procedure. Rather, they were interested in the substantive values of their clients, and it was argued (although less overtly) that if underrepresented groups gained access and were listened to, then substantive decisions would change and there would be a redistribution of benefits. The third level of the claim addresses the broader societal goals of changing the distribution of power in important public and private decision-making processes. The structure of decision making in America would be democraticized, the voices of the underrepresented would now be heard where decisions are being made, and the alliance between government and vested interests would be checked. In terms of basic American political theory, institutional pluralism, as noted by Theodore Lowi and others, would be countered by a revival of pluralism. There would be "New Voices for New Constituencies."[64]

[64] The title of the Ford Foundation pamphlet setting forth its program for supporting public interest law.

Quite naturally, there is debate as to what pluralism means and how power is to be measured. It is claimed, for example, that whether pluralism exists can be analyzed in terms of who, in fact, exercises power in actual decisions. Others claim that this is too constricted a view and that one also has to look at who controls the agenda; the elite may prevent issues from arising. A third view claims that even the second view does not go far enough; structures and institutions in society may be so dominant that grievances are not even felt by the oppressed or underrepresented.[65] Social-reform groups' law-reform activity is supposed to revitalize pluralism whichever view is taken as to how power is exercised in American society. The direct effects of law reform activity gain access to the decision-making procedure, and the indirect effects raise consciousness, diminish quiescence, cue expectations, and change the national agenda. What do the case studies and theoretical framework tell us about this most ambitious claim? There are many definitions of pluralism; for purposes of analysis, I will use the definition and analysis of Phillippe Schmitter (1974) in his article, *Still the Century of Corporatism.* Schmitter contrasts pluralism with its principal alternative "corporatism." Pluralism and corporatism are not distinct systems of government in real life; rather, in their ideal types, they represent end points on a continuum, and there are many forms of pluralism as well as corporatism in between. Moreover, corporatism is not peculiarly the province of regimes considered fascist. Societal corporatism (as Schmitter uses the term) appears in many western liberal countries such as Sweden, Switzerland, France, Canada, and Great Britain. It is very close to, if not exactly what, Lowi and other scholars call institutionalized pluralism in the United States.

For purposes of analysis, I start with Schmitter's ideal types.

> Corporatism can be defined as a system of interest representation in which the constituent units are organized into a limited number of singular, compulsory, non-competitive, hierarchically ordered and functionally differentiated categories, recognized or licensed (if not created) by the state and granted a deliberate representational monopoly within their respective categories in exchange for observing certain controls on their selection of leaders and articulation of demands and supports [p. 93-94].

At first glance, it may seem that this definition is far-fetched as applied to the United States; in fact, however, much of what Lowi (1969) describes as the developing reciprocal relationships between vested interest groups, such as agriculture, and government (to name only one prominent example), fit Schmitter's definition of societal corporatism. In the latter half of the nineteenth century, the Grange movement, a

---

[65] The three views of power in pluralism are analyzed in Lukes (1974), Baratz (1977), and Dolbeare (1969, pp. 258–263).

militant organization, reflected the discontent of farmers, and, in the course of time, was instrumental in obtaining important regulatory regulation plus many government services that aided marketing operations. The Grange was superseded by an even more militant organization, the Farmers Alliance, which turned the agrarian movement into a political movement. But by the turn of the century, after the movement was largely absorbed into the Democratic Party, agricultural organization moved into its "third" and present stage. Aside from the American Farm Bureau Federation, the only important national organization, agriculture organized around commodities, became concerned strictly with business problems, and established close relations with government. With the passage of time, 10 or so self-governing systems of policymaking for particular commodities emerged, built upon a close relationship between the agricultural interest group, a bureau in the federal Department of Agriculture, and a congressional committee. Each system was duplicated at the local level with a policymaking committee composed of local farmers primarily interested in the particular commodity of their area. The government uses these organizations to administer the various farm programs, thereby strengthening the organization and its internal structure. Through the distribution of government benefits, the organization is able to meet competition and the leadership is able to maintain its position in the face of internal challenge. As a natural result, the alliance has become extremely conservative and protective of its special interest, repeatedly defeating all efforts at reform. According to Lowi (1969), agriculture learned that the best way to maintain the established patterns of the organization was to use government. Interest groups have converted "governments into additional means of system maintenance for groups rather than for society at large. Government sponsorship and maintenance of organized groups has become a very important aspect of contemporary democratic ideology [p. 49]."[66] The other examples that Lowi uses are trade unions and business organizations; they illustrate the same point, namely, that the needs of organizational maintenance become entwined with the goals of organizations, and that alliances are forged with government to preserve established positions. In this way, what Lowi calls institutional pluralism, instead of being receptive to social change, becomes supportive of the status quo.

The fit between Lowi's examples and Schmitter's definition of societal corporatism is fairly close. There is a limited number of associational interests that participate; outsiders are excluded by the group that is already dealing with the government and is aided by the

[66] See also Dolbeare (1969, pp. 258–263).

government. Singular is only a matter of degree; in some instances, only one economic interest will be in partnership, but probably in most cases, there will be industry leaders and trade association representatives. The extent to which membership is compulsory is also a matter of degree, but if dissent is suppressed, and the receipt of benefits depends on participation in particular programs, members of the industry will be compelled to join the organization or suffer economic loss. Noncompetitive, hierarchically ordered, functionally differentiated, representational monopoly, and controls on leadership are also evident. Recognition by the state can either come about through law, or through informal continuous dealings where the industry "captures" the regulatory agency.

Corporatism, as noted, appears in a variety of social and political contexts, ranging from Sweden and Switzerland, on the one hand, to Mussolini's Italy and Salazar's Portugal, on the other. Because of its diversity and dispersion among so many countries in so many different political cultures, there is, quite naturally, uncertainty as to why corporatism develops as well as whether it is inevitable. Schmitter argues that corporatism is a necessary condition of advanced capitalism, that when the state assumes responsibility for the management of key segments of the economy, of necessity, it is to its advantage to enter into stable arrangements with key private producers. The successful formulation and implementation of public economic policy (and hence the survival of the regime) depends on information and cooperation of the regulated interests which, in turn, benefit for the reasons already indicated.

Social-reform groups are the opposite of vested, economic interests; instead of powerful, selective incentives, which maintain the organization, they seek collective goods and face free riders, which weaken the organization. How, then, can it be argued that they will evolve into the societal corporatist model?

Before answering that question, it is necessary to define pluralism more precisely. Although pluralism shares several characteristics with societal corporatism (for example, the importance of organized representation), there are important differences. Schmitter defines pluralism (ideal type) as follows:

> Pluralism can be defined as a system of interest representation in which the constituent units are organized into an unspecified number of multiple, voluntary, competitive, nonhierarchically ordered and self-determined (as to type or scope of interest) categories which are not specially licensed, recognized, subsidized, created or otherwise controlled in leadership selection or interest articulation by the state and which do not exercise a monopoly of representational activity within their respective categories [p. 96].

Where social-reform groups that use law reform activity will locate on the pluralism–corporatism continuum will depend on how they survive and maintain themselves in the future.

The analysis so far has stressed the great difficulty that social-reform groups will have in capitalizing on procedural access gained by the law reformers; and that access and the ability to persuade requires social-reform groups to have considerable staying power and to mobilize and continue to mobilize the technical and professional resources necessary to avoid passive co-optation. The requirements needed to capitalize on access are little different from the requirements needed to overcome other unfavorable variables in activity by social-reform groups. Groups that formally have access also face free riders, the distribution of benefits and costs has not been altered, the bureaucratic contingency may still be technically complex or require long-term field-level discretion, and, because participation will most likely be of low visibility, the law reformers will probably drift away.

It would be a mistake, however, to conclude from this analysis that the current wave of law-reform activity by social-reform groups will simply fade away because of its inherent, structural weaknesses. There are several reasons that promise to keep it alive. One, for example, is its political appeal. It has been noted that environmental, consumer, and currently to a lesser extent, civil rights, seem to be good politics. Ambitious legislators, congressmen, senators, governors, and even recent presidents, have seized consumer and environmental issues.[67] A great deal of legislation has been enacted and, from time to time, vigorous leaders of social-reform groups and advocates have been appointed to key administrative positions. The supports for the constitutional values of access are relatively cheap. Consumer and environmental protection legislation do not impose much of a demand on governmental budgets and apparently have a high political pay-off. All of the measures of publicly financed public interest law groups do not amount to a great deal of money, at least as compared with any other government program of any consequence. Even far-reaching ideas, such as the Nader utility check-off, will not cost the states any money.

A second reason indicating survival is that the social-reform groups, and especially the law reformers, are not unaware of their structural difficulties, and concerted efforts are being made to institutionalize sources of outside resources. The most promising source of support will probably be various forms of public financing, with con-

---

[67] It is because of the legislative victories that some commentators mistakenly believe that social-reform groups are no longer underrepresented in American society. See, for example, Stewart (1977) and compare with Wilson (1974, p. 135).

tinued support from foundations. A third, is the varied effort of some
social-reform groups to publicly institutionalize their base of support;
the most prominent example is that of the Nader groups, which seek to
have established statewide consumer groups to participate in utility
rate-making financed by check-offs from utility bills. So far, no state
has passed the necessary legislation, but the effort continues.

These supports combine with the legitimated demands of the
social-reform groups for access. Although the Supreme Court has
retreated from the Warren court days, the basic legal symbols of
fairness and access are now fixed in our political culture, and the argument will be over details, such as the technicalities of standing, and the
proper allegations of interests and injuries.

The chances are, then, that various kinds of public and some foundation support will be available to support social-reform groups' law-
reform activity, and that the legal and political affirmation of the goals
of the groups and the law reformers will be sufficient to maintain purposive incentives. The question to be asked is what effect will this support for social-reform groups have on the issues of pluralism?

To the extent that the law reformers and leaders of social-reform
groups are successful in seeking a stable institutionalized source of outside resources, the characteristics of the social-reform groups will
change. As Wilson and McCarthy and Zald argue, purposive organizations, to survive, become staff-led and dependent primarily on outside
resources. The leadership will be able to avoid the strictures of Olson's
free rider but only at the cost of dependency on the outside funding
source. The groups, in short, will become hierarchically organized.
Moreover, to the extent that the law reformers are the ones who successfully raise the outside resources, the social-reform groups will
become increasingly dependent on the organizational needs of the law
reformers. Again, it is a question of degree. Some social-reform groups
are only shells now; they are paper organizations, in fact, and whatever
impact they make is solely due to the efforts of the law reformers. This
is probably the situation with many mental health, health, and other
low-income and minority organizations. Other social-reform groups are
still maintained by purposive incentives, but even these groups lack the
resources to pursue goals through the legal system or meaningfully participate in the decision-making forums that have been opened to them.
Absent some radical transformation in American political culture, the
most likely prognosis for these purposive organizations is that they will
continue to exist, marshal political support from time to time, and help
in consciousness-raising, but that they will also continue to lack the
resources to engage government agencies and their economic adver-

saries over the long haul. Even partial success in this latter endeavor will depend on the fund-raising efforts of the law reformers. The groups that survive, then, may not only become staff-led but also lawyer-led. It will be the success of obtaining outside funding that will move social-reform groups along the continuum from pluralism to societal corporatism.

The clearest example of the push to societal corporatism is government funding of law-reform activity by social reform groups that provides funds to regulatory agencies to finance citizen participation in their proceedings. Some important agencies (for example, the FTC) already finance such participation, others are considering such a move, and this will probably develop into a more general trend. The demands for citizen participation have been legitimated and are now part of the political culture. There is political pressure on government to consult with citizen groups and to respond to their demands, formal procedures have opened up, and there are demands to finance participation or at least give the appearance of sincere consultation. Whereas the government cooperates with economic interests to improve the success of its regulatory programs, here, the government cooperates with social-reform groups to legitimate its decision-making processes. Legal symbols now demand procedural fairness on the part of government, and government is responding to these demands.

With the implementation of financing citizen participation, all or most of Schmitter's definition of societal corporatism will be met. The groups are already hierarchically organized (or will become so). A principal source of their law-reform resources will come from government agencies who will have discretion to pick and choose since agencies will not be required to finance every group that wants to appear before it. Instead, vague, discretionary rules will authorize financing for "legitimate" groups that speak for a constituency. But if a group is staff-led, who does it speak for? Government agencies may grant access to a wide variety of groups, but they will tend to finance those groups that meet the agency's legitimation needs but, at the same time, do not cause too much trouble. They will try to finance groups whose leaders and lawyers will give the appearance of satisfying the legal symbols of fairness but who also will be reasonable and willing to meet the agency's needs for compromise and accommodation.

To the extent that the agencies are successful in picking and choosing the recipients of their funds, existing groups will be favored over new groups, existing leadership of the groups will be supported, and dissent within the represented groups will be discouraged (not recognized or financed by the agency). Law reformers and group leaders will be strengthened in their dealings with the membership (if it exists) insofar as the agency will give them information not otherwise available. It will give them important symbols of access and participation, various tangible concessions might be made, depending on the circumstances and the issues, and, probably most important, the agency will provide the financial resources to keep the law reformers going and probably the group leaders as well. In Schmitter's terms, there will be a monopoly of representation by an hierarchical group, supported by the state, and, to a large extent, explicitly or implicitly controlled by the state.[68]

The extent to which the societal corporatism model will apply will depend on a number of factors, and certainly one of them is the nature of the social-reform group itself. One would expect that the NAACP and the Sierra Club would exercise more independent roles than a local consumer organization or a poverty group. The former have more independent resources and more of a claim to be heard (and financed) before a particular agency in their fields. The government would exercise less direct and indirect control over these organizations.

There are proposals for other funding mechanisms. Will they also push law-reform activity by social-reform groups along the continuum from pluralism to societal corporatism? The other hoped-for principal source of funding is from the organized bar; specifically, law reformers are urging state bar associations to turn over a portion of their dues to support public interest law firms. Although no state bar association has done this, the plan would also include the establishment of an independent committee or board to administer the fund and to preserve the independence of the grantees. There are other funding proposals—for example, the establishment of a national group with foundation, private gifts, and perhaps some public funds, to fund public interest law firms.

These proposals would lessen the immediate problem of government agencies more or less directly controlling the selection of the law reformers, but, basically, they would not do much to stem the drift toward societal corporatism. A centralized dispenser of funds, whether on a national or state level, would accelerate trends toward hierarchical, monopolistic, social-reform groups that would be led by staffs and professionals. Nothing in the alternative proposals deals with the tendency of purposive organizations to become staff-led if they are to survive. If the staff wants to continue law-reform activity, it will have to engage those law reformers who will be seeking grants from the

---

[68] See Trubek (1977). Social-reform groups "operate much like any other organization . . . and consequently, once formed, they operate as though organizational survival were the primary goal [McCarthy and Zald, 1977, pp. 1212, 1226]."

funding sources. Moreover, the law reformers will also retain their current monopolistic position. In reality, if state bar associations get into the business of financing law-reform activity, the chances are that only one or a small number of firms will be established in any given state. If a national group is formed, there may be even less firms. The small number of law-reform firms will continue to influence the social-reform groups to the needs of the law reformers. Finally, it may be that under these alternative funding arrangements, the law reformers will find themselves more restricted than they now are concerning substantive matters. State and local bar associations are led by elite lawyers who have as clients the enemies of social-reform groups and law reformers. In the past, there have been occasions where lawyers for clients sued by social-reform groups have tried to exert pressure on the law reformers through the funding sources (foundations). There is no reason to assume that these tactics will automatically cease; in fact, there is probably every reason to assume that they will increase through networks in the bar associations.[69]

One of the definitions of corporatism is direct or indirect sponsorship, recognition, and control by the state. Formally, bar association and/or private national group sponsorship of law reformers fall outside of the definition. Nevertheless, all the other elements of the definition will be found as law-reform activity by social-reform groups evolves. The distinction between selection and influence by the organized profession and/or a national group, also composed of elites, and government sponsorship is not as great as between government selection and autonomous groups envisaged under a pluralist system. On the pluralist–societal corporatist continuum, social-reform groups and law reformers would still be much closer to the corporatism end.

The analysis, then, leads to three choices for social-reform groups. In their natural state of evolution, they will rise, be active for awhile, languish, and either wither and die or turn into staff-led organizations. If they choose to pursue their goals through the use of law reformers, the process of conversion to a staff-led group and an increased dependency on law-reformer professionals may actually accelerate. Under this arrangement, there will be two alternatives depending on the energy and success of the law reformers. One likely alternative is

---

[69] There are a few bar association supported public interest law firms, the most famous one supported by the Beverly Hills Bar Association. It had a stormy career and was subject to the pressures described in the text and finally ended. See Handler, Hollingsworth, and Erlanger (1978).

There is some effort to create foundation supplied matching endowments for public interest law firms; the firms would make their contributions primarily through attorney fee awards. To the extent that firms would be able to support themselves through such mechanisms, they would be independent of government agencies, bar associations, and foundations.

formal, but not very significant participation in the decision-making procedures. Because the groups will either be abandoned by the law reformers (who will turn to other endeavors) or be unable to raise sufficient resources, they will be passively co-opted. The other alternative is that they will actively participate as part of a system of societal corporatism. Pluralism will not be revived. Rather, institutionalized pluralism will be modified to take into its fold the new interest groups, as, in a prior day, it took in and socialized farmers and organized labor. Socialization is often a reciprocal relationship, and to the extent that social-reform groups are successful in establishing a meaningful bargaining relationship with government and private sources of decision making, substantive outcomes should be changed, at least somewhat. There will be more of a concern for the position that the groups represent, but, because such groups will be closer to societal corporatism than pluralism, the same questions that Lowi and others raise as to other vested interest groups must also be raised for the new partners. Just as we now ask who organized farmers and labor speak for in their partnership with government, we will also ask who organized environmentalists, consumers, civil rights leaders, and their lawyers speak for.

Societal corporatism, at least according to Schmitter and others, is the dominant trend of government in the postliberal, capitalist state. It is present in many Western European countries, Canada, and the United States, and law-reform activity by social-reform groups will not be able to alter this development. Depending on the strength of the social-reform groups, substantive outcomes may be different or new forms of symbolic reassurance may appear. But whatever the result, decision making will not have been democratized a great deal.

Schmitter, and others, have proposed another alternative direction. They look at the rise in demands of social-reform groups as posing a threat to the structure of societal corporatism, which may eventually result in a more democratic, responsive system. In Schmitter's (1974) words:

> Established, societally corporatist systems are also facing new tensions which they, too, seem incapable of resolving. They are being bombarded with demands for more direct and authentic forms of participation, undermining both the stability of their established internal hierarchies of authority and their claims to democratic legitimacy. More importantly, they are being bypassed with increasing frequency by broad social movements on the one side and specific spontaneous protest actions on the other . . . Here, the prospective associational answer is certainly *not* further societal corporatization, *nor* a reversion to past pluralism, *nor* even less a regression to state corporatism, but may be some experimentation with the sort of dispersed,

nonspecialized, nonhierarchic "hived-off," voluntaristic units, autonomously responsible for allocating their values and resolving their conflicts . . . .[p. 127].[70]

This literature, however, is singularly lacking in any mention of the problems dealt with in this monograph. There is no discussion of the characteristics of social-reform groups, the incentives and disincentives for mobilization, the effects of the distribution of benefits and costs on mobilization, what it means to convert purposive incentives and consciousness-raising into the enactment of laws and the day-to-day struggles with bureaucracy. The structures of the advanced state of capitalism are in place—massive public bureaucracies and large, powerfully organized economic, social and political interests—and have to be confronted not only once, or twice, but over the long haul. These are the brutal facts facing "dispersed, nonspecialized, nonhierarchical, voluntaristic units," and just how, in the real world are they going to mount this kind of campaign? Existing evidence is not very promising. Ralph Nader and Common Cause (which do not use law reformers very much) appear to be unique, but still are facing difficult times in fund raising and maintaining momentum. The United Farm Workers, which also used nonlitigation techniques, blossomed for awhile, attracted outside elite resources, but when the attention of the elites slackened so, too, apparently, have the fortunes of that organization (Jenkins and Perrow, 1977). The fortunes, or misfortunes, of many other social-reform groups have been discussed throughout this monograph. In short, the theoretical and empirical information indicates the hope that the increase in social-reform groups will overcome the bureaucratic, hierarchical state is still in the realm of wishful thinking.[71]

Social-reform groups have turned to law reformers and the legal system because they are weak. The powerful rarely need the courts; they can exert their influence in politics, administration, and the private market. The issues that the social-reform groups and the law reformers are confronting are serious and important. They are seeking to curb the most powerful economic interests and to obtain social justice for despised, discriminated individuals and groups in American

[70] Scheingold (1974, chap. 9) also implies that legal rights activities have the most promise in mobilizing grass roots organizations that can eventually change political structures.

[71] Compare Lynd and Alperovitz (1973) with review of Gerald Chaliand's *Revolution in the Third World* (Viking 1977) in Steel (1977). Piven and Cloward (1977) take a different approach. They argue that mobilization (the escalation of direct action) is much more effective for lower-income social-reform groups than organization. However, in only one chapter (dealing with the National Welfare Rights Organization) do they discuss the problems of maintaining incentives and that discussion is used to demonstrate their point about the futility of trying to organize poor people. They never deal explicitly with the problem of translating gains derived from direct action into long-term gains.

society. Not under any circumstances would these groups obtain victories easily. In their state of powerlessness, they have sought the help of young and activist lawyers and pressed their claims in the courts and before administrative agencies. They have made modest gains. In carefully chosen situations, they have been able to accomplish direct, tangible results for their members. In other situations, although the evidence is less clear, indirect benefits have probably also accrued. And, then, as to be expected, there have been failures. But at its core, by turning to the legal system, social-reform groups have appealed to traditional institutions, and their claims for social justice have been based on traditional American constitutional values. It should come as no surprise, then, that law-reform activity by social-reform groups will not result in any great transformation of American society. Instead, it is, at its most successful level, incremental, gradualist, and moderate. It will not disturb the basic political and economic organization of modern American society.

References

Alford, R. 1975. *Health care politics: Ideological and interest group barriers to reform.* Chicago, Ill.: University of Chicago Press.

Anderson, F. R. 1973. *NEPA in the courts: A legal analysis of the national environmental policy act.* Baltimore, MD.: Johns Hopkins University Press.

Andrews, R. N. 1976. Agency responses to NEPA: A comparison and implications. *Natural Resources Journal, 16,* 301–308.

Arrow, K. 1972. Models of job discrimination. In A. Pascal (Ed.), *Racial discrimination in economic life.* Lexington, Mass.: P.C. Heath-Lexington Books.

Auerbach, J. S. 1976. *Unequal justice: Lawyers and social change in modern America.* New York: Oxford University Press.

Automotive News. 1968. December 9, p. 6.

Automotive News. 1970. August 17, p. 39.

Appleton, A. 1974. Pipeline construction—a status report. Mimeographed, Friends of the Earth, May 15, 1974.

Ayres, B. D. 1974. *New York Times.* November 11, 1974.

Ayres, R. E. 1975. Enforcement of air pollution controls on stationary sources under the clean air amendments of 1970. *Ecology Law Quarterly, 4,* 441.

Baratz, M. S. 1977. Book review. *American Journal of Sociology, 82,* 1165.

Becker, G. 1971. *The economics of discrimination.* Chicago: University of Chicago Press.

Bell, D. A. 1976a Book Review. *Emory Law Journal, 25,* 779.

Bell, D. A. 1976b. Serving two masters: Integration ideals and client interests in school desegregation litigation. *Yale Law Review, 85,* 470.

Bickel, A. M. 1962. *The least dangerous branch.* Indianapolis, Ind.: Bobbs Merrill.

Blinder, A. S. 1973. Wage discrimination: Reduced form and structural estimates. *Journal of Human Resources*, 8, 436–455.

Boyer, B. 1972. Alternatives to administrative trial-type hearings for resolving complex scientific, economic, and social issues. *Michigan Law Review*, 71, 111.

Capowski, J. J. 1976. Introduction to the welfare issue. *Cornell Law Review*, 61, 663.

Chamberlin, J. 1974. Provision of collective goods as a function of group size. *American Political Science Review*, 68, 707–716.

Cloward, R. A., and Elwan, R. 1966. Advocacy in the ghetto. *Transaction*, December 1966.

Cloward, R. A., and Piven, F. F. 1966. A strategy to end poverty. *The Nation*, May 2.

———. 1977. *Poor people's movements.* New York: Pantheon.

Connolly, W., (Ed.). 1969. *The bias of pluralism.* New York: Atherton.

Cortner, H. J. 1976. A case analysis of policy implementations: The national environmental policy act of 1969. *Natural Resources Journal*, 16, 323.

Davis, T. P. 1973. Legislative restriction of creditor powers and remedies: A case study of the negotiation and drafting of the Wisconsin consumer act. *Michigan Law Review*, 72, 3.

Davis, T. P. 1976. Citizen's guide to intervention in nuclear power plant siting: A blueprint for Alice in nuclear wonderland. *Environmental Law*, 6, 621–650.

Danielson, M. N. 1976. *The politics of exclusion.* New York: Columbia University Press.

Demkovich, L. E. 1976. Consumer leaders hope that Carter will go to bat for them. *National Journal*, 49, 1738.

Demkovich, L. E. 1977a. Consumer report/Consumer groups see end in sight after long fight over agency. *National Journal*, 5, 174.

Demkovich, L. E. 1977b. Consumer focus/Six—count 'em—six consumers. *National Journal*, 11, 394.

Demkovich, L. E. 1977c. Consumer report/New equal credit regulations are creating new headaches. *National Journal*, 10, 354.

De Toledano, R. 1975. *Hit and run: The rise and fall? of Ralph Nader.* New Rochelle, N.Y.: Arlington House.

DiMento, J. F. 1977. Citizen environmental litigation and the administrative process: Empirical findings, remaining issues and a direction for future research. *Duke Law Review*, 1977, 409–448.

Dolbeare, K. M. 1967. *Trial courts in urban politics; state court policy impact and functions in a local political system.* New York: Wiley.

Dolbeare, K. M. 1969. *Power and change in the United States: Empirical findings and their implications.* New York: Wiley.

Dolbeare, K. M., and Hammond, P. E. 1971. *The school prayer decisions.* Chicago: University of Chicago Press.

Doolittle, F., and Wiseman, M. 1976. *The California welfare reform act: A litigation history.* Berkeley, Cal.: University of California Institute of Business and Economics Research, Work Paper No. 71, August.

Dreyfus, D. A., and Ingram, H. M. 1976. The national environmental policy act: A view of intent and practice. *Natural Resources Journal*, 16, 243–248.

Dworkin, R. 1977. Why Bakke has no case. *New York Review*, 24, 11.

Edelman, M. 1964. *The symbolic uses of politics.* Urbana, Ill.: University of Illinois Press.

Edelman, M. 1974. The political language of the helping professions. Institute for Research on Poverty, Discussion Paper 195–74. University of Wisconsin, Madison.

Edelman, M. 1975. Symbolism in politics. In L. Lindberg et al. (Eds.), *Stress and contradiction in modern capitalism.* Lexington, Mass.: Lexington Books.

Edwards, H. T., and Zaretsky, B. L. 1975. Preferential remedies for employment discrimination. *Michigan Law Review, 74,* 1.

Energy Report. 1976. The never ending controversy over the Trans-Alaska pipeline. *National Journal,* July 31, 1080.

Farley, R. 1977. Trends in racial inequalities: Have the gains of the 1960s disappeared in the 1970s? *American Sociological Review, 42,* 189–208.

Findley, R. W., and Plager, S. J. 1974. State regulation of non-transportation noise: Law and technology. *Southern California Law Review, 48,* 209.

Fireman, B., and Gamson, W. A. 1978. Utilitarian logic in the resource mobilization perspective. In M. N. Zald and J. D. McCarthy (Eds.), *The dynamics of social movements: Resource mobilization, tactics and social control.* New York: Sage Publications.

Fiss, O. 1971. The Charlotte–Mecklinburg case: Its significance for northern school desegregation. *University of Chicago Law Review, 38,* 697.

Friedman, L. M. 1975. *The legal system: A social science perspective.* New York: Russell Sage Foundation.

Friedman, L. M., and Macaulay, S. 1977. *Law and the behavioral sciences.* Indianapolis, Ind.: Bobbs, Merrill, (2nd ed.).

Friesema, P., and Culhane, P. J. 1976. Social impacts, politics, and the environmental impact statement process. *Natural Resources Journal, 16,* 339–353.

Galloway, L. T., and McAteer, J. D. 1977. Testimony before the subcommittee on environment, committee on interior and insular affairs, U.S. House of Representatives on H.R. 2. Washington, D.C.: United States Government Printing Office.

Gamson, W. 1975. *The strategy of social protest.* Homewood, Ill.: The Dorsey Press.

Gardner, J. 1973. Consumer report/New product safety commission adopts "tough but reasonable" approach to its job. *National Journal, 38,* 1391.

Gellhorn, W. 1967. Poverty and legality: The law's slow awakening. *William and Mary Law Review, 9,* 285.

Glazer, N. 1975. *Affirmative discrimination: Ethnic inequality and public policy.* New York: Basic Books.

Gorey, H. 1975. *Nader and the power of everyman.* New York: Grosset and Dunlap.

Green, M. I. 1975. *The other government: The unseen power of Washington.* New York: Grossman.

Greenberger, M., and Gutmann, D. 1977. Legal remedies beyond Title VII to combat sex discrimination in employment. In Joint Economic Subcommittee, Subcommittee on Economic Growth and Stabilization, *American women workers in a full employment economy.* Washington, D.C.: U.S. Government Printing Office.

Gusfield, J. R. 1963. *Symbolic crusade: Status politics and the American temperance movement.* Urbana, Ill.: University of Illinois Press.

Hall, R. H. 1972. *Organization, structure, and process.* Englewood Cliffs, N.J.: Prentice-Hall.

Halpern, C., and Cunningham, J. 1971. Reflections on the new public interest law: Theory and practice at the Center for Law and Social Policy. *Georgetown Law Journal, 59,* 1095–1126.

Hamilton, J. 1972. Procedures for the adoption of rules of general applicability: The need for procedural innovation in rulemaking. *California Law Review, 60,* 1276.

Handler, J. F. 1966. Controlling official behavior in welfare administration. *California Law Review, 54,* 479.

Handler, J. F. 1973. *The coercive social worker: British lessons for American social services.* New York: Academic Press.

Handler, J. F. Forthcoming. *Protecting social service clients: Legal and structural constraints on discretion.* New York: Academic Press.

Handler, J. F., Edgar, G., and Settle, R. F. 1978. Public interest law and employment discrimination. In B. Weisbrod, J. Handler,and N. Komesar (Eds.), *Public interest law.* Berkeley, Cal.: University of California Press.

Handler, J., Ginsberg, B., and Snow, A. 1977. The public interest law industry. In B. Weisbrod, J. F. Handler, and N. Komesar (Eds.), *Public interest law.* Berkeley, Cal.: University of California Press.

Handler, J. F., and Hollingsworth, E. J. 1971. *The deserving poor: A study of welfare administration.* New York: Academic Press.

Handler, J. F., Hollingsworth, E. J., and Erlanger, H. 1978. *Lawyers and the pursuit of legal rights.* New York: Academic Press.

Hart, H. 1975. *New Times*, January 10, p. 42.

Hartman, C. 1974. *Yerba Buena: Land grab and community resistance in San Francisco.* San Francisco: Glide Publications.

Harvard Law Review. 1973. Note, right to treatment. *Harvard Law Review, 86,* 1292.

Harvard Law School Record. 1969. Vol. 49, no. 3.

Horowitz, D. L. 1977. *The courts and social policy.* Washington, D.C.: The Brookings Institution.

James, M. 1973. *The people's lawyers.* New York: Hale, Rinehart and Winston.

Jenkins, J. C., and Perrow, C. 1976. Insurgency of the powerless: Farm workers movements (1946–1972). *American Sociological Review, 42,* 249–268.

Jones, J. E. 1970. The bugaboo of employment quotas. *Wisconsin Law Review, 70,* 341.

Jones, J. E. 1976a. The development of the law under Title VII since 1965: Implications of the new law. *Rutgers Law Review, 30,* 1.

Jones, J. E. 1976b. The transformation of fair employment practices policy. In Federal policies and worker status since the thirties. Industrial Relations Research Association, University of Wisconsin, Madison.

Katz, J. 1977. Cover-up and collective integrity: On the natural antagonisms of authority internal and external to organizations. *Social Problems, 25,* 3–17.

Kazanjian, P. C. 1972. Preparing for the law: A look at the new breed. *Student Law Journal, 17.*

Kirchheimer, O. 1961. *Political justice: The use of legal procedure for political ends.* Princeton, N.J.: Princeton University Press.

Kirp, D. L., Boss, C., and Kurilof, R. 1974. Legal reforms of special education: Empirical studies and procedural proposals. *California Law Review, 62,* 40.

Kirp, D. L., and Yudof, M. G. 1974. *Educational policy and the law.* Berkeley, Cal.: McCutchan Publishing Co.

Kirshten, D. 1977. Paperwork is having a big impact on environmental statements. *National Journal, 29,* 1119.

Komesar, N. 1978. Housing, zoning, and the public interest. In B. Weisbrod, J. Handler, and N. Komesar (Eds.), *Public interest law.* Berkeley, Cal.: University of California Press.

Komesar, N., and Weisbrod, B. 1978. The public interest law firm: A behavioral analysis. In B. Weisbrod, J. Handler, and N. Komesar (Eds.), *Public interest law.* Berkeley, Cal.: University of California Press.

Kotz, N., and Kotz, M. L. 1977. *A passion for equality; George A. Wiley and the movement.* New York: W. W. Norton and Co.

Ladinsky, J. 1970. Law, legal services and social change: A note on the OEO legal services program. Institute for Research on Poverty Discussion Paper 85–70. University of Wisconsin, Madison.

Large, D. W. 1972. Is anybody listening? The problem of access in environmental litigation, *Wisconsin Law Review, 72,* 229.

Leaf, P. J. 1978. The medical marketplace and public interest law. In B. Weisbrod, J. Handler, and N. Komesar (Eds.), *Public interest law.* Berkeley, Cal.: University of California Press.

Leflar, R. B., and Rogol, M. H. 1976. Consumer participation in the regulation of public utilities: A model act. *Harvard Journal of Legislation, 13,* 235.

Leone, R. 1972. Public interest advocacy and the regulatory process. *The Annals, 400,* 46.

Lewis, A., and *The New York Times.* 1964. *Portrait of a decade: The second American revolution.* New York: Random House.

Liroff, R. A. 1976. *A national policy for the environment.* Bloomington, Ind.: University of Indiana Press.

Lomax, L. E. 1971. *The Negro revolt.* New York: Harper and Row.

Lowi, T. J. 1969. *The end of liberalism.* New York: W. W. Norton and Co.

Lowi, T. J. 1971. *The politics of disorder.* New York: Basic Books.

Lukes, S. 1974. *Power: A radical view.* London: Macmillan.

Lynd, S., and Alperovitz, G. 1973. *Strategy and program.* Boston: Beacon Press.

McAteer, J. D. 1975. The use of closure orders and notices of violation under the federal coal mine Health and Safety Act of 1969—the necessity for stringent enforcement. *West Virginia Law Review, 77,* 689.

McCarthy, J. D., and Zald, M. N. 1973. *The trend of social movements in America: Professionalization and resource mobilization.* Morristown, N.J.: The General Learning Press.

McCarthy, J. D., and Zald, M. N. 1977. Resource mobilization and social movements: A partial theory. *American Journal of Sociology, 82,* 1212–1241.

McCloskey, R. G. 1972. *The modern supreme court.* Cambridge, Mass.: Harvard University Press.

McNeil, K. E. 1973. Citizens as brokers: Cooptation in an urban setting. Unpublished Ph.D. dissertation, Vanderbilt University.

Marine, G. 1969. *The black panthers.* New York: The New American Library.

Marks, F. R. 1972. *The lawyer, the public, and professional responsibility.* Chicago, Ill.: American Bar Association.

Maslow, J. E. 1974. Is Title VII sinking? *Juris Doctor, 4,* 28.

Mayhew, L. 1975. Institutions of representation: Civil justice and the public. *Law and Society Review, 9,* 401.

Mechanic, D. 1962. Sources of power of lower participants in complex organizations. *Administrative Science Quarterly, 7,* 349–364.

Moonan, W., and Goldstein, T. 1972. The new lawyers. In R. Gross and P. Ostermal (Eds.), *The new professionals.* New York: Simon and Schuster.

Moynihan, D. P. 1969. *Maximum feasible misunderstanding.* New York: Free Press.

Mueller, M. 1969. Nader: From auto safety to a permanent crusade. *Science, 166,* 980.

Myers, H. R. 1975. Federal decisionmaking and the Trans-Alaska Pipeline. *Ecology Law Quarterly, 4,* 915.

Nadel, M. V. 1971. *The politics of consumer protection.* Indianapolis, Ind.: Bobbs Merrill.

Nader, R. 1965. *Unsafe at any speed.* New York: Grossman.

The New York Times. 1976. April 15, p. 1, col. 1.

The New York Times. 1977a. March 14, p. 1, col. 1.

The New York Times. 1977b. November 14. Consumer aides find U.S. jobs are frustrating, p. 1.

Nickel, J. W. 1975. Preferential policies in hiring and admissions: A jurisprudential approach. *Wisconsin Law Review, 75,* 534.

Nuclear Energy Policy Study Group. 1977. *Nuclear power issues and choices.* Cambridge, Mass.: Ballinger.

Oberschall, A. 1973. *Social conflict and social movements.* Englewood Cliffs, N.J.: Prentice-Hall.

O'Brien, D. J. 1974. The public goods dilemma and the "apathy" of the poor toward neighborhood organization. *Social Service Review, 48,* 229–244.

Olson, M., Jr. 1965. *The logic of collective action.* Cambridge, Mass.: Harvard University Press.

Orfield, G. 1969. *The reconstruction of southern education: The schools and the 1964 civil rights act.* New York: Wiley and Sons.

Pederson, W. F. 1975. Formal records and informal rulemaking. *Yale Law Journal, 85,* 38.

Peterson, P. E., and Greenstone, J. D. 1977. Racial change and citizen participation: The mobilization of low-income communities through community action. In R. Haveman (Ed.), *A decade of federal antipoverty programs.* New York: Academic Press.

Piven, F. F., and Cloward, R. A. 1971. *Regulating the poor: The functions of public welfare.* New York: Pantheon.

Piven, F. F., and Cloward, R. A. 1977. *Poor people's movements: Why they succeed, how they fail.* New York: Pantheon.

Plager, S., and Handler, J. F. 1966. The politics of planning for urban development: Strategies in the manipulation of public law. *Wisconsin Law Review, 63,* 724.

Rabin, R. L. 1970. Implementation of cost-of-living adjustment for AFDC recipients: A case study in welfare administration. *University of Pennsylvania Law Review, 118,* 1143.

Rabin, R. 1976. Lawyers for social change: Perspectives on public interest law. *Stanford Law Review, 28,* 207–261.

Robinson, T. 1970. The making of administrative policy: Another look at rulemaking and adjudication and administrative reform. *University of Pennsylvania Law Review, 118,* 485.

Rodgers, H. R., 1973. Law as an instrument of public policy. *American Journal of Political Science, 17,* 638.

Rodgers, H. R., and Bullock, C. 1972. *Law and social change: Civil rights laws and their consequences.* New York: McGraw-Hill.

Rosenheim, M. K. 1976. Notes on helping: Normalizing juvenile nuisances. *Social Service Review, 50,* 179.

Rubenstein, L. S. 1976. Procedural due process and the limits of the adversary system. *Harvard Civil Rights-Civil Liberties Law Review, 11,* 48.

Sabatier, P. 1975. Social movements and regulatory agencies: Toward a more adequate—and less pessimistic theory of "clientele capture." *Policy Sciences, 6,* 301–342.

Sager, L. 1969. Tight little islands: Exclusionary zoning, equal protection and the indigent. *Stanford Law Review, 21,* 767.

Salisbury, R. 1969. An exchange theory of interest groups. *Midwest Journal of Political Science, 13,* 1.

Sanford, D. 1976. *Me and Ralph: Is Nader unsafe for Detroit?* Washington, D.C.: The New Republic Book Company.

Sarat, A., and Grossman, J. 1975. Courts and conflict resolution: Problems in the mobilization of adjudication. *American Political Science Review, 69,* 1200–1217.

Sax, J. L., and DiMento, J. F. 1974. Environmental citizen suits: Three years' experience under the Michigan environmental protection act. *Ecology Law Quarterly, 4,* 1–10.

Scheff, T. J. 1961. Control over policy by attendants in a mental hospital. *Journal of Health and Human Behavior, 2*, 93–105.

Scheingold, S. A. 1974. *The politics of rights: Lawyers, public policy, and political change.* New Haven: Yale University Press.

Schmitter, P. 1974. Still the century of corporatism. *The Review of Politics, 85*, 112.

Shields, G., and Spector, L. S. 1971. Opening up suburbs: Notes on a movement for social change. *Yale Law Review of Law and Social Action, 2*, 300.

Silberman, C. E. 1964. *Crisis in black and white.* New York: Random House.

Sitkin, P. 1973. Welfare law: Narrowing the gap between congressional policy and local policy. In United States Joint Economic Committee, Subcommittee on Fiscal Policy, *Issues in Welfare Administration.* Washington, D.C.: United States Government Printing Office.

Sive, D. 1977. Forward: Roles and rules in environmental decision-making. *Iowa Law Review, 62*, 637.

Smith, J. 1976. Communities, associations, and the supply of collective goods. *American Journal of Sociology, 82*, 291–308.

Snow, A., and Weisbrod, B. 1978. Consumerism, consumers, and public interest law. In B. Weisbrod, J. Handler, and N. Komesar (Eds.), *Public interest law.* Berkeley, Cal.: University of California Press. (chap. 14).

Snyder, D., and Kelly, W. R. 1978. Strategies for investigating violence and social change: Illustrations from analysis of racial disorders and implications for mobilization research. In M. N. Zald and J. D. McCarthy (Eds.), *The dynamics of social movements.* New York: Sage Publications.

Sovern, M. 1966. *Legal restraints on racial discrimination.* New York: Twentieth Century Fund.

Steel, R. 1977. Russia, the West, and the rest. *The New York Review, 24*, 19.

Stewart, R. 1975. The reformation of American administrative law. *Harvard Law Review, 88*, 1667.

Stewart, R. 1977. The development of administrative and quasiconstitutional law in judicial review of environmental decisionmaking: Lessons from the clean air act. *Iowa Law Review, 62*, 713.

Sullivan, R. 1977. Inquiry links "institutional indifference" to deaths of 7 at Bronx mental facility. *The New York Times*, June 10, p. B5M.

Swanston, W. 1972. Washington pressures/Consumer Federation on America waging spirited battle for survival. *National Journal, 28*, 1126.

Thain, G. J. 1978. Non-law public interest advocacy groups: A case study of two groups with similar goals. In B. Weisbrod, J. Handler, and N. Komesar (Eds.), *Public interest law.* Berkeley, Cal.: The University of California Press.

Thurow, L. 1969. *Poverty and discrimination.* Washington, D.C. The Brookings Institution.

Trubek, D. M. 1976. Law and the politics of justice: Rethinking the open suburbs movement. Unpublished manuscript, University of Wisconsin, Madison.

Trubek, D. M. 1977a. Allocating the burden of environmental uncertainty: The NRC interprets NEPA's substantive mandate. *Wisconsin Law Review, 77*, 747.

Trubek, D. M. 1977b. Book review, Council for Public Interest Law: Balancing the scale of justice: financing public interest law in America. *Wisconsin Law Review, 77*, 303.

Trubek, D. M. 1978. Environmental defense 1: Introduction to interest group advocacy in complex disputes. In B. Weisbrod, J. F. Handler, and N. Komesar (Eds.), *Public interest law.* Berkeley, Cal.: University of California Press.

Trubek, D. M., and Gillen, W. J. 1978. Environmental defense 2: Examining the limits of interest group advocacy in complex disputes. In B. Weisbrod, J. Handler, and N. Komesar (Eds.), *Public interest law*. Berkeley, Cal.: University of California Press.

Trubek, L. G., and Trubek, D. M. 1978. Effective consumer advocacy in government: Filling the void. *The Public Interest*, 4, 4.

Truman, D. 1959. The American system in crisis. *Political Science Quarterly*, 74, 481–497.

Turk, A. 1976. Law as a weapon in social conflict. *Social Problems*, 23, 277–291.

United States Civil Rights Commission. 1961. Staff report, political participation. *Education*, 2, 177–178.

United States Civil Rights Commission. 1959, p. 131.

United States Civil Rights Commission. 1963. Staff report. *Public Education* (December), 1–5.

United States Congress. 1973. Hearings before the general subcommittee on labor of the House committee on education and labor. *Black lung benefits eligibility (oversight)*. Washington, D.C.: United States Government Printing Office.

United States Congress. 1976. Hearing before the sub-committee on energy and power of the committee on interstate and foreign commerce. Ninety-Fourth Congress, Second Session, Serial No. 94–125. Washington, D.C.: United States Government Printing Office.

United States Council on Environmental Quality. 1976. *Environmental impact statements: An analysis of six years' experience by seventy federal agencies*. Washington, D.C.: United States Government Printing Office.

United States General Accounting Office. 1976. *Trans-Alaska oil pipeline—progress of construction through November 1975*. Washington, D.C.: United States Government Printing Office.

United States Senate. 1972. Hearings before the sub-committee on labor of the Senate committee on labor and public welfare. Ninety-Second Congress, Second Session. Black lung legislation, 1971–1972. Washington, D.C.: United States Government Printing Office.

United States Senate. 1977. Committee on Governmental Affairs. Study on federal regulation, public participation in regulatory proceedings. Washington, D.C.: United States Government Printing Office.

Vanderwicken, P. 1971. The angry young lawyers. *Fortune*, September.

Vogel, D., and Nadel, M. 1977. Who is a consumer: An analysis of the politics of consumer conflict. *American Politics Quarterly*, 5, 27–56.

Vose, C. 1972. *Constitutional change*. Lexington, Mass.: Lexington Books.

Wark, L. G. 1971. Consumer report/Nader campaigns for funds to expand activities of his consumer action complex. *National Journal*, 38, 1904.

Welch, C., and Walter, L. 1975. Interest groups, ideology and the costs of participation. *Rocky Mountain Social Science Journal*, 12, 81.

Welles, C. 1966. Accusers: Detroit botches its job. *Life Magazine*, 60, 40.

Wexler, S. 1970. Practicing law for poor people. *Yale Law Journal*, 79, 1049.

Wickelman, A. F. 1976. Administrative agency implementation of the national environmental policy act of 1969: A conceptual framework for explaining differential response. *Natural Resources Journal*, 16, 263–279.

Wilson, J. 1977. Social protest and social action. *Social Problems*, 24, 469–481.

Wilson, J. Q. 1973. *Political organizations*, New York: Basic Books.

Wilson, J. Q. 1974. The politics of regulation. In J. W. McKie (Ed.), *Social responsibility and the business predicament*. Washington, D.C.: Brookings Institution. Pp. 135–168.

Yale Law Journal. 1975. Comment, The Wyatt case: Implementation of a judicial decree ordering institutional change. *Yale Law Journal, 88,* 1338.

Young, L. 1972. A chink in Nader's armor? *The New Republic,* September, 11.

Zemansky, G. M. 1976. *Environmental non-compliance and the public interest during the construction of the Trans-Alaska Pipeline.* Fairbanks, Alaska: Fairbanks Environmental Center, Mimeographed.

Subject Index

Institute for Research on Poverty
Monograph Series

Vernon L. Allen, Editor, *Psychological Factors in Poverty*

Frederick Williams, Editor, *Language and Poverty: Perspectives on a Theme*

Murray Edelman, *Politics as Symbolic Action: Mass Arousal and Quiescence*

Joel F. Handler and Ellen Jane Hollingsworth, *"The Deserving Poor": A Study of Welfare Administration*

Robert J. Lampman, *Ends and Means of Reducing Income Poverty*

Larry L. Orr, Robinson G. Hollister, and Myron J. Lefcowitz, Editors, with the assistance of Karen Hester, *Income Maintenance: Interdisciplinary Approaches to Research*

Charles E. Metcalf, *An Econometric Model of the Income Distribution*

Glen G. Cain and Harold W. Watts, Editors, *Income Maintenance and Labor Supply: Econometric Studies*

Joel F. Handler, *The Coercive Social Worker: British Lessons for American Social Services*

Larry L. Orr, *Income, Employment, and Urban Residential Location*

Stanley H. Masters, *Black–White Income Differentials: Empirical Studies and Policy Implications*

Irene Lurie, Editor, *Integrating Income Maintenance Programs*

Peter K. Eisinger, *Patterns of Interracial Politics: Conflict and Cooperation in the City*

David Kershaw and Jerilyn Fair, *The New Jersey Income-Maintenance Experiment, Volume I: Operations, Surveys, and Administration*

Fredrick L. Golladay and Robert H. Haveman, *The Economic Impacts of Tax–Transfer Policy: Regional and Distributional Effects*

Morgan Reynolds and Eugene Smolensky, *Public Expenditures, Taxes, and the Distribution of Income: The United States, 1950, 1961, 1970*